HOW THE
EUCHARIST
CAN SAVE CIVILIZATION

HOW THE
EUCHARIST
CAN SAVE CIVILIZATION

R. JARED STAUDT, PHD

TAN Books

Gastonia, North Carolina

Cover design by Jordan Avery

Cover image: Jules Breton, *The Blessing of the Wheat in Artois*, 1857, oil on canvas / commons.wikimedia.org.

Interior images: *Sacrament of the Last Supper* © 2022 Salvador Dalí, Fundació Gala-Salvador Dalí, Artists Rights Society (p. 272). All other interior images are public domain.

Library of Congress Control Number: 2022945125

ISBN: 978-1-5051-2820-8
Kindle ISBN: 978-1-5051-2821-5
ePUB ISBN: 978-1-5051-2822-2

Published in the United States by
TAN Books
PO Box 269
Gastonia, NC 28053
www.TANBooks.com

To my wife, Anne, in thanksgiving
for our Eucharistic life together

"If any one eats of this bread, he will live for ever; and the bread which I shall give for the life of the world is my flesh."
—*John 6:51*

Contents

Foreword

Before joining Dr. Staudt in the discussion of how the Eucharist can save civilization, we should ask ourselves whether civilization is worth saving.

What exactly is civilization?

According to Wikipedia, it is "any complex state society characterized by a social hierarchy . . . a perceived separation from and domination over the natural environment . . . urbanization (or the development of cities), centralization, the domestication of both humans and other organisms, specialization of labor, culturally ingrained ideologies of progress and supremacism, monumental architecture, taxation . . . and expansionism."[1] At this point, we could be forgiven for questioning whether we still see civilization as something that is good and worth defending. How many of us would fight for civilization if we thought that we were fighting for the increasing complexity of the state and its social hierarchy? How many of the agrarians among us would fight for a civilization that defined itself as being separate from the natural environment and as seeking to dominate it? How many of us would fight for incessant urbanization, centralization, and the passive domestication of ourselves alongside the

---

[1] Wikipedia, s.v. "Civilization," last modified June 15, 2022, 17:54, https://en.wikipedia.org/wiki/Civilization.

domestication of other organisms? How many of us had realized that being civilized was the willingness to make ourselves cattle in the service of increasingly complex social hierarchies? How many of us thought that civilization was marked by the sort of "specialization of labor" that had reduced human work to that of a disposable cog in an increasingly large and complex mechanism? How many of us guessed that civilization was defined by culturally ingrained progressivism and other supremacist ideologies? How many of us perceived that taxation was civilized and that increasing taxation was therefore and presumably a mark of increasing civilization?

If this is indeed "civilization," we would be justified in hoping that civilization would go to hell and equally justified in believing that it was already in the process of going there.

We would, however, be wrong to abandon civilization because of such woefully awry definitions of it. Having seen how civilization is defined on the internet (the one thing to rule them all and in the darkness bind them), let's distinguish between such a definition and the Christian understanding of what it is to be civilized.

True civilization is a culture animated by the transcendental trinity of the good, the true, and the beautiful. The authentic presence of goodness is love and its manifestation in virtue. The authentic presence of truth is to be seen in the culture's conformity to reason, properly understood as an engagement with the objective reality beyond the confines of egocentric subjectivism. The authentic presence of the beautiful is a reverence for the beauty of creation and creativity, properly perceived in the outpouring of the gratitude and wonder which is the fruit of humility. A society informed and animated by such a culture is truly civilized.

A civilized man is not animated by a desire to shape himself into an image of his "self," which is itself unknowable, but by a willingness to allow himself to be shaped into an image of the perfect Person beyond himself. Responding to Christ's trinitarian description of Himself as the Way, the Truth, and the Life, a civilized man surrenders himself to the Way of Virtue (Love), the Truth of Reason, and the Life of Grace (Beauty). In short and in sum, civilization manifests itself in the conforming of the will of man to the will of the Giver of all goodness, truth, and beauty.

What is civilization? It is the conforming of the heart of humanity to the Heart of Christ, even if, as was the case with pre-Christian cultures, the unknown Christ was present in goodness, truth, and beauty and not in His Incarnate Presence. All other definitions of civilization are not only wrong but ultimately uncivilized.

Once we perceive this Christian understanding of civilization, it is evident, as Dr. Staudt illustrates in this splendid book, that the Eucharist can save civilization because the sacramental Presence of Christ is the very heart of civilization itself. As John Senior observed, "Christendom, what secularists call Western Civilization, is the Mass."[2] Christopher Dawson, in *Religion and the Rise of Western Culture*, said much the same thing, albeit less sweepingly: "The preservation and development of . . . liturgical tradition was one of the main preoccupations of the Church in the dark age

---

[2] Senior, *The Restoration of Christian Culture* (Ignatius Press), 15–16.

that followed the barbarian conquest, since it was in this way that the vitality and continuity of the inner life of Christendom which was the seed of the new order were preserved."[3]

It is through this liturgical tradition and through the grace of the sacraments that the life and light of Christ are made manifest in human culture. The Eucharist is, therefore, together with the other sacraments, the spiritual conduit through which Christ becomes present in history. This Christ-life made present in the sacraments is the very light by which we see and the life by which we live.

As Cardinal Ratzinger reminds us, "One is Church and one is a member thereof, not through a sociological adherence, but precisely through incorporation in this Body of the Lord through baptism and the Eucharist."[4] Furthermore, as Ratzinger explains, it is through this Eucharistic presence that Christ is present in His Church:

> The Eucharistic Presence in the tabernacle does not set another view of the Eucharist alongside or against the Eucharistic celebration, but simply signifies its complete fulfillment. For this Presence has the effect, of course, of keeping the Eucharist forever in church. The church never becomes a lifeless space but is always filled with the presence of the Lord, which comes out of the celebration, leads us into it, and always makes us participants in the cosmic Eucharist. What man of faith has not experienced this? A church without the Eucharistic Presence is somehow dead, even when

---

[3] Dawson, *Religion and the Rise of Western Culture*, 43.
[4] Ratzinger, *The Ratzinger Report*, 47.

it invites people to pray. But a church in which the
eternal light is burning before the tabernacle is always
alive, is always something more than a building made
of stones. In this place the Lord is always waiting for
me, calling me, wanting to make me "Eucharistic." In
this way, he prepares me for the Eucharist, sets me in
motion toward his return.[5]

Although Cardinal Ratzinger's words refer to the presence
of the Eucharist in individual tabernacles in individual
churches, they also apply to the Eucharistic presence in the
Church herself throughout all the centuries, from the first
to the last. Taking the cardinal's words and applying them
to history, we can say that history "never becomes a lifeless
space" as long as the Eucharist is present "but is always filled
with the presence of the Lord." The presence of the Eucharist in history makes history itself and all those participating
in it "participants in the cosmic Eucharist." It makes time
a participant in eternity. It makes the past and the future
coeval with God's omnipresence. History "without the
Eucharistic Presence is somehow dead." It is Christ, present
in the Sacrament, who gives life. It is He who makes all
things new—and all things beautiful. It is His Eucharistic
Presence in all ages which, as J. R. R. Tolkien proclaimed,
is "the one great thing to love on earth": "Out of the darkness of my life . . . I put before you the one great thing to
love on earth: the Blessed Sacrament. . . .There you will find
romance, glory, honor, fidelity, and the true way of all your
loves upon earth, and more than that: death: by the divine

---

[5] Ratzinger, *The Spirit of the Liturgy*, 90.

paradox, that which ends life, and demands the surrender of all, and yet by the taste (or foretaste) of which alone can what you seek in your earthly relationships (love, faithfulness, joy) be maintained, or take on that complexion of reality, of eternal endurance, that every man's heart desires."[6]

Joseph Pearce

---

[6] Carpenter, *The Letters of J. R. R. Tolkien*, 53–54.

Introduction

Source and Summit
of the Christian Life

"Come to me, all who labor and are heavy laden,
and I will give you rest" (Mt 11:28).

O f all the problems that we face today, what is the most destructive? There are so many things we could list: the decline of the family, political division, disease, poverty, and war. "We want God!" This was the answer chanted by the crowd of more than a million people gathered in Warsaw to welcome Pope Saint John Paul II back home when Poland still suffered Communist oppression. With all the suffering and challenges they bore, the Poles still recognized the fundamental problem facing a secular world: the absence of God. If God is most important for human flourishing, turning away from Him presents the greatest problem the world could ever face.

Pope Saint Paul VI called our distance from God the "drama of our time," framing it as a "split between faith and culture."[1] God has become absent from our culture because we have built a self-sufficient world based on science and technology

---

[1] Pope Paul VI, *Evangelii Nuntiandi*, no. 20.

that thinks it has no need of the divine. Pope Benedict XVI pointed out that this split enters also into the lives of Christians who, even if they attend Mass, still "live as though God did not exist."[2] He called this a kind of practical atheism, a secularism that undermines the Christian life by holding faith as "irrelevant to daily life." Many Catholics live no differently than pagans except for fulfilling their Sunday obligation. They keep their faith private rather than sharing it with the world.

The Eucharist, however, manifests God's radical presentness to us, not as an idea or remote divine being, but as coming to each one of us personally. Secularism ultimately fails because we need God to be happy and complete. God wants to help us, to be a part of our life, not to impose Himself on us but to live within us, helping us to become truly alive and truly happy. The Eucharist is not simply a belief. It is an encounter, an abiding communion with the living God, who is meant to shape us both inwardly and outwardly in our entire life. We need the presence of God physically with us, abiding in us, and shaping everything that we do. The Eucharist is something to be lived, a mission and plan that will lead us toward true happiness and fulfillment.

As members of an individualistic culture, we prize our independence. Enhancing the fallen tendency we inherited through original sin, we are inclined to rely even less on God and more on ourselves. We all know, however, that we are broken, that material things do not satisfy us, and that we do not really understand our own lives. Jesus invites us to experience healing and rest and to find meaning in Him. He is the one who gives

---

[2]   Pope Benedict XVI, General Audience, November 14, 2012.

us what we so desperately need and cannot find anywhere else. He invites us into communion with Him: "Abide in me, and I in you. As the branch cannot bear fruit by itself, unless it abides in the vine, neither can you, unless you abide in me. I am the vine, you are the branches. He who abides in me, and I in him, he it is that bears much fruit, for apart from me you can do nothing" (Jn 15:4–5). On our own, we falter. With Christ, we will see fruit blossom in our lives, not only for ourselves, but for those around us. Attached to the vine, we will flourish and can share the fruit that Jesus grows in us with others. Yes, the Eucharist is both our life and "the life of the world" (Jn 6:51).

And therefore, the Eucharist needs to extend beyond our Sunday obligations to become the foundation for our entire lives and for our civilization. The Blessed Sacrament can set a spiritual fire aflame in our secular culture, giving it life by rekindling the sacred within it. Because God is our maker and redeemer, we simply cannot be happy and fulfilled without Him. The branches wither without the vine. The Eucharist is the answer to our culture's problems, and as it brings healing and life into us, it also sends us out into the world as agents of this transformation. If we allow it, the Eucharist truly can save our civilization, bringing renewal from the inside and eventually growing to build an entire way of life.

Encountering Jesus in the Eucharist

The Eucharist forms the center of Catholicism—the heart of the Church's faith and life—because it makes Jesus present to us every day within the Mass. Despite its absolute importance, the frequency with which Catholics experience the Eucharist can make it easy to overlook its supernatural power. It can be helpful to take time to reflect anew on the Eucharist and its ability to draw us into an encounter with God. Jesus presents Himself to us in the Eucharist as the source of an ongoing revelation of His identity and a way of drawing us, His disciples, into a deeper friendship. We can see this happening from the first moments of the Church.

For instance, on the day of the Resurrection, two disciples journeyed from Jerusalem to the town of Emmaus and began talking with a stranger along the way. They discussed the recent death of Jesus, and the stranger explained the prophecies from the Old Testament that pointed to the suffering and death of the Messiah. The evangelist Luke describes the culmination of this encounter:

> So they drew near to the village to which they were going. He appeared to be going further, but they constrained him, saying, "Stay with us, for it is toward evening and the day is now far spent." So he went in to stay with them. When he was at table with them, he took the bread and blessed, and broke it, and gave it to them. And their eyes were opened and they recognized him; and he vanished out of their sight. They said to each other, "Did not our hearts burn within us while he talked to us on the road, while he opened to us the scriptures?" (Lk 24:28–32)

Luke shows us the way that Jesus makes Himself present and known to us after His resurrection. The disciples could not recognize Jesus in the world any longer, but they encountered Him in the breaking of the bread, which completed their contemplation of Scripture (which is continued in the liturgies of the

Word and the Eucharist during the Mass). After His death and
resurrection, Jesus remains present to His Church, although He
manifests Himself in a new way through the sacrament of His
body and blood. And because He is present to us in this way,
He continues to act, sometimes speaking to us and calling us in
dramatic ways. This dynamic presence can be seen in the life of
Saint Giles, who was celebrating a Mass for the emperor Charlemagne, particularly in reparation for his sins. As depicted by an
anonymous painter, in answer to the saint's prayers, Jesus sent an
angel down to the altar to reveal a hidden sin of the emperor in
order to bring him to full repentance. Through the celebration
of the Eucharist, Jesus is not distant from His Church, as He
directs and guides it from within. The Eucharist will change our
lives if we allow its graces to penetrate our minds and hearts.

Master of Saint Giles, *The Mass of Saint Giles*, c.1490–1500

This living Eucharistic presence enlivens the Church by drawing us into an encounter with Christ, shining light into our dark world. The Mass provides an antidote to our brokenness, sin, and suffering, giving us a healing balm that restores our life. Saint Elizabeth Ann Seton provides a powerful example of the Eucharist's transforming effect in our lives, as it drew her to the Catholic faith while sojourning in Italy. Imagine her pain, becoming a widow in a foreign country without family nearby, feeling deep pain and isolation, alone with her five children. She sought solace in prayer and began attending Mass at a local parish. She was struck by the deep piety expressed toward the Eucharist, and she discovered, to her surprise, God's presence speaking to her there. She had found a new center, a place of refuge, and she embraced the Catholic faith. Saint Elizabeth Ann Seton discovered not only the heart of the Catholic faith in the Eucharist but the heart of reality itself: the God who made us has come into the world and given Himself for us.

Jesus entered the world, born of the Virgin Mary, two thousand years ago, and He continues to do so at each Mass, showing His great desire to enter into communion with us. Jesus offers this intimacy to each of us. Like Saint Elizabeth, it was during a dramatic moment when I came to know Jesus through His real presence in the Eucharist. I was thirteen years old and had just switched over to Catholic school after a traumatic incident in public school. The parish priest, in welcoming me to the school, invited me to serve at the early morning Mass on the anniversary of his ordination. Although I had received my first Communion, I was not a practicing Catholic, and this was the first Mass I had attended in some time. That dark morning, I encountered Jesus in the Eucharist and received a call to enter into friendship with Him. Jesus manifested His true presence to me, and I felt a clear invitation to follow Him. My life changed at that moment, as Jesus made it clear that I had found my true home and purpose in Him.

The Eucharist in the Plan of Life

Although this book focuses on how the Eucharist shapes life and culture, it is important to begin with some definitions. What do Catholics believe about the Eucharist and the Mass? The Eucharist is the sacrament of Jesus Christ's body and blood. A sacrament, in turn, is a visible sign of an invisible, spiritual reality. It not only symbolizes that reality but, as an efficacious sign, a sacrament actualizes this spiritual reality by making it tangibly present. The sacraments use signs to manifest how God's grace flows through them. Water, the physical sign (or matter) of Baptism, represents the cleansing of sin, and when combined with the form (the words prayed), it actually does cleanse. The signs of the Eucharist, bread and wine, symbolize that God wants to feed us, and when the form is spoken over them by the priest, they truly become the body and blood of Christ. Catholics do not believe that the Eucharist symbolizes Jesus; rather, Catholics believe that the bread and wine really and substantially become His body and blood, making Him present during the Mass.

Catholic belief in the sacraments makes a truly remarkable claim: that God uses material means to bring about supernatural transformation. He uses material means because He made us as material-spiritual beings (or body-soul unities) who learn even the most profound truths through our senses. In establishing the sacraments, Jesus drew upon the whole history of Israel, fulfilling its ritual and deepening it as a means of transmitting grace. It is only in Jesus's gift of Himself on the cross, removing our sin and bestowing new life on us, that the logic of the sacraments can be seen. When approached in faith, the sacraments unite us to Jesus's saving work, becoming a means of remembrance, presence, and grace.

God also has a plan for each person within the overarching story of salvation history. He established the sacraments to accompany and guide us throughout life, marking our major transitions, growth, and mission. Rogier van der Weyden captures this spiritual journey in his famous altarpiece of the seven sacraments, depicted as stations throughout a church with the cross at the center. Within this sacramental order that guides our life, we must first receive Baptism. This sacrament bestows on us the grace of salvation—the forgiveness of sin and the infusion of God's life—along with the gift of adoption, which offers a share in Jesus's own sonship. These graces are strengthened in Confirmation, which offers a renewed outpouring of the Holy Spirit. The Eucharist completes initiation into the Christian life by enabling regular communion with God and providing the spiritual food needed to nourish the soul. When sin wounds this communion, it can be renewed in the sacrament of Penance (or confession), as well as the Anointing of the Sick, which prepares us for eternal life in the midst of sickness and death. Finally, there are two sacraments of mission that draw those called into service of the Church. The sacrament of Holy Orders, by which men participate in Christ's own headship and service, provides access to and oversight of all the sacraments. Matrimony serves the Church by bringing forth new believers and then nurturing that Christian life within the walls of the domestic Church.

Rogier van der Weyden, *Seven Sacraments Altarpiece*, 1445–50 (side panels altered in size for uniformity)

The Eucharist stands as the greatest of the seven sacraments because it not only communicates God's grace but makes the Son of God truly present to us in tangible fashion. The word "Eucharist" means "thanksgiving," continuing the prayer of thanks that Jesus offered to the Father at the Last Supper, the night before His suffering and death on the cross. During a meal with His disciples, He celebrated the first Eucharist by offering His body and blood in sacrifice under the form of bread and wine to be eaten. In the Eucharistic celebration, known as the Mass, this offering of Jesus is remembered in a way that makes His action present through the ministry of the priest. Thus, the Eucharist constitutes our supreme act of worship by enabling us to share in Christ's offering of Himself on the Cross. The Mass also enables us to enter into communion with the Son of God, receiving His body, blood, soul, and divinity, the divinity He shares with the Father and the Holy Spirit. The deepest reality of the Eucharist, therefore, is communion with the Triune God: resting in the bosom of the Father, through Christ, and in the Holy Spirit.

How the Eucharist Shapes Culture

The Eucharist forms the heart of Catholic culture as the vital center that inspires and animates the life of Catholics. Without it, culture would simply comprise a collection of outward forms built up by our best efforts. Through the Eucharist, Christian culture becomes an outpouring of the divine life into our own lives that, when accumulated across the lives of believers, takes root also in communities. The word "culture" may sound complex or arcane, but it could be defined simply as a "shared way of life." It is made up of the beliefs, relationships, practices, customs, and societal structures that give a communal sense of identity and purpose. It can exist on a micro level within a family, school, parish, or local community, as well as on a macro level for a region, a country, or groups of nations, becoming a civilization, a higher form of culture that shapes education, economics, and politics. It can also exist within religious groups that share beliefs and practices even when dispersed across distinct ethnic or national cultures. Culture is a fundamental necessity for human life. We need to live in communion with others and jointly pursue common goods, both earthly and spiritual.

As Catholics, we can live our faith more easily with the help of others and by instantiating it within concrete practices. Aidan Nichols helps us to consider this by contrasting the Middle Ages to our own culture: "It is surely clear that the medieval Christian at prayer was supported culturally by a whole way of life. . . . By comparison, the contemporary Christian experiences an absence of God in the world today."[3] He refers to our culture as a spiritual desert that makes it difficult to sustain faith and prayer because of the lack of any general support and the existence of so many obstacles. We can feel like the faithful in Achille Beltrame's depiction of a church during the First World War, trying to stay focused on Jesus even as everything gives way around us.

Achille Beltrame, *Christ Wounded by Bombs*, 1918

---

[3]   Nichols, Christendom Awake, 204.

The historian Robert Lewis Wilken makes a case for why we need Christian culture to sustain faith. He defines culture as "the pattern of inherited meanings and sensibilities encoded in rituals, law, language, practices, and stories that can order, inspire, and guide the behavior, thoughts, and affections of a Christian people."[4] Flowing from this understanding, he asks, "Can Christian faith—no matter how enthusiastically proclaimed by evangelists, how ably expounded by theologians and philosophers, or how cleverly translated into the patois of the intellectual class by apologists—be sustained for long without the support of a nurturing Christian culture?" He asks this rhetorical question to highlight the fact that our culture is missing the fertile soil where faith can grow and flourish. Our deficient soil points us to a pressing need to recover a Christian culture, even on the micro level, to support the life of faith. Wilken argues that "nothing is more needful today than the survival of Christian culture, because in recent generations this culture has become dangerously thin." Yes, Christian culture has become too thin, and Catholics urgently need to begin living their faith more robustly than ever before. If not, our Christian culture will wilt and be overtaken by a pagan society.

A consideration of culture may help us understand why it is so difficult to live the faith and why so many people fall away from it. They are experiencing the split between how they live and what they believe, a split that can run right through us. It is true that Jesus did not come to earth

---

[4]   Robert Louis Wilken, "The Church as Culture," *First Things*, April 2004, https://www.firstthings.com/article/2004/04/the-church-as-culture.

to form a new culture, understood as a distinctive way of eating, dressing, and living for one ethnic group or nation. Rather, He proclaimed the Kingdom of God, a new radical inbreaking of God's presence in the world through His own entrance into it. Jesus's mission, however, should transform culture, shaping how Christians live in the world by bringing us into communion with God. Jesus's teaching on culture could be summarized with His words from the Sermon on the Mount: "Seek first his kingdom . . . and all these things [such as eating, drinking, and dressing] shall be yours as well" (Mt 6:33). Christian culture flows from faith, seeking to put God first and to live in accord with that faith.

Pope Benedict XVI offers a powerful example from history to demonstrate this point. Following the collapse of the Roman Empire, Benedictine monks left the world and entered the monastery to seek God (*quaerere Deum*) and unintentionally—through their dedication to the word and to their work—laid the foundations for a whole new civilization in Europe built around this search.[5] Christians create culture not by making culture the goal but by putting God first in life and ordering everything else to Him. Culture draws what we believe and how we live together. For this reason, Pope Saint John Paul II challenged us by pointing out that "a faith that does not become culture is a faith not fully accepted, not entirely thought out, not faithfully

---

[5] See Pope Benedict XVI, "Meeting with Representatives from the World of Culture," Collège des Bernadins, Paris, September 12, 2008, https://www.vatican.va/content/benedict-xvi/en/speeches/2008/september/documents/hf_ben-xvi_spe_20080912_parigi-cultura.html.

lived."[6] Faith is not abstract belief, but rather, it is meant to shape the everyday life of Christians, living out what we believe concretely in communion with others. Worship should be at the heart of our culture, shaping our thoughts, how we spend our time, the space in which we live and pray, and how we form relationships.

Putting God first provides a sound basis for forming the material elements of culture as well. Faith stimulates our work and prayer so that through them, we can guide the world to reach toward its true goal, found only in God. We need to look at Christian culture especially though the lens of the Eucharist because it is the center of the Christian life. Within it, spirit transforms matter, God enters the world, and creation offers back to the Creator a prefect work of prayer and sacrifice, offering to the Father a gift of infinite value. God draws our own work into this sacrifice, sanctifying our humanity and life, and shapes our life and work through it. According to the same logic, the Eucharist transforms not only our soul but our entire life, as we incarnate its fruits in our family life, work, and leisure. Christian culture as a whole becomes sacramental, an expression of the divine bursting forth from God's entrance into the world.

Can the Eucharist Save Civilization?

Can we save civilization? The question itself can seem overwhelming when we look at the magnitude of the world's problems. It is hard enough to come to terms with the problems in one's own life. Who can save civilization? There is

---

6   Pope John Paul II, *Christifideles Laici*, no. 59.

only one person ultimately who can do it: God, who has made Himself present to us in the Incarnation and continues to do so in the Eucharist. He is the answer and remedy for every problem that society and man faces. The difficulty is, however, that Jesus does not necessarily want to save civilization. He does not care about all of the structures that we have built up *per se*. He cares about each and every soul living in the world. He did not come into the world for the sake of civilization. He came into the world for our sake.

He does want us, through the power of His grace, to do our part in serving others and building up a world that focuses more on what truly matters. As we have seen in Jesus's teaching on the Sermon on the Mount, if we focus on God first, then everything else will fall into place. The Eucharist can help us to save the world, although not in the way we may expect. We should not care about civilizations for their own sake—the power and wealth of nations—but as a vehicle for making the world more human in the truest sense: a civilization of love that promotes the true flourishing of the human person. It is not that civilization doesn't matter. It is true, of course, that a good civilization should help us to live a good life and a bad one will do the opposite. Christians do, therefore, need to work to transform the world in Christ. Salvation, however, remains our first priority, and only through union with Christ will our work have effect in changing the world.

It may sound overly pious to point to the Eucharist as the means of healing and rebuilding civilization, although what could serve as a more powerful source than God's own presence in the world? The Mass, therefore, lays out its own plan for renewal. The Eucharist literally contains what is most needed for renewal—in our own lives, yes, but also for our society. It is a real plan. How did Christians withstand the Roman Empire? How did we rebuild culture in the Dark Ages? What stood in the center of the culture of Christendom? Why has the Church not simply died out under the persecutions of countless modern revolutions, like so many had predicted? In all of these cases, there is the same answer, one which we could still say to the world, quoting Jesus's enigmatic saying to His disciples: "I have food to eat of which you do not know" (Jn 4:32). This is the food that gives life, a life that the world does not know about but which it desperately needs.

The Eucharist is the greatest force for change. It can and will alter us into other Christs for the world. We are not simply individuals, however, no matter how much the world tells us that we are autonomous. By eating this hidden food, God changes us so that we can, in turn, change the world, spreading the Gospel to every corner of society, not for the glory of the Church or any nation, but for the good of all people. Civilization is not simply the external mechanisms of a society. It is made up of all those living within it. Civilization can be saved by changing and transformation those living within it, by a creative minority or the conversion of multitudes. By transforming our lives, He will begin the work of transforming our family, our parish, our work, and, over time, even our civilization.

A Eucharistic Revival: Immersed in the
Source and Summit of the Christian Life

The Eucharist truly provides life for our soul and our way of life, or "culture." It is not enough to believe in the Eucharist, or even to receive this sacrament regularly. Jesus wants the Eucharist to reshape our humanity, to transform who we are and how we live every day, and even to save our civilization. This book, therefore, proposes how Catholics can *live* the Eucharist. Nothing is more important for the Christian life than living with, in, and through Jesus, flowing from our Eucharistic encounter and communion with Him. The Church expresses the supreme importance of the Eucharist by calling it "the source and summit of the Christian life." The phrase may be often quoted, but it is important to ask what it truly means and how it applies to life. The Eucharist is the source through which God comes into the world, the summit in our ongoing encounter with Christ at the Mass, and the heart of the Christian life that emerges from this encounter. Jesus comes within our souls to transform us so that we in turn may shape the world with the grace He gives us. This book contains three parts that will explore the Eucharist in these three dimensions.

First, it examines the source in how Christ has manifested His presence throughout history in the culture of Israel and the Church. This first section uses the story of salvation history to examine how Jesus established the Eucharist as the source of the spiritual life in communicating His presence to the world. It demonstrates how the Eucharist perfects humanity's religious nature through the covenants of the Old Testament and by the Word becoming flesh, which continues to shape the Church's life. Second, it presents the summit, the way in which the faithful come into contact with this presence through the Mass and sacraments to transform our lives. It looks at how the Eucharist forms the summit of the Christian life through the communion with God it offers. It describes how heaven breaks forth into the world through the Mass, making the sacrifice of Christ present, drawing believers into a communion of love and requiring serious preparation to form the right disposition to receive Christ. And third, it details the Christian life, the way in which we live in response to this encounter, transforming the world and building up culture and civilization. This last part presents how the Eucharist constitutes the heart of the Christian life, the animating impulse of the life of the disciple. It explains how the Eucharist shapes the Christian life by forming a Christian culture, shaping time through prayer, extending into the world, and guiding all actions through charity.

These parts or sections could also be described through the words "recognize," "receive," and "respond." First, it is important to recognize the truth of the Eucharist and how God presents it within the story of salvation history. Second, the Christian encounters its reality in prayer, receiving it sacramentally within the Mass. Third, it shapes the Christian life, making it a response to Jesus's presence within the sacrament of His love. This response should be the beginning of a revolution to reorder all things in our lives and, consequently, in the world. The Eucharist should form the basis for a whole way of life that also includes a way of seeing.

The Eucharist shapes the Christian imagination, leading the believer to see all things differently, not just some things. To foster this renewed perspective, this book will present many images within its narrative that capture a Eucharistic and sacramental vision ordered toward the building up of Christian culture.

It is important to note that this book will be appear during the three-year Eucharistic revival led by the United Stated Conference of Catholic Bishops (USCCB). The Church in the United States was rocked by a 2019 Pew survey that revealed only one third of Catholics in the country believed in the true presence of Jesus in the Eucharist. The bishops realized that after decades of declining church attendance, ineffective catechesis, and a breakdown of the Christian life, something must be done. Under the leadership of Bishop Andrew Cozzens, the USCCB released the following plan:

> Over three years, every Catholic diocese, parish, school, apostolate, and family is invited to be a part of renewing the Church by enkindling a living relationship with the Lord Jesus Christ in the Holy Eucharist. This Revival launches on the Feast of Corpus Christi, June 19, 2022. Over the next three years, dioceses will host Eucharistic Congresses and processions. Parishes will increase or begin Eucharistic Adoration. There will be a revival of faithful adherence to the liturgical norms in all their richness—the *ars celebrandi*. Families and friends will gather in small groups to learn and pray together. Filled with the flame of charity from the reception of Jesus in the Eucharist, missionary disciples will go to the

margins, recognizing the mystery of Jesus' presence in the poor. All of this will culminate in the first National Eucharistic Congress in the United States in almost fifty years.[7]

The Eucharist is *literally* the lifeblood of the Church, for Christ's very body and blood flows through those who receive Him worthily. Hopefully, this three-year effort will spark longer-term renewal leading to stronger faith in Jesus's Eucharistic presence and a life lived in accord with it. Belief is tied to practice. Sadly, it is hard to believe in Jesus's true presence when we do not act like He is truly present, and His presence does not seem to change our lives.

The book's particular contribution can be seen in applying the doctrine and spirituality of the Eucharist toward forming a Christian way of life or culture with the Blessed Sacrament at its center. A Christian civilization will be only as strong and vibrant as its devotion to the Eucharist. This book also forms a short guide for understanding, entering into, and living through the Eucharist. Its key contention focuses on how the Eucharist must shape how we live and order all we do to God in thanksgiving and for His glory. If we as Christians respond to this call, it will not only change our own lives but also reverberate throughout the world and become a source of hope for our civilization.

---

[7]   National Eucharistic Revival, "About the Revival," accessed 3/19/22, https://eucharisticrevival.org/about/#about-the-revival.

PART I

The Source: The Foundations of Christian Culture

The Eucharist is the living and transforming presence of Jesus in the world. More than a symbol or even a doctrine, it makes Christ's body and blood present on earth in tangible fashion. We call it the source of the Christian life because through it, Jesus draws us into communion with Him. Likewise, Christian culture flows from it as the transforming source for how we live in the world, continuing our communion with God in all the details of life. Catholics believe that grace builds upon nature. Taking this principle seriously helps us to recognize the way God reveals Himself to us and saves us, working in and through our nature to elevate and perfect it. The same could be said for culture. Faith cannot exist in isolation from culture; rather, faith builds upon it, taking root in how we live in order to sustain us. Our faith cannot exist in a vacuum; it takes up our humanity and cultural life to heal and perfect them.

There is a paradox latent within Catholic culture, however. The Kingdom of God is not found in eating and drinking, as Saint Paul says (see Rom 14:17), and yet it is only in the spiritual eating and drinking of the Eucharist that we have life (see Jn 6:53). God cannot be contained by any earthly reality, even as He enlivens the details of our life and gives them meaning through communion with Him. The divine food and drink of the Eucharist truly form Christian culture and give deeper meaning to everything that we do, including our ordinary eating and drinking. As Saint Paul explains, "So, whether you eat or drink, or whatever you do, do all to the glory of God" (1 Cor 10:31). Everything we do should express our faith because Jesus sanctified the physical world and human life in the Incarnation. He uses human language and the fruits of human culture to communicate and achieve His mission. Likewise, He uses the food and drink of His presence to extend the Incarnation into the life of his followers. The Eucharist unlocks the dynamics of culture, truly perfecting nature, creating the deepest community, and making the goal of human life, God Himself, present on earth.

The first section of this book examines the foundations of Christian culture in relation to the Eucharist. Its four chapters take for their organization the four major components of culture identified by the great historian Christopher Dawson. A culture consists in (1) a particular place and environment, which serves as its natural foundation, (2) a group of people united by familial and societal bonds, (3) social practices and institutions that shape how people live, and (4) the religious and moral beliefs that guide the ultimate direction of a culture.[1] Following these four components, the first chapter begins with the natural world as

---

[1]   Dawson, *The Age of the Gods*, xiii–xiv.

the foundation for all human culture, looking at how the Eucharist is rooted in the natural world. The second chapter examines how God called one particular people to be His own and established cultural and religious practices for them, which foreshadowed the Eucharist in many ways. The third chapter presents the Incarnation as the center of human history, forming a mystical body of believers that comprises the core social reality of the Christian life, giving rise to distinctive Christian practices. The fourth chapter looks at how belief in the true presence of the Eucharist led to a theology and spirituality centered on the Holy Eucharist, placing the sacrament as the center of Christian culture and civilization.

1

Nature and Culture:
Soil for Supernatural Food

E ven if we must eat to survive, we also love to eat. In addition to nourishing us, food draws us together and literally adds flavor to life. Given its centrality, it should not be surprising that God uses food to engage us. The Eucharist is a sacred meal, making Jesus present to us in a tangible way as He gives us Himself to eat and drink. Like the Incarnation—the Son of God taking on flesh—the Eucharist makes God accessible, reaching us in a way that speaks to our nature and our experience. Grace builds upon nature, and so even as we explore the theology of the Eucharist, we need to start with its foundations in the world and within our own nature. Most fundamentally, we can recognize the Eucharist as food and drink that gathers the community together to celebrate. It not only builds upon nature but also includes the works and customs of human culture. In this chapter, we will look at how the Eucharist builds upon our nature as rational, eating beings who meet God through physical signs.

Why We Eat

Have you ever wondered why we eat? It may be necessary to sustain the body, to be sure, but we eat for other reasons as well. We are not simply animals, as rational and spiritual beings. We express our inner life in everything that we do, including how we eat. We eat for social reasons just as much as for bodily ones. Food unites us, forming a center for family life and serving as a touch point for conversation and friendship. Not only that, food and drink have played a central role in religion from the beginnings of history, making a sacrifice of the things that we need to sustain us, as well as using them as a means of celebration through religious festivity.

The story of the Eucharist arises out of the story of mankind, bound up with salvation history stretching from Genesis to Revelation. God created humanity with a view toward the Eucharist, knowing it would fulfill our ultimate destiny of entering into communion with Him. God created us not only in His image but also as a physical sacrament in the world. As physical beings, we express the interior life of the soul through our outward actions. The human person is a unity of body and soul who manifests inner thoughts and desires through outward, bodily action. The body should express the inward beauty and love of the person to others, making our communication and action a source of communion. This extends even to how we eat.

Human beings are icons of God, and our bodies are sacraments of the soul's life in the world. This sacramentality reaches to the outward actions of human life. Eating and drinking, therefore, entail more than simple nourishment of the body. Leon Kass shows this in his book *The Hungry Soul* as he looks at how the etiquette and rituals related to eating have shaped communal life and constitute an important force in civilization: "The meal taken at table is the cultural form that enables us to respond simultaneously to all the dominant features of our world: inner need, natural plentitude, freedom and reason, human community, and the mysterious source of it all. In humanized eating, we can nourish our souls even while we feed our bodies."[2] Eating aims to sustain the soul along with the body.

In the Bible's sacramental vision, earthly realities symbolize hidden, spiritual ones. This includes drinking, which God uses to express blessing and joy.[3] According to the Psalms, God gives "wine to gladden the heart of man" (Ps 104:15). In Psalm 23, God provides a banquet in which the psalmist notes His abundant generosity: "my cup overflows" (Ps 23:5). Drinking is also a sign of thanksgiving and praise: "I will lift up the cup of salvation and call on the name of the LORD" (Ps 116:13). The abundance of wine offers an image of the bounty of the earth and God's blessing of His people within it. God reveals to us how eating and drinking relate to our spiritual nature and should even draw us into worship. In establishing the Eucharist, God provides spiritual food for the soul's nourishment. This shows how worship fulfils us as a complete person. God communicates His grace in a way that touches our nature, with its materiality and senses—touch, smell, and taste—perfecting us as rational animals, not disembodied angels.

---

[2] Kass, *The Hungry Soul*, 228.
[3] For how this includes beer, see Staudt, *The Beer Option*.

Alexander Coosemans's still life *The Allegory of the Eucharist* vividly portrays the Eucharist's dependence upon food and the culture needed to fashion it into bread and wine. The painting captures the great beauty of nature's contribution to our spiritual eating and the way in which God perfects this natural foundation. Cooseman's addition of flowers and other fruits indicates how the Eucharist leads nature into its greatest moment of praise to its creator.

Alexander Cooseman, *The Allegory of the Eucharist*,
late 17th century.

Christianity opposes any dualism that would pit soul against the body, because God made us as sacramental beings. God established the sacraments to shape the growth of human life in a way that follows its natural development, as the soul matures like the body. Aquinas speaks of Baptism as corresponding to birth, Confirmation to bodily growth, the Eucharist as providing continuing nourishment, confession and Anointing strengthening in sickness, and Marriage and Holy Orders as perfecting communal life.[4] God established the sacraments to guide the overall development of the person, including our social nature, showing how grace builds upon nature. God's grace confirms the wisdom of the natural order, while elevating it to the supernatural life of friendship with Him.

Cult, Culture, and Cultivation

The story of salvation history does not exist in a vacuum. It builds not only upon human nature, as we have seen, but also upon the surrounding culture of the Ancient Near East from which God called the Israelite people. God taught the Israelites to think and worship in ways that made sense to them, while also moving them beyond the limits of pagan culture. Most importantly, He spoke to them in a personal way, revealing Himself as the one God, the Creator who made the world and who stands wholly beyond it. He made the material world, though He Himself is beyond the material; He created the plants and animals that humanity eats

---

[4]   St. Thomas Aquinas, *Summa Theologiae* (*ST*), part III, question 65, article 1.

and sacrifices, even as He has no need to be sustained by them. He is Spirit, ultimate goodness, and true perfection, revealing Himself as the great "I AM."

God speaks to reveal Himself, and His speech expresses order—the wisdom and intelligence that underlie all of creation, as we see in the days of the first creation story. God spoke, and it was made. He also created man and woman in His image with the power of speech, making them capable of dialogue with Him. Speech demonstrates how God calls man and woman to cooperate with His work of creation, as Adam names the animals in the second creation story, showing His dominion over them. The power of speech becomes fundamental not only for creation but also for God's recreation, as this effective power serves as the foundation of the sacraments as well. Creation remains subject to God's wisdom and power, for when Jesus speaks, "This is my body," it comes to be. In the sacraments, natural symbols meet human speech, expressing its form, manifesting God's continued power over His creation.

In addition to speech, work expresses the mission God gave to the first man and woman: "And God blessed them, and God said to them, 'Be fruitful and multiply, and fill the earth and subdue it; and have dominion'" (Gn 1:28). We can see the same command more concretely in the creation of Adam: "The LORD God took the man and put him in the garden of Eden to till it and keep it" (Gn 2:15). God did not make the world in static completion, because He intended humanity to play a role in its perfection. This entails providing for our material needs—including procuring food and drink—that entails the physical work of shaping the earth.

This mission also includes building culture to provide for all of the social and spiritual practices that lead to a complete way of life.

Culture entails the perfection of the goods of nature and human life to form a complete way of living. The Second Vatican Council affirms that "man comes to a true and full humanity only through culture, that is through the cultivation of the goods and values of nature."[5] It forms a necessary part of life in working together to form society in order to both realize basic necessities and pursue the highest goods. Earthy things, however, must be ordered toward the glory of God, which is made clear when God establishes the "rest" that culminates His work of creation. Rest points us to the reality that work finds its ultimate purpose in worship, extending beyond man's efforts. Human culture, as a way of life, finds its heart in religion because it is only the divine that provides the deepest perspective on what truly matters and how everything else should be organized to reach the transcendent goal of life. Creation and human life were ordered toward a good beyond themselves, one that can only be realized in the supernatural life of God.

The public worship of liturgy (literally "the work on behalf of the people") expresses the deepest thrust of culture by providing public and communal expressions of worship. Even in the ancient, pagan world, liturgy provided a foundation for civil life by ordering society to the divine and providing the richest expression of communal life and festivity. For early Christians, the Mass constituted the central act of

---

[5] Second Vatican Council, *Gaudium et Spes*, no. 53.

worship, enabling them to enter into a supernatural society of the people of God. This new way of celebration shaped time differently by ordering the week around the Lord's Day and inspiring service to neighbor by sharing the fruit of their work in the charity that flowed from the Eucharist (as we see in Acts 2 and 4). As the Christians broke the bread of Christ's body, they shared their own bread with the poor. The monks continue to witness to the original radicality of Christian culture by forming a way of life centered on prayer. Saint Benedict called his monks to focus above all on the *Opus Dei*, the work of God, that would give life to the community and their cultural mission of work within the monastery and to those without through hospitality. As the title of John Rogers Herbert's painting indicates, the monks' prayer becomes their work (*laborare est orare*), perfecting God's creation through the extension of the worship into work. The monastery seems to fit within a natural setting, perfecting it and enabling it to give greater glory to God.

John Rogers Herbert, *Laborare Est Orare*, 1862

The Eucharist, therefore, builds upon the nature and history of humanity's religious and cultural life. It makes use of the fruits of culture and offers them in sacrifice to bring about communion with God. It draws upon God's creation—wheat and fire, grapes and yeast—as well as their development through work, by making them into bread and wine. The Eucharist requires cultivation and craft, as it uses the products of human culture, which draw upon and perfect the natural world. In the Eucharist, God accepts the offering of these gifts and supernaturally transforms them into spiritual realities, the body and blood of Christ. Thus, we find in the Eucharist the full perfection of nature and culture as they reach their true goals of giving honor to God and bringing about communion with Him.

Food in the Fall

The story of creation teaches us the essential truths of creation and humanity, while also pointing to a fundamental disorder that has crept into human life, distorting our relationship with nature, one another, and God. Interestingly, in Genesis's account of the Fall, the first sin occurs through eating. The devil, in undermining the goodness of humanity, sought to supplant the right order of physical things to human reason and the soul's order to God. He played on the weakness of humanity's physical nature, pitting obedience against the allurement of a physical temptation: "So when the woman saw that the tree was good for food, and that it was a delight to the eyes, and that the tree was to be desired to make one wise, she took of its fruit and ate; and she also gave some to her husband, and he ate. Then the eyes of both were opened, and they knew that they were naked; and they sewed fig leaves together and made themselves aprons" (Gn 3:6–7). In this act of eating, Eve followed the devil in putting herself before God in deciding for herself what was good or evil. As depicted by Tintoretto, Eve draws Adam into her sin, sharing the forbidden fruit in a deadly meal. Instead of using food properly for communion, it becomes an act of rebellion that ruptures the original harmony of creation.

Tintoretto, *The Temptation of Adam*, 1550

This act of disobedience flips the universe upside down. The command to abstain from eating the fruit signifies the need to put God before the gift of His creation. Adam and Eve, however, subordinated God to a physical object, desired for its outward delight and the appeal of gaining knowledge. God, however, is the one to bestow wisdom, just as He provides the fruit of the earth; it cannot be grasped and taken but must be accepted at the proper time. Adam and Eve could have eaten the fruit of all other trees, which, significantly, included the tree of life, through which God had given them freedom from corruption. By grasping what lay beyond their proper reach, they lost the rest of the fruit of the garden, including the tree of life that they no longer deserved.

Spurning God's gifts, our first parents fell subject to a number of curses. Adam and Eve, along with their descendants—now without the protection of the garden—would suffer the grind of daily life at enmity with creation, in spiritual warfare with the serpent, experiencing the pains of labor from work and childbirth, and falling into rivalry and division between themselves. In the Fall, all of humanity lost the original holiness and justice that orders human life to God and creates a right ordering within the person and with one another. Instead, life became marked by concupiscence, the desire for material things, a fixation on lesser goods above higher ones. This created pride and disorder, putting one's own desires before God and others, as well as a breakdown of peace and communion. Society lacked the communal order of right worship to unite people in seeking the highest good together.

Concupiscence now shapes how we eat and drink by creating an attachment to the pleasure found in material things meant to serve the body. Gluttony and drunkenness provide stark examples of this slavery to material goods, using them for selfish pleasure rather than for giving glory to God and for entering into communion with others. Even more seriously, idolatry makes a false offering of natural things, turning away from the worship of the true God and toward material ends. Idolatry seeks to bribe or manipulate false gods into providing protection or favors, continuing Adam and Eve's futile attempt to grasp control of the divine. God did not abandon humanity to this distortion, however. In working out His plan of redemption, God returns eating and drinking to right order and uses them within a renewed worship. In the book of Revelation, God indicates that He will restore the fruit lost in the Fall: "To him who conquers I will grant to eat of the tree of life, which is in the paradise of God," with "its twelve kinds of fruit" (Rv 2:7; 22:2). God promises the ultimate perfection of humanity, including our need for food. In preparation for the complete restoration of heaven, God established a supernatural food, using bread and wine to offer His own divine life as food.

2

Feeding a Holy People:
Celebration and Memory
in the Old Testament

How does food form community? Food unites people not simply by fulfilling a physical necessity; it gathers people together for fellowship, celebration, and even worship. Even though the Fall led to isolation and conflict, God responded by restoring unity through a new culture that would foster communion with Him. God established a new people, His chosen nation, to stand against the fallen practices of the world and to prepare for the coming of the Savior. While the last chapter looked at the foundations of culture in nature, this chapter will present how God established one particular culture by forming His own chosen people. In forming the nation of Israel, God feeds His people miraculously and teaches them how to relate to Him in worship in order to establish communion. Worship constituted the center of Israel's life, foreshadowing the coming sacrifice of the Eucharist through covenants, ritual, and religious feasts. In many ways, the Old Testament points to Jesus's establishment of the Eucharist that will bring about a new covenant for God's people.

Food within Israel's Covenant

After the Fall left humanity in isolation, unmoored from its Creator and from communion with one another, God set in motion a whole movement to restore unity by forming a holy people. Just as the first sin arose through eating, so did this restoration draw upon food as a source of communion, celebration, and worship. Food's role can be seen in the first moment of religious worship in the Bible: the story of Cain and Abel. Both brothers offer food in sacrifice, as Abel brought choice portions of his possessions, "firstlings of his flock and of their fat portions," while Cain offers "the fruit of the ground" (Gn 4:4, 3). By emphasizing the quality of Abel's sacrifice, the text implies that Cain skimped in his sacrifice. Indeed, God told Cain that he did not do well in his offering. This misdirected worship, not honoring God in proper fashion, leads, also, to the first bloodshed of the Bible, as brother turns on brother. Turning away from God leads to disorder in human relationships, a reality magnified with the rise of society (as Cain founds the first city). Cain's descendants only increased in wickedness, falling into idolatry.

Idolatry reverses the order of Creation, turning our attention to created things over the transcendent. God made the world to lead us to Him, as we see in Saint Paul's Letter to the Romans: "Ever since the creation of the world his invisible nature, namely, his eternal power and deity, has been clearly perceived in the things that have been made" (Rom 1:20). The world should glorify God, drawing humanity into a cosmic liturgy, with man at the center, offering its first fruits back to the Creator. Worshipping the signs rather than their Creator turns humanity downwards toward the world and inward, remaining focused on oneself. Stuck in pride and subject to demonic influence, pagan ritual sought to manipulate and control the mysterious force underlying nature rather than embracing a humble service of God. The Tower of Babel provides the best evidence for a broken culture, which sought to storm the heavens through man's own efforts.

God responded to this prideful idolatry not with destruction but with renewal, including the cleansing waters of the Flood. Rather than storming the world by force, He quietly issued an invitation to one man, Abraham, chosen as the father of a new nation. Through this people, God established a new way of life centered on friendship with Him and guided by true worship. To restore culture, it was necessary first to put things right with God. From Abraham's obedience, breaking from his family and city, a new community could emerge to give public expression to God's commandments and worship. The new people of Israel would be founded on faith, following from Abraham's initial trust, entering into a covenant with God. It was God's own initiative and promises that founded this people, calling Israel to abide in covenantal fidelity by maintaining proper worship and moral uprightness.

What did Israel need for the establishment of this new culture? First, it needed an identity given to it by God as a chosen people to whom He uniquely revealed Himself. Israel was entrusted with a great responsibility in receiving this knowledge. Second, this identity gave them a mission, their deepest purpose. In response to God's call, they were entrusted with a priestly function in returning material goods to their right order to God, using them to glorify God, not to pursue their own honor and pleasure. Third, they needed a place to live, for land was necessary in order to sustain their culture and for the material goods needed to worship God. And fourth, Israel required particular practices to give shape to their way of life as a holy people. God provided all of these things over time, although we can see a clear beginning in the covenant He enacted with Abraham. God speaks to Abraham of his identity as the father of this new nation; He asks him to make a sacrifice of animals; He promises him the holy land; and He speaks of the actions of his descendants and how they will be liberated from slavery. The promised land provides a concrete symbol of the covenant itself: "On that day the LORD made a covenant with Abram, saying, 'To your descendants I give this land'" (Gn 15:18). Like Eden, God intended it as a place of protection and to serve as a kind of temple to manifest His presence in the world.

Flowing from the land, food cannot be forgotten in the formation of this new culture. Essential to the formation of any covenant was the religious ritual that would bind people together, including oaths and sacrifice. To seal this pact, a covenant meal would be celebrated as a sign of unity and friendship. The clearest biblical example of this can be seen in the covenant enacted between Isaac and Abimelech: "'We see plainly that the LORD is with you; so we say, let there be an oath between you and us, and let us make a covenant with you, that you will do us no harm, just as we have not touched you and have done to you nothing but good and have sent you away in peace. You are now the blessed of the LORD.' So he made them a feast, and they ate and drank" (Gn 26:28–30). We see a similar pattern of covenant ritual in Abraham's life, most prominently in his encounter with the priest-king of Salem, Melchizedek, the first of many instances of the sacrifice of bread and wine. Bread, as a daily staple, stands for food itself, the blessing of the land that comes from God's providence. Wine serves as an even stronger sign of God's blessing, bringing more joy and celebration than water. Together they constitute a sacred meal, offered in an unbloody manner, symbolizing communion through shared food and drink. Melchizedek, a priest-king chosen by God and not by any tribal inheritance, offers this blessing to Abraham in a way that foreshadows the Passover, the bread of the presence, and Jesus's own offering at the Last Supper.

A meal also features prominently in one of Abraham's most profound encounters with God as he waits upon the Lord who appeared to him in the form of three men (see Gn 18). Even though God had promised Abraham an heir through Sarah, the patriarch tried to force its fulfillment by fathering the son of promise through Hagar, taking her as a concubine. In response, the Lord gave Abraham circumcision as a penitential sign of the covenant and appeared to him shortly afterward by the Oakes of Mamre to renew the promise of the true heir. Although three travelers visit Abraham, he speaks to them singly as "the Lord" and offers them "a morsel of bread" and prepares a calf for them to eat. God visits Abraham and renews the promise in the context of a meal. The Russian iconographer Andrei Rublev clearly captures both the Trinitarian and Eucharistic dimensions of the scene. The three angels, while identical in their features, can be distinguished by their clothing. The angel representing the Son is seated in the center, gazing at the Father, with the head of the sacrificed calf before him, representing his own future sacrifice and Eucharistic flesh, which is the focus of the Holy Spirit, who transformed the gifts through His presence. The image beautifully portrays the fellowship we have with the Trinity through the Eucharist.

Andrei Rublev, *The Trinity*, early 15th century

The sacrifice and communion offered to Abraham were incomplete, however. In Abraham's final test, God asked him not to withhold his son but to make an offering to Him, challenging his faith in God's promise to raise up a nation through his offspring. Isaac himself carries the wood up the mountain, Mt. Moriah (which tradition places as the site of the future Temple). When Isaac asks about the sacrifice, Abraham rightly answers that God Himself would supply the ram for a sacrifice, which He does at the very moment that Abraham raises his knife. God clearly points to a more perfect sacrifice to come that He Himself would supply. Through Abraham's willingness to offer his beloved son, God provides a sign that He will provide His only Son, His beloved one, as the perfect sacrifice, which will be made accessible to God's people through another covenant meal.

God formed Israel as a people by establishing a covenant with them, sealed by ritual sacrifice and festive meals. Worship, more than anything else, united them as a distinct people devoted to the one, true God. Sacrifice, in particular, manifests God's preeminence over created goods. It also united Israel in common ritual action and the festive meals that arose from its sacrifice. Israel's worship and ritual continued to renew its covenantal relationship with God, as can be seen in circumcision, the initiation into the community of God's chosen people. Through ritual action, the covenant was remembered and accepted on a personal level to enter into and share in its blessings.

The Central Feast of Israel's Redemption

Israel's core identity solidified in its redemption from slavery. Within two generations of Abraham, Israel lived in exile from the promised land. In ending Israel's slavery in Egypt, God clearly made Himself known not simply as the God of the covenant of Israel's ancestors, Abraham, Isaac, and Joseph, but as the One who transcends all other beings: "I AM." This name shows God to be the fulness of life—Being and life itself—who will give Israel a share in His life by saving and nourishing them. The act of liberation from slavery manifests God's supremacy over pharaoh and the gods of Egypt, whom He humbles through the plagues, teaching Israel that He is the supreme Lord of all. As God's plan for their liberation unfolds, we see how the foundational elements of covenant in sacrifice and meal are drawn into Israel's salvation.

God established a central feast to enact Israel's salvation and to serve as a commemoration for future generations. The Passover constituted the key event that formed Israel as a nation, establishing it as a people redeemed from slavery. Gathered in the home marked with the blood of a lamb, safe from the angel of death afflicting the Egyptians, the family ate a meal that included the flesh of the sacrificed lamb, bitter herbs, unleavened bread, and, according to Israelite tradition, four cups of wine. The lamb was slain in the place of the firstborn sons, with its blood as a sign of God's mercy and its flesh consumed as a household. It was necessary to eat the flesh of the lamb, not simply to sacrifice it, as an act of partaking of the victim who died on behalf of the family.

The Passover manifests that God offers His covenant as an act of mercy, offering ritual signs as a way of entering into and abiding within it. The importance of the Passover event transcended the night of the tenth plague. As we see in the week-long celebration of the feast of unleavened bread, begun by

Passover, it served as an annual opportunity for each family to remember and experience ritually the redemption offered by God to Israel. "This day shall be for you a memorial day, and you shall keep it as a feast to the LORD; throughout your generations you shall observe it as an ordinance for ever. . . . And you shall observe the feast of unleavened bread, for on this very day I brought your hosts out of the land of Egypt: therefore you shall observe this day, throughout your generations, as an ordinance for ever" (Ex 12:14, 17).

The festivity of Israel's redemption must be celebrated by following generations because they too needed to experience its fruits: the formation of Israel as God's chosen people with the laws and liturgical life that flowed from the Exodus. As a sign that the Passover begins a new life for Israel, God stated that the annual Passover feast would begin its new year. Time would revolve around the central feast of Israel's identity as God's chosen and redeemed people, shaping an enduring and concrete memory.

God continued to feed His people, even after the festival had ended. Giving His people food and drink show His lordship and care, serving as a sign of how their culture depended directly on Him. After crossing the Red Sea, God miraculously provided drink, making bitter waters sweet and even drawing it forth from the rock. He offered food as well, giving Israel both meat and manna, the bread that came down from heaven. This miraculous food, a "fine, flake-like thing," one of the clearest foreshadowings of the Eucharist, not only fed Israel but manifested the presence of God: "I have heard the murmurings of the people of Israel; say to them, '. . . you shall be filled with bread; then you shall know that I am the LORD your God'" (Ex 16:12). Not only caring for their bodily needs, God sought to create trust by providing this food, revealing Himself as the true head of His people, even though the Israelites would continue to groan and rebel throughout their forty-year sojourn. Christians recognized in manna a clear sign of the Eucharist, as Dutch painter Bouts depicted in host-like form, with God providing bread from heaven. In response, he depicts how the Israelites gather it reverently to respect its divine origin. As Jesus made clear in John 6, however, the new manna, His own flesh, will greatly exceed the old.

Dieric Bouts, *The Gathering of Manna*, 15th century

God redeemed the Israelites from slavery, although He then had to teach them what to do with their freedom. The Law, in particular, would give His chosen people their defining character as a nation, teaching them how to live and worship. At Mt. Sinai, the Lord, acting as king and lawgiver, bestowed the Ten Commandments, the key ordinances of justice, along with liturgical rituals. Moses sealed the covenant with his people, once again using blood: "And Moses took the blood and threw it upon the people, and said, 'Behold the blood of the covenant which the LORD has made with you in accordance with all these words'" (Ex 24:8). Like the Passover, this sealing of the covenant mediated by Moses culminated in a meal, eaten before the Lord: "They saw the God of Israel; and there was under his feet as it were a pavement of sapphire stone, like the very heaven for clearness. And he did not lay his hand on the chief men of the people of Israel; they beheld God, and ate and drank" (Ex 24:10–11). At Sinai, we see how the enacting of a new covenant drew together guidance on how to live, worship, and celebrate.

The Mosaic covenant taught Israel how to worship God through visible actions and signs, understood as a shadow of the true worship of heaven. In instructing Moses how to set up the tabernacle, the meeting place of God in the wilderness, God told him to follow the model He showed to him, which the Letter to Hebrews calls "a copy and shadow of the heavenly sanctuary" (Heb 8:5). Using visible signs, God manifested heaven to Israel and called them to an encounter with Him. God established within Hebrew culture a manifestation of His own divine glory. The story of Exodus serves as a pivotal moment in God's plan to establish a more perfect communion with Him through sacrifice and meal, opening the heavenly sanctuary to His people.

The Liturgical Life of Israel

The creation of Israel as a chosen people helps us to glimpse the true heart of culture. More than ethnicity, language, or location, culture arises out of a common belief and ritual. Religion truly forms the heart of culture because it unites people in the pursuit of the highest good, one that should bring peace and order within the community. God established the nation of Israel as a kingdom of priests endowed with a liturgical culture to abide in a right relationship with Him and to serve as agents for the sanctification of the world. Worship truly was the center of their culture, shaping daily life and providing an annual rhythm through the liturgical cycle of feasts.

On the holy mountain of Sinai, God gave the Israelites three central feast days to revive their memory and to teach them how to relate rightly to God, offering Him the fruits of Israel's work:

> Three times in the year you shall keep a feast to me. You shall keep the feast of unleavened bread; as I commanded you, you shall eat unleavened bread for seven days at the appointed time in the month of Abib, for in it you came out of Egypt. None shall appear before me empty-handed. You shall keep the feast of harvest, of the first fruits of your labor, of what you sow in the field. You shall keep the feast of ingathering at the end of the year, when you gather in from the field the fruit of your labor. (Ex 23:14–16)

These feasts—Passover, Pentecost, and the Feast of Booths—would serve as times for the entire people to gather and worship, reaffirming their identity in relationship with God. Israel's worship would also shape each individual day at the tabernacle (the tent of God's presence and forerunner of the Temple), which contained the ark, the table for the bread of the presence, and the lampstand of six branches and seven lights.

The bread of presence (or showbread), which God commanded to be set "on the table before me always" (Ex 25:30), provides another important foreshadowing of the Eucharist. To show forth His presence in the tabernacle, God chose bread and wine rather than animal sacrifice, with unleavened bread and bowls of wine being laid out on an altar before the holy of holies. As Brant Pitre points out, the word "presence" would most literally be translated as the bread of the "face."[6] Mysteriously, the altar of presence would be taken out for the people to see during Israel's feasts, when God commanded Israel to gather in His presence or "to see his face." In addition, the tabernacle also contained an altar for the sacrifice of burnt offerings and, further outside of the inner areas, an altar of incense, a bronze basin for washing, and a broader court. This division of areas would continue in the building of the Temple. In order to minister in this holy place, men would have to be set apart and anointed as priests and would need to dress in a sacred and priestly manner. The connections to Catholic worship should be clear, with God's presence manifested through bread and wine,

---

[6] Pitre, *Jesus and the Jewish Roots of the Eucharist*, 121.

making present the sacrifice of Christ's own flesh, which has washed us clean of our sins, and which we approach through the ministry of priests and accompanying solemnity, such as incense.

Israel's ritual worship sought to overcome idolatry by directing earthly goods rightly to God.[7] The priests, drawn from the tribe of Levi, led Israel through many forms of sacrifice, some ordered to atone for sin and others for thanksgiving and peace. These offerings included animal sacrifices (burnt, peace, and sin offerings), grain (cereal), wine, and *shekar* (translated as "strong drink," a beer-like substance). Sacrifice could also create communion and fellowship, as peace offerings entailed eating and rejoicing before the Lord (see Dt 27:7) and the offering of thanksgiving would involve eating unleavened cakes. In this way, Israel offered their goods to the Lord, showing His preeminence and ordering earthly things to Him. It also formed a pattern of worship that shaped their life, with daily, sabbath, monthly, and festival offerings, offering each in "its due season" (see Nm 28). In his great tapestry design, "The Triumph of the Eucharist," Peter Paul Rubens devoted a whole scene to Old Testament sacrifice, seeing in the animal and grain sacrifice a sign of the

---

[7]   The ordering of Israel's worship to overcome idolatry can be seen in the timing of the revelation of detailed ritual instruction. God commanded more detailed sacrifice following the worship of the golden calf. Initially, it seems, Israel would have relied upon the priesthood of the firstborn in the family, but in response to this idolatry, God enacted a new priesthood through the tribe of Levi, the tribe of Moses that had largely remained faithful by refusing to worship the golden calf. This hereditary priestly tribe would lead Israel in worship, attempting to keep Israel from falling into idolatry again by practicing the sacrifices commanded by the Lord.

Eucharistic sacrifice of Christ's flesh in the form of bread. The new sacrifice would bring God's presence to earth in a definitive way, symbolized by Ruben's depiction of the ark of the covenant in the top right of the tapestry.

Peter Paul Rubens, *The Sacrifice of the Old Covenant*, 1626

Prayer, especially through a pattern of liturgical ritual, helped shape the Israelites' distinctive and holy way of life and led them to encounter God in His dwelling place. To direct this liturgy, God gave His priests specific commands related to purity along with others who stood before His presence. These commands reveal how God requires a break from normal life, a setting apart in ritual purity, that points to a further call to holiness. Ultimately, the Israelites were called to live a life distinct from the world. Israel's holiness should renew the world itself, something we can see concretely in how Israel treated the land given by God. Although humanity lost the life of paradise in the Garden, Israel received a mission to renew creation and care for the poor through a cycle of Sabbath days and years, a participation in God's own rest that points to the very purpose of creation itself. Every seven years, God commanded Israel to leave the land fallow and allow the poor to eat its fruit. The jubilee year after a Sabbath of Sabbath years (the fiftieth year) entailed a release of all debtors and slaves. The weekly Sabbath day and cycle of Sabbath years pointed Israel to something greater than their own work—the eternal rest of God—that called them to trust in God to provide for all their needs.

God formed a distinct culture in Israel, one guided by a unique form of worship that rejected idolatry and immorality. Worship, since it brings us into relation with God, should always remain the priority—over work, political success, and even life itself. Israel continued to struggle with this reality, however. After settling into the promised land, Israel remained tempted to turn away from the worship given to them by God to embrace the idolatry of its neighbors, forgetting the feasts and profaning the Sabbath. To refocus Israel's attention and to foster unity of worship, the tabernacle became permanently fixed in the Temple in Jerusalem, set in motion by David and built by his son Solomon. Here, Israel gathered to celebrate the three great feasts, as well as the festival of the First Fruits, Trumpets, and the Day of Atonement. The Temple provided a place that shaped the Isrealites' consciousness, teaching them that God dwelt in their midst and that they had a duty to serve Him there.

The Temple reminded them that God was close to them and called them into a communion with Him.

The worship of the Mosaic covenant, however, could not fulfill perfectly its ultimate objective of making Israel into a holy and priestly people, bound in close friendship with God and witnessing to the surrounding nations. Because of the Israelites' repeated infidelity to God, He withdrew His presence from the Temple, manifested in the shekinah cloud, and sent Judah into exile, while the northern tribes of Israel were scattered and destroyed. The Jews did not preserve the memory of the covenant faithfully; they did not abide the Sabbath days and years and had fallen into an outward observance of ritual that missed the heart. Therefore, God promised a new covenant through the prophet Jeremiah: "I will put my law within them, and I will write it upon their hearts" (Jer 31:33). The Lord also promised that He Himself would come to the Temple (see Mal 3:1) and He Himself would shepherd them and feed them (see Ez 34), bringing about a new redemption of His people akin to the exodus of old (see Is 43). In coming to His people, God promised to initiate a new feast in Jerusalem for the salvation of His people, redeeming them not just from earthly slavery but from death itself:

> On this mountain the LORD of hosts will make for all peoples a feast of fat things, a feast of wine on the lees, of fat things full of marrow, of wine on the lees well refined. And he will destroy on this mountain the covering that is cast over all peoples, the veil that is spread over all nations. He will swallow up death for ever, and

the Lord GOD will wipe away tears from all faces, and the reproach of his people he will take away from all the earth; for the LORD has spoken. It will be said on that day, "Lo, this is our God; we have waited for him, that he might save us. This is the LORD; we have waited for him; let us be glad and rejoice in his salvation." (Is 25:6–9)

The coming of a new Messiah (the anointed king) would fulfill these great prophecies and enable Israel to serve as a light to all the nations. God would renew His people, enabling them to worship in spirit and truth and to be gathered from all the nations into the Church, the new Israel. God would take up the foundation He laid in Israel of calling a people to Himself grounded in worship of the true God. He would feed His people not simply with the flesh of a lamb or even with miraculous bread from heaven; He would give them His own life to eat.

3

The Incarnation:
The Abiding Center of All Things

Why did God make the world or call a chosen people to Himself? He did not simply make us to exist alongside of Himself but to come to a deep and abiding supernatural union with Him. To bring this about, the Word of God, the one through whom the world was created, entered into His creation and took on flesh. The Word became flesh to teach us, save us, and, ultimately, feed us with His very self. The Eucharist is Christ, the one who died on the cross for us in a new Passover, giving to us His flesh and blood to eat and drink. In establishing the Eucharist, Jesus, the incarnate Word, did not disregard the culture of Israel, as He took it up and transformed it. Christians build upon the legacy of Israel by maintaining a liturgical culture of prayer and worship that forms how we relate to God. The Creator came into His creation, embracing human life and culture, making it His own and expressing Himself through it. God uses the goods of human culture—human words, relationships, and actions—to establish a new way of life. Christian culture consists essentially, even today, in the continuing presence of the Son of God in the world, made accessible through the physical signs of the sacraments. This presence draws a new people together, a new Israel, not a single race, but a mystical body of believers.

The Incarnation: An Interior and Cultural Revolution

More than anything else, the Eucharist concerns presence. The God who is completely beyond all things and who cannot be comprehended or contained in any way, the One who made the universe and holds it into being, entered into His creation to transform it from within. Even with all the blessings that God had given His chosen people, He still longed to give them something much greater. God did not simply form Israel to live as a nation among other nations, even with its Temple dedicated to divine worship; He wanted Israel to become His temple, embodying His presence in the world itself. He would bring this about by coming to His people to establish a more direct communion by feeding them with His own divine life, establishing His presence within them.

The Incarnation—the Son of God's enfleshment—truly set off a spiritual revolution in the world. Jesus entered the world for a rescue mission, divinizing human life from within. Rather than seeking the meaning and purpose of our existence blindly by ourselves, the Word of God shone His light into our darkened world and sought us out. John's Gospel describes this vividly: "The light shone in the darkness," he said, because "the Word became flesh and dwelt among us" (Jn 1:5, 14). In the Greek original, the words "dwelt among" literally mean that He "pitched

His tent among us." This tent, Jesus's humanity, is the new tabernacle where we meet God, the place of God's presence in the world and the new Temple. Although the nativity was a quiet and humble event, which few noticed, Sandro Botticelli's painting "Mystic Nativity" shows its monumental importance. You can see heaven breaking into the earth above the simple cave stable, with quite an

Sandro Botticelli, *Mystic Nativity*, 1500

audience of angels dancing in celebration. They know that everything had changed when God came into His own to reclaim it and transform it for Himself. Other altarpiece paintings emphasize the Eucharistic implications of the nativity—that Jesus was born in Bethlehem, which means the house of bread, and was laid in the manger, a place of eating—and show the baby Jesus's flesh presented as a gift for the world. Even with Botticelli's cosmic background, you can still see the shepherds led by the angels to adore Jesus, whose flesh is being revealed to the world. They imitate Mary's own adoration of her Son, as if He is being presented to them on the altar of sacrifice, anticipating how He will give His flesh for the life of the world.

If the Incarnation makes God present on earth, then the Eucharist continues this presence so that the Word becomes flesh for us at every Mass. In taking on our flesh, the Word established a bridge between God and humanity, overcoming the abyss that arose since the Fall. Although humanity had turned its back on God, making Him seem far off and inaccessible, the Son drew so near to us that we could even see and touch Him. He manifested God in the world as a perfect icon of the Father, enabling humanity to reclaim its own identity as made in His image and likeness. Although Adam and Eve had grasped after God, wanting to seize the divine life, Jesus offered this life to us freely, drawing God down to our humanity so that we could, in turn, be lifted up to Him. The Incarnation brought about a spiritual revolution, recreating humanity from within, with the divine life acting as a leaven, a leaven that continues its transforming work in His Eucharistic presence.

This interior revolution has broad implications for our understanding of nature and culture. God's entrance into the world affirms and elevates the goodness of creation, reclaiming the world as His tabernacle. The Incarnation makes the material world an expression of God Himself, as He takes human nature as His own and dwells within the world. It also shapes the way in which we engage nature, using it to build a sacramental culture. The work of culture seeks to make an inhospitable wilderness into an ordered garden, bringing order and beauty to the natural world through human artifice. God has sanctified this work, suffusing His own divine life into it through His labor (the Creator continuing His work on earth). God sanctified the world as He humbled Himself to walk over its soil, eat food, wear clothing, and build with wood and stone. By elevating these ordinary goods of life, Jesus enabled culture to take on a supernatural character, suffused from the inside with a new divine principle. By imitating Jesus, Christians animate the work of culture through their prayer, enabling it to take on a heavenly orientation—working not just for sustenance but for the glory of God.

We can identify a tension within a Catholic approach to culture, however. If God came to earth to lead us to heaven, we could ask if the Incarnation made culture less important. Israel, for instance, had been so focused on the gift of a physical place—the promised land—and cherished their physical descent from Abraham. Jesus initiates a people born not of flesh and blood but of God (see Jn 1:13), seemingly relativizing one of the key aspects of culture. Rather than organizing His followers into a distinct nation living in a physical location, Jesus's disciples live as exiles and pilgrims on earth. On the other hand, culture becomes more important through the Incarnation because God's presence in the world bestowed a sacramental dimension upon it. The physical world, human relationships, and culture become in Christ a means of reaching God, a means of charity. Most especially, the sacraments embody this affirmation of culture in a supreme way, as Jesus established them as a physical means, drawing upon the works of culture, for communicating His divine life and grace to us.

The Incarnation stands at the center of all history as its great turning point. All that came before prepared the universe for the entrance of its Creator. All that follows must be seen as a working out, through many difficulties, of the spiritual restoration it initiated. At the heart of this restoration stands Jesus's abiding physical presence in the world. His own flesh, both when He walked on this world and now hidden in the Eucharist, offers the greatest leaven for transforming the world. He offers this flesh as a gift to heal and sanctify His followers, changing them from within by uniting them to His body. Jesus's presence in the world constitutes the "good news," a radical message of great joy, but also one that should inspire awe and wonder. The Creator who revealed Himself to Israel as the great I AM, too awesome even to be named, has become man and enables Himself to be seen, heard, touched, and even to be eaten.

Jesus Feeds His People

The Incarnation changes everything, giving the world and human life their deepest meaning, and leads us to see everything differently through a sacramental lens. God's coming into the world and taking on flesh reveal how spiritual realities require physical manifestation. Everything takes on a deeper significance by God drawing close and sanctifying it. This certainly includes human life itself, which God affirmed in a fundamental way by joining it to Himself. In choosing to reveal Himself to us through our own humanity, God granted a higher dignity to everything on earth. The interior change He works in us does not take us away from our humanity but enables us to appreciate its goodness more fully. Because we are material and social beings, we need to express our faith and relationship with God in outward and physical ways. All the details of our life matter to God and should be ordered to God to give Him glory, and this right ordering then opens up the path to our own happiness, the deepest fulfillment of our being,

The sacramental vision of life also applies to how we eat and drink. God uses these outward actions as a sign of salvation and as a means of drawing us into communion, as we see in Jesus's own teaching and ministry. Jesus spoke of His teaching as new wine, which required new wineskins. The new creation He inaugurates, making us into new wineskins, goes hand in hand with the new food and drink of His flesh and blood with which He wants to fill us. This nourishment renews our humanity by creating a new internal vigor to follow Christ. Having been reborn, we cannot simply keep eating and drinking the same mundane things. Jesus will provide the food and drink we need—a new bread from heaven and a water from the rock of our hearts that, when softened, wells up to eternal life. To give this food and drink, Jesus inaugurated a new liturgical feast, proclaiming a holy year—a jubilee—"to release captives" and also to celebrate the coming of the kingdom of God.

As with any real celebration, the wedding feast of salvation requires food and drink, which Jesus will provide from His very self. To show the celebratory nature of His mission, Jesus performed His first miracle, beginning His public ministry, at a wedding feast at Cana. Read simply, Jesus responds to the needs of the hosts by providing for their lack of wine, saving them from embarrassment. More mystically, however, we see the rich significance of the transformation of water into wine. The wine points to Jesus's hour that He mentions in the passage, the hour when He will pour out His blood on the cross. As gruesome as it may sound, this act carries a marital significance because on the cross, Jesus gives Himself to His bride, the Church. From this gift of His body and blood on the cross would also come the gift of the Eucharist, bringing about a complete union with His bride. We also can recognize at Cana the same kind of transubstantiation (one thing becoming another) that happens in the Eucharist, showing Jesus's power in miraculously providing the drink needed for the wedding feast of the kingdom. The entire miracle witnesses to the festal nature of salvation, teaching us that our salvation is a love story in which God marries His people.

Jesus began His ministry by providing a supernatural drink. Many Jews hoped the Messiah would bring earthly prosperity, and the devil played on this expectation by tempting Jesus to focus on producing tangible results to satisfy human needs. The devil tempted Jesus to focus primarily on providing for bodily sustenance, when he said,

"Command these stones to become loaves of bread" (Matt 4:3). Jesus replies, however, that "man does not live by bread alone," as the body must become subordinate to the good of the soul (Mt 4:4). Although the kingdom does not consist of ordinary food, Jesus does direct us to pray in trust that the Father will provide us with bread. In the Our Father, we pray for our "daily bread," the daily sustenance we need. The prayer means more, however, as Jesus wants us to pray for the bread that will truly satisfy our souls. We translate the Greek word *epiousion* as "daily," although its meaning is much more mysterious and profound, literally meaning "super-substantial." Even though we need ordinary food every day to survive, expressed by the prayer for bread, God wants to give us a "super-substantial" bread to feed us for the journey to heaven. In this sense, the Our Father clearly speaks of the Eucharist: asking the Father to feed us with a supernatural and heavenly bread.

Jesus, as the good shepherd who feeds His sheep, provides both ordinary and supernatural bread to His flock. On two different occasions, moved with pity, Jesus fed large crowds by multiplying loaves and fish.[8] He performed this miracle at the time of the Passover and foreshadowed the Last Supper by taking the bread, breaking it, and blessing it. The flesh of fish is added to the bread perhaps as a sign that through the bread of the Eucharist, Jesus will offer His own flesh to eat. Immediately following this miracle, Jesus enters the synagogue at Capernaum,

---

[8] The crowds, recognizing the great miracle and having been satisfied in body, at least, caved into the temptation of looking to Jesus as the earthly Messiah and sought to crown Him king. They see the miraculous supply of food as a sign that a new Moses has arrived.

where He reveals in more detail the true food that He wants to provide. Unlike the loaves that were just consumed, Jesus teaches them to desire a more satisfying food, namely Himself: "I Am the bread of life." Jesus referred to Himself as the new manna or bread from heaven that he would give.

> Your fathers ate the manna in the wilderness, and they died. This is the bread which comes down from heaven, that a man may eat of it and not die. I am the living bread which came down from heaven; if any one eats of this bread, he will live for ever; and the bread which I shall give for the life of the world is my flesh. . . . Truly, truly, I say to you, unless you eat the flesh of the Son of man and drink his blood, you have no life in you; he who eats my flesh and drinks my blood has eternal life, and I will raise him up at the last day. (Jn 6:49–51, 53–54)

These words startled the crowd and even caused some of Jesus's followers to abandon Him. Not only did they sound cannibalistic, they also entailed the drinking of blood, which was strictly forbidden in the Law: "You shall not eat the blood of any creature, for the life of every creature is its blood; whoever eats it shall be cut off" (Lv 17:14). Some Christians, even today, try to explain away His words, because Jesus said, "the words that I have spoken to you are spirit and life" (Jn 6:63). Nonetheless, He did not tell His disciples to come back and not to worry, as if eating His flesh was simply an image or allegory. He emphasized, rather, the reality of His statement, using the word "indeed": "For my flesh is food indeed, and my blood is drink indeed. He who eats my flesh and drinks my blood abides in me, and I in him" (Jn 6:55–56). He allowed the scandal of His words to remain because eating His flesh was central to His mission of inaugurating a new Passover, with Himself as the new Paschal lamb, the source of "spirit and life" in us.

Jesus institutes the new Passover—the Paschal Mystery of His death and resurrection—beginning at the Last Supper, itself a Passover meal.[9] This new Passover meal contained many elements of the original, though it also diverged in significant ways. Using the traditional format and prayers, Jesus established a new covenant in His blood and offered His own body and blood to be consumed as the means of entering into this covenant. Just as the Passover lamb must be sacrificed and then eaten, so Jesus offered His own body and blood, offered on the cross, to be consumed within the context of a ritual festive meal. He states clearly in offering the bread and wine, "this *is* my body," and "this *is* the blood of the new covenant," bringing His words of being the bread of life into reality. Juan de Juanes's depiction of the Last Supper shows clearly how Jesus is giving Himself to His disciples through the bread and

---

[9] Despite debates surrounding its timing, Jesus clearly celebrated a Passover meal with His disciples before His death: "I have earnestly desired to eat this Passover with you" (Lk 22:15). It appears that He celebrated it without the eating of a lamb (which nowhere is mentioned in the Gospels), because He would offer Himself as the Passover lamb during the official Passover celebration. Pope Benedict XVI explains how "the paschal *haggada,* the commemoration of God's saving action, has become a memorial of the Cross and Resurrection of Christ—a memorial that does not simply recall the past but attracts us within the presence of Christ's love. Thus, the *berakah,* Israel's prayer of blessing and thanksgiving, has become our Eucharistic celebration in which the Lord blesses our gifts— the bread and wine—to give himself in them" (Homily, April 5, 2007).

wine offered during the Passover meal, lifting up the unleavened bread while pointing to His breast. The painting captures the unity between the bread offered and Jesus Himself, clearly pointing to this moment as a gift and invitation.

Juan de Juanes, *The Last Supper*, c. 1560

Jesus established a sacrificial meal to perpetuate the new covenant within His Church. The three synoptic Gospels all make clear the enduring nature of this new covenant ritual through Jesus's command to His disciples to "do this in memory of me." Like the annual Passover meal, Jesus directs the Church to maintain a ritual memory of the events of salvation. This memory does not arise simply from remembering past actions but from a liturgical presence that makes the historical events present to us. As an action that renews the new covenant, the Eucharistic celebration constitutes the Church as the new chosen people, called together to be a priestly nation. The new Passover serves as the key Christian feast that celebrates and enacts our salvation. We participate in this salvation by consuming the Passover lamb, Jesus Himself, who gave His life in our place, saving us from eternal death.

John's Gospel, which although it does not specifically relate Jesus's words of institution for the Eucharist, gives a deeper explanation of their significance in the Last Supper Discourse. He describes the reality of the Eucharist as communion through abiding in Jesus and as living as a branch of His vine: "Abide in me, and I in you. As the branch cannot bear fruit by itself, unless it abides in the vine, neither can you, unless you abide in me. I am the vine, you are the branches. He who abides in me, and I in him, he it is that bears much fruit, for apart from me you can do nothing" (Jn 15:4–5). Abiding in Jesus is not an abstract concept, because in the Eucharist, Jesus comes to dwell in us. We receive the sap of the vine at that moment so that it can invigorate us and fill us with divine life. In this communion, we become as one with Jesus and, therefore, with His Father: "If a man loves me, he will keep my word, and my Father will love him, and we will come to him and make our home with him" (Jn 14: 23). By giving His whole self to us in the Eucharist and the entire life of the Trinity, Jesus has given us the greatest gift. A gift that allows us to abide in Him and to live our lives in divine communion.

Jesus's words "this is my body given for you" and "this is the blood of the new covenant" come to fulfillment on the cross. The Paschal lamb was sacrificed, and from His side, blood and water came forth. John stops his Gospel to assure us that he witnessed this event, "he who saw it has borne witness—his testimony is true," (Jn 19:35) and comes back to it strongly in his first letter: "This is he who came by water and blood, Jesus Christ, not with the water only but with the water and the blood. And the Spirit is the witness, because the Spirit is the truth" (1 Jn 5:6–7). From His pierced side, Jesus offers not only water for the forgiveness of sins but also life, the very blood of the Savior. By giving us His blood to drink, which the Old Testament recognized as life, Jesus offers a direct share in His own life and spirit.

Jesus's Abiding Presence

The Paschal Mystery—Jesus's great work of redemption in offering His life for us—is not something that has been left in the past. His death and resurrection mark a new beginning, initiating an even deeper communion with us. The disciples, nonetheless, want to cling to the way things were before. We see this desire in the request of the two travelers walking with Jesus to Emmaus on the day of the Resurrection: "Stay with us" (Lk 24:29). Although they did not recognize Him at first, these words speak for all of us, expressing our desire to remain in His presence. Jesus did not reveal Himself to them openly, but only in the breaking of the bread. This shows Jesus's desire to remain with His followers in a new way: through a sacramental, Eucharistic presence. During the Last Supper discourse, Jesus said mysteriously that it would be better for us if He went away (see Jn 16:7). How could that possibly be? The Eucharist shows us why. Jesus will not just exist physically near us, as He did with His disciples on earth. He will enter within us and dwell in us as His temple in the world, animating us with His own Spirit to remain with us in the most intimate way possible.

The Resurrection enables this new mode of presence, as Jesus's body is no longer bound by the limits of earthly existence, as He walks through locked doors and can appear and disappear suddenly. He maintains a real living body, however, as Jesus asks for food to eat to prove the reality of His bodily resurrection (see Lk 24:41–43). Although Jesus leaves the disciples at the Ascension, seeming to be further removed, He remains closer to them than ever in His Eucharistic presence. The disciples need a new way of seeing to recognize this presence, trusting in faith that Jesus stays faithful to His word

Jan Steen, *Supper at Emmaus*, 1668

in giving His body and blood to them. This new mode of presence is captured well by the Dutch Catholic artist Jan Steen, who shows the disciples at Emmaus in the moment when Jesus became known to them in the breaking of the bread. Jesus may have vanished from their sight, although He remained with them, still reaching out toward them. Steen shows how Jesus reaches out to them in their grief to console and enlighten them.

The disciples did not act as if they had been abandoned; rather, they continued to follow Jesus confidently, even to death. He remained present to them through the breaking of the bread. Jesus's command to "do this in memory of me" laid the foundation for Christian culture, giving the Church its key practice that shaped its memory, identity, and mission. We looked in the two previous chapters at the natural foundation for the Eucharist—in the cultivation of bread and wine—and also in the gathering of a chosen people who devote themselves to the worship of the true God. We now see them coming together within the new way of life of the Church, a community dedicated to preserving the memory of Jesus's saving actions and to the ritual that enables communion with Him. The Eucharist forms the central practice of the Church, its *raison d'etre*, or "reason for being," that continues Jesus's presence in the world, ensuring that it should remain on earth for all time. Christian culture, therefore, arises from the practices established by Jesus Himself that enable the Church to abide in His presence and to draw others into this communion.

The Church has continually celebrated the Eucharist from the earliest moments of her existence. In fact, the Acts of the Apostles gives us a blueprint of Christian culture, centered on the breaking of the bread. Already on Pentecost Sunday, the first believers enter into the central practices of Christian culture:

So those who received his word were baptized, and there were added that day about three thousand souls. And they devoted themselves to the apostles' teaching and fellowship, to the breaking of bread and the prayers. And fear came upon every soul; and many wonders and signs were done through the apostles. And all who believed were together and had all things in common; and they sold their possessions and goods and distributed them to all, as any had need. And day by day, attending the temple together and breaking bread in their homes, they partook of food with glad and generous hearts, praising God and having favor with all the people. And the Lord added to their number day by day those who were being saved. (Acts 2:41–47)

From the beginning, the Church shaped the life of Christians. Baptism opened the Christian life to them, and they were nourished by word and sacrament. Their communion with Christ flowed into the fellowship and charity they practiced toward one another. This description of early Christian life mentions the breaking of bread twice, showing the Eucharist's centrality for the community. And because of the Eucharist, these believers lived countercultural lives filled with contagious joy.

The reality that Jesus founded a Eucharistic Church can be seen in the life of the early Christian community. The Church *is* Eucharistic because of its essence as the mystical body of Christ, an ongoing sacrament of Jesus's presence in the world, constituted around the altar. Saint Paul learned the mystical unity of Jesus and His disciples vividly when Jesus told him that by persecuting His followers, he was persecuting

Jesus Himself (see Acts 9:5). Paul explained this connection in detail in his First Letter to the Corinthians, particularly in chapters 10 and 11 that show how we become one with Christ: "The cup of blessing which we bless, is it not a participation in the blood of Christ? The bread which we break, is it not a participation in the body of Christ? Because there is one bread, we who are many are one body, for we all partake of the one bread" (1 Cor 10:16–17). Jesus bestows His own divine Spirit upon believers and gives them His body to eat, literally making them one spirit and body with Him. In this way, the Eucharist forms the Church as the body of Christ, for by consuming Christ, we become one with Him and all those joined to Him, creating a bond more profound than any nation or ethnicity. This spiritual unity in faith and communion provides a strong foundation for Christian culture, giving a common life and purpose to Christ's followers.

4

A Eucharistic Church:
Christ's Body in the World

Just as religion forms the heart of culture throughout history, so the Eucharist animates Catholic culture as its living center. The Eucharist extends the Incarnation of the Word made flesh by constituting the Church as Christ's body in the world. The Eucharist helps us to understand the reason for the Church's existence: to cherish and guard Jesus's presence in the world and to foster communion around it for the salvation of souls. If Christian culture forms around the Eucharist, then we should be able to see this clearly throughout Church history. Although Christians live within the various cultures of the world, the Church has her own culture that sustains the life of believers. She establishes the most perfect culture on earth because it reaches to and actualizes supernatural goods within it. This culture arises by remembering, proclaiming, and celebrating Jesus's sacramental presence. The Church expresses her Eucharistic faith in the liturgy, doctrine, theological texts, poetry, and lives of the saints.

The Growth of a Eucharistic Church

In the Church's history, we see clearly that the successors of the apostles were faithful to Jesus's command to "do this in memory of me." A continuous story connects the community described in Acts of the Apostles to the Church of today, united in an unbroken memorial of the Eucharist. Although some Christians claim, repeating the assertions of the Reformation, that the Bible is sufficient to constitute and govern a church, they miss the historical and unbroken reality of Christ's living body in the world. Jesus did not provide a written blueprint for His Church to be taken up in some distant future, because He established a living communion to continue His presence in the world. We have testimony from the apostolic era and from the apostles' direct successors on the nature of the early Christian community and the central role of the Eucharist within it.

The Catholic and Orthodox churches have preserved an unbroken succession of bishops from the apostles. Preserving the teaching and tradition of the apostles, passing on what they received from Jesus, entails a key aspect of the Church's mission. Saint Paul speaks of tradition in a dynamic way, referring to what he received in relation to the Eucharist and also its forward motion in anticipating the Lord's return:

> For I received from the Lord what I also delivered to you, that the Lord Jesus on the night when he was betrayed took bread, and when he had given thanks, he broke it, and said, "This is my body which is for you. Do this in remembrance of me." In the same way also the cup, after supper, saying, "This cup is the new

covenant in my blood. Do this, as often as you drink
it, in remembrance of me." For as often as you eat this
bread and drink the cup, you proclaim the Lord's death
until he comes. (1 Cor 11:23–26)

The Church has remembered, proclaimed, and celebrated
this without ceasing from the time of the Last Supper. We
can receive the Eucharist only because it has been handed
down faithfully through the centuries to today, making it
our most prized and sacred inheritance.

Jesus gave the apostles the authority to teach, to heal, to
forgive sins, to baptize, and to celebrate the Eucharist. This
mission had to be continued after their deaths, and, at the
beginning of Acts, the apostles had to decide how to replace
Judas. In Saint Peter's speech, we can see how the Eucharist shaped the choice of succession, seeking someone "who
ate and drank with him after he rose from the dead" (Acts
10:41), showing the crucial importance of communion with
Jesus. They continued to select their own cooperators and
successors to perpetuate the Eucharist, as we see in Saint
Paul's letters to Timothy and Titus, whom he appointed as
bishops, and Mark's work assisting Peter. We have an unbroken line of succession that can be traced historically from
the time of the apostles down to the Church today, preserving Jesus's presence in the Eucharist.

What the earliest Christians believed about the Eucharist
is not a mystery lost to time. We have testimony from early
Church Fathers who knew the apostles and were formed by
them on the Eucharist's centrality in the life of the Church.
As Christians quickly established the Lord's Day, Sunday,

as a new Sabbath and day of the Eucharist, a burgeoning Eucharistic culture formed around the breaking of the bread according to the Acts of the Apostles. We have testimony that shows that the outline of the Mass was set very quickly, that reception of the Eucharist was accompanied by fasting and the forgiveness of sin, and that the Eucharist was brought to the sick and imprisoned to strengthen them. Although belief in Christ's true presence was articulated clearly early on, the Church guarded this teaching and did not openly discuss the details of the sacraments, a practice called the *disciplina arcana*. This secrecy itself provides a sign of the importance of the Eucharist to the early community, guarding the sacrament from profanation and ridicule.

The earliest testimony to the Eucharist outside of the Bible may come from an ancient catechism, known as the Didache (Greek for "Teaching"), from the late first century.[10] In it we find already the name Eucharist being used, Greek for "thanksgiving," the term we still use for the sacrament today. This points back to Jesus, who gave thanks at the Last Supper, and to our own Eucharistic thanksgiving to the Father for our own salvation. We also see elements of the Mass emerging, with the priest presiding over Eucharistic prayers and the congregation responding with familiar prayers such as "Amen," the Our Father, "hosanna" to the holy one who comes, and "the power and glory are yours." The Didache also testifies to other Eucharistic practices of the community: "But every Lord's day gather yourselves

---

[10] It was rediscovered only in the last 150 years and dated between the years AD 60 and 120.

together, and break bread, and give thanksgiving after having confessed your transgressions, that your sacrifice may be pure. But let no one that is at variance with his fellow come together with you, until they be reconciled, that your sacrifice may not be profaned. For this is that which was spoken by the Lord: 'In every place and time offer to me a pure sacrifice; for I am a great King, says the Lord, and my name is wonderful among the nations'" (Malachi 1:11).[11]

The community exercised oversight and authority over who could partake of the Eucharist, requiring baptism beforehand, insisting upon proper preparation, and pointing to the necessary oversight of bishops, priests, and deacons.

This hierarchical oversight proved crucial for creating a unified community and culture. Written shortly after the Didache, Saint Ignatius of Antioch's letters (c. 100) offer a unique glimpse into the Church he refers to as "Catholic." Ignatius, who perhaps was a disciple of both Peter and John, recognized the intrinsic connection between the authority of the bishop, the celebration of the Eucharist, and the unity of the Church: "Let that be deemed a proper Eucharist, which is [administered] either by the bishop, or by one to whom he has entrusted it. Wherever the bishop shall appear, there let the multitude [of the people] also be; even as, wherever Jesus Christ is, there is the Catholic Church."[12] Ignatius also recounted that there were some in the early Church who rejected the true presence of Jesus in the Eucharist and fell into heresy: "They abstain from the Eucharist and

---

[11] Riddle, "The Didache," ch. 14.
[12] Roberts, "The Epistle of Ignatius to the Smyrnaeans," ch. 8.

from prayer, because they confess not the Eucharist to be the flesh of our Saviour Jesus Christ, which suffered for our sins, and which the Father, of His goodness, raised up again. Those, therefore, who speak against this gift of God, incur death in the midst of their disputes."[13] Remarkably, we find in this letter the first clear attestation of the Church's belief in the true presence of Jesus in the Eucharist. Because of Jesus's presence, Ignatius sees eternal life as proceeding from the fellowship gathered around the bishop and experienced at the altar: "If anyone be not within the altar, he is deprived of the bread of God."[14] The Catholic Church is characterized by unity as received from the Eucharist and in turn watched over authoritatively by the bishop.

The dignity of the human person also found affirmation in the Eucharist. In the ancient world, many sects and philosophical theories denied the goodness of the body. Crucial to a Catholic way of thinking and seeing, however, stands the sacramentality of the human person as a unity of body and soul. Like both the Incarnation and the Eucharist, humanity communicates its spiritual nature through exterior expression. Saint Irenaeus of Lyons, originally from Smyrna where he knew Saint Polycarp, himself a disciple of Saint John the Evangelist, used the Eucharist to affirm the goodness of the body and God's creation against the Gnostics, who sought

---

[13]   Roberts, ch. 7.

[14]   Roberts, "Letter to the Ephesians," ch. 5. He says in chapter 7 of his "Letter to the Romans": "I have no delight in corruptible food, nor in the pleasures of this life. I desire the bread of God, the heavenly bread, the bread of life, which is the flesh of Jesus Christ, the Son of God, who became afterwards of the seed of David and Abraham; and I desire the drink of God, namely His blood, which is incorruptible love and eternal life."

to attribute them to an evil demiurge or creator. Irenaeus professes humanity's creation by the Word, who Himself took on flesh, offered that flesh on the cross, and continues to offer His flesh to nourish the body and soul of Christians in the Eucharist: "When, therefore, the mingled cup and the manufactured bread receives the Word of God, and the Eucharist of the blood and the body of Christ is made, from which things the substance of our flesh is increased and supported, how can they affirm that the flesh is incapable of receiving the gift of God, which is life eternal, which [flesh] is nourished from the body and blood of the Lord, and is a member of Him?"[15]

If the bread and wine, after they have "received the Word of God, becom[e] the Eucharist, which is the body and blood of Christ," so the Christian becomes transformed into Christ through this gift.[16] God affirms the goodness of human nature in so many ways, including nourishing our flesh with His own.

These testimonies make clear that early Christians had a strong faith in the Eucharist, seeing it as the source of God's life in them. They needed this strength since they received ridicule (including accusations of cannibalism) and even deadly persecution for their faith and dedication to the Eucharist. Attending Mass could easily lead to martyrdom. Nonetheless, Christians would mark their doors with a fish, the symbol of Christ, and risk their lives to gather to celebrate the Eucharist. One example of the early Church's use

---

[15] St. Irenaeus, *Against Heresies*, Bk 5, ch. 2.
[16] St. Irenaeus, Bk 5, ch. 2.

of the fish as a symbol for the Eucharist can be seen in the Catacomb of Saint Callixtus, where it is placed alongside little loaves of bread. The catacombs, underground burial chambers, served as the first public site where the Eucharist was celebrated, and they contain other images related to the Eucharist, such as the Last Supper.

Loaves and Fish, St. Callixtus Catacombs

Saint Justin Martyr, an apologist of the second century, actually wrote to the emperor Antoninus Pius about the year AD 155 to defend Christians. Even though they rejected the belief in pagan gods, Justin said that they were not guilty of atheism (a common accusation against Christians), for they believed in the true God who created everything. He also defended believers against the charge of cannibalism, as rumors claimed that Christians gathered at night to consume flesh and blood. He described in basic outline the nature of Christian prayer, including the Mass, where Christians consume the Eucharist "not as common bread and common drink." Just as the Word of God has taken flesh, so "the food which is blessed by the prayer of His word, and from which our blood and flesh by transmutation are nourished, is the flesh and blood of that Jesus who was made flesh."[17] Justin points to a change that happens at Mass. The food is trans-mutated or transformed into the flesh and blood of Jesus, and a similar change happens to the Christians who receive this spiritual food.

Explaining the nature of their secret gatherings, Justin described that Christians gather from all around on Sunday to read the Scriptures and for instruction. "Then we all rise together and pray, and, as we before said, when our prayer is ended, bread and wine and water are brought, and the president in like manner offers prayers and thanksgivings, according to his ability, and the people assent, saying Amen; and there is a distribution to each, and a participation of that over which thanks have been given, and to those who are absent a portion is sent by the deacons."[18] The Eucharist was important enough that even those who were absent needed to receive it. The earliest Christians believed in the real pres-ence of Jesus in the Eucharist, who makes His redemptive power present to the believer in this communion with Him. This living reality was worth sacrifice and even death. It shaped the life of the community and gave Christians their identity as members of the Body of Christ.

---

[17] Justin Martyr, "First Apology," ch. 66.
[18] Justin Martyr, ch. 67.

Culture Follows Belief: The Development of Theology

The Eucharist gave birth to a Christian culture in the life of the first Christians as they lived in accord with their strong faith in Christ's presence. Of the four elements of culture—land, people, practices, and belief—Christopher Dawson saw that belief gave the greatest unity, organization, and purpose to a group of people. Christians maintained their central practice of the Eucharist, uniting them to the Church, because of their belief in Christ's true presence within it. It is belief that shapes culture more than anything else and that gives rise to all the shared institutions, practices, and customs that make up a way of life. The Church's belief in the Eucharist would not change over time—as the early Church clearly believed in Christ's true presence—even though the articulation of its theology would develop in clarity and depth.

The Eucharist has been celebrated without fail from the time of the Last Supper, even as, through the centuries, the Church's understanding of this reality grew, expanded, and developed in continuity. Saint John Henry Newman described most clearly how an idea can remain the same and yet develop in the articulation of its details and implications. Newman sees the Church's doctrine, including the Eucharist, as all contained in seed in Christ's revelation to the apostles: "If Christianity is a fact, and impresses an idea of itself on our minds and is a subject-matter of exercises of the reason, that idea will in course of time expand into a multitude of ideas, and aspects of ideas, connected and harmonious with one another, and in themselves determinate and immutable, as is the objective fact itself which is thus represented."[19] The Church's understanding of the mysteries she celebrates has deepened, and she has provided clearer doctrinal statements to help the faithful to assent to the truths of the faith. There are a few major stages in the development of the Church's articulation of the theology of the Eucharist.

The first major stage of the theology of the Eucharist assumed a liturgical character in catechesis and preaching. The Church developed a rigorous process of initiation into the Church called the baptismal catechumenate that lasted over a period of years. The catechumenate was a time of mentorship and formation, with Lent serving as a time of intense prayer and preparation to receive the sacraments at the Easter Vigil. The details of the sacraments were taught only after they had been received, as part of the *disciplina arcana*, a protective secrecy on the precise details of the nature and celebration of the sacraments. Even preaching had to maintain this practice, as catechumens were present for the first part of the liturgy, called the Liturgy of the Catechumens, before being dismissed at the recitation of the Creed, when the Liturgy of the Faithful would begin. After the Easter Vigil, the newly initiated were given detailed explanations of the sacraments they had received in a period called mystagogy. This mode of explanation clearly follows the Church's maxim of *lex orandi, lex credendi*—the law of that which is to be prayed is the law of

---

[19] Newman, *Essay on the Development of Christian Doctrine*, 55.

that which is to be believed—with theology flowing from the Church's worship.

One example of these mystagogical discourses comes from Saint Cyril of Jerusalem (313–86), whose five talks to the newly initiated on the sacraments complete the eighteen catechetical discourses given during Lent to prepare for sacramental initiation. After explaining Baptism and Confirmation, he tells the newly initiated that they need faith to see beyond the outward forms of the Eucharist: "Consider therefore the Bread and the Wine not as bare elements, for they are, according to the Lord's declaration, the Body and Blood of Christ; for even though sense suggests this to you, yet let faith establish you. Judge not the matter from the taste, but from faith be fully assured without misgiving, that the Body and Blood of Christ have been vouchsafed to you."[20] Saint Ambrose, leading his own neophytes in Milan, gives the same assurance, teaching that grace has more power than nature: "Perhaps you will say, I see something else, how is it that you assert that I receive the Body of Christ? And this is the point which remains for us to prove. And what evidence shall we make use of? Let us prove that this is not what nature made, but what the blessing consecrated, and the power of blessing is greater than that of nature, because by blessing nature itself is changed."[21] Ambrose's teaching offers a deeply biblical foundation for the Eucharist, drawing upon Old Testament types, and seeks to lead the neophytes toward a deeper reception of the sacraments.

---

[20] St. Cyril of Jerusalem, "Catechetical Lecture 22."
[21] St. Ambrose, "On the Mysteries," ch. 9, no. 50.

Further theological development arose from the cathedral and monastery schools of Europe that laid the foundation for the university. Ordered toward the preservation and dissemination of Scripture and the Church Fathers for prayerful study, these schools eventually established a new method of study called scholasticism, drawing from the logical rigor of classical philosophy. Blessed Lanfranc and his student Saint Anselm (1033–1109), both of them serving as monks, abbots, and archbishops of Canterbury, helped develop this method of applying philosophical reasoning to questions of faith. Scholastic theology would lead to increased clarity on the nature of the Eucharist and the Mass, especially through the writings of Saint Thomas Aquinas. Scholastic methodology arose to strengthen understanding of faith, including being able to answer the objections of heresy. The denial or distortion of faith that comes from heresy actually helps the Church to develop doctrinal clarity by demanding the formulation of clearer teaching.

In the case of the Eucharist, Berengar of Tours (999–1088), a master at the school of Chartres, denied the substantial presence of Jesus's body and blood in the sacrament, leading to a heresy later known as Stercoranism. He held that the substance of the bread and wine remain after the consecration, while Jesus's presence within them is of a spiritual nature. This controversy led to the first recorded use of the word "transubstantiation" by Hildebert de Lavardin, archbishop of Tours (although the reality behind this term can be seen earlier). In the face of this theological error, the Church had to clarify that the reality of the Eucharist consists in the bread and wine truly becoming the body and blood Christ. Philosophical terms like "substance" assisted the Church in thinking through matters of faith. Substance is what a thing is, and the Church affirmed that the "thing" of the Eucharist is not bread and wine but Jesus's own flesh and blood.

Alongside this doctrinal clarity, we see a corresponding development of the arts. Central to the culture of Christendom was the instantiation of faith into visible realities of social structures and artisanship. The belief in Christ's real and substantial presence was bolstered by one popular artistic depiction of Christ's appearance during a Mass celebrated Pope Saint Gregory the Great. In response to a scoffing woman present there, the saint prayed that Jesus would make His true presence known to her, and Jesus miraculously appeared on the altar for all to see. The scene captured the imagination of medieval artists, whose depictions sought to make the reality of transubstantiation clear, that Christ is really, truly present. This is a crucial matter of faith and at the heart of the Church's life, not a mere theological squabble. This particular version of *The Mass of Saint Gregory* by Hans Baldung shows Christ appearing in dynamic fashion, almost as if he were dancing, showing the dramatic way that Christ's makes Himself available to His faithful. His presence clearly invites a stronger response of faith and devotion, which enables the believer to enter into communion with Him.

Hans Baldung, *The Mass of Saint Gregory*, 1511

The deepening theological understanding of Jesus's true presence in the Eucharist laid the foundation for the Church's official adoption of the term "transubstantiation" at the Fourth Lateran Council in 1215. Further strengthening the reality that culture flows from belief, Lateran IV decreed that the faithful must receive Communion at least once a year at Easter after a Lenten confession. Here is the council's Eucharistic teaching:

> There is one Universal Church of the faithful, outside of which there is absolutely no salvation. In which there is the same priest and sacrifice, Jesus Christ, whose body and blood are truly contained in the sacrament of the altar under the forms of bread and wine; the bread being changed (*transsubstantiatio*) by divine power into

the body, and the wine into the blood, so that to realize the mystery of unity we may receive of Him what He has received of us. And this sacrament no one can effect except the priest who has been duly ordained in accordance with the keys of the Church, which Jesus Christ Himself gave to the Apostles and their successors.[22]

Saint Thomas Aquinas, born ten years after the council, would become the great theologian of transubstantiation. In his great masterpiece the *Summa Theologiae*, he used Aristotelian metaphysics to describe the nature of substance and how the sacramental change occurs through a miracle of grace. He describes why the bread must cease to be bread in order for Christ to become really and substantially present in the Eucharist. Christ's body does not cease to be in heaven, nor does it move down from heaven by physical motion. It is only through a substantial change of the bread and wine into His body and blood that His presence is possible: "Now a thing cannot be in any place, where it was not previously, except by change of place, or by the conversion of another thing into itself. . . . And consequently it remains that Christ's body cannot begin to be anew in this sacrament except by change of the substance of bread into itself. But what is changed into another thing, no longer remains after such change."[23] Something cannot be two things at once. The Eucharist is either bread or Christ's body. For the one to become the other, a miraculous change must occur, bringing about a new sacramental

---

[22] The Fourth Lateran Council (1215), Canon 1, in Schroeder, *Disciplinary Decrees of the General Councils*.
[23] *ST* III, q. 75, a. 2, c.

mode of presence by which Christ, who remains in heaven, becomes substantially present to us in the Eucharist.

But before you think this theology represents the logic chopping of an intellectual, we see, once again, how theology brings forth artistic expression. Aquinas expresses his faith in the Eucharist also as a poet, composing hymns for the newly established feast of Corpus Christi, such as the "Tantum Ergo": "Down in adoration falling / this great sacrament we hail! / Over ancient forms of worship / newer rights of grace prevail. / Faith will tell us Christ is present / when our human senses fail." Aquinas is a doctor of the Eucharist, teaching most deeply about transubstantiation while also guiding us in our praise of Christ's presence in adoration. In fact, poetry can capture the truth of things more profoundly and beautifully than abstract reasoning. Although we need clarity of thought, which is indispensable for the Church, it is Aquinas's poetry that leads the faithful in their praise of the reality of Christ's Eucharistic presence as they sing his verse in benediction.

Finally, in the last major stage of theology, we find a deeper awareness of the Eucharistic nature of the Church in response to an overemphasis on the individual. For many in the modern world, the Eucharist has been reduced to a symbol of Christ's presence within one's soul, undermining any sense of a Eucharistic life and culture. Holding to a merely symbolic presence would view the Eucharist as a general expression of faith in Christ as opposed to insisting on the particulars of belief, practice, adherence to authority, and membership in a visible community. From our brief survey of Church history, a disembodied and individualistic belief in the Eucharist clearly opposes the Incarnation—Christ's actual and ongoing presence in the flesh—and its continuing presence through the sacramental reality of the Church. The Eucharist is not an idea or mere symbol, because within it, Christ takes flesh within the life of the community, requiring the faithful adherence of one's entire life. The Eucharist does not simply concern God and one's own soul in isolation. We need the Church to experience the Eucharist because Christ gathered a visible community to Himself and entrusted to its leaders the sacramental memory of His presence. Receiving the Eucharist entails being physically united to Christ as a member of His body in the world—the Church.

The denial of Jesus's substantial presence in the Eucharist did not gain much traction in the Middle Ages, although it became a central tenet of the Reformation. Rather than a genuine reform of the Church—bringing it back to its original purity—the Reformation occurred as a revolution, a challenge to the received tradition of the Church's doctrine, sacraments, and way of life. So-called reformers, such as Luther, Zwingli, and Calvin, railed against the Mass as a sacrifice and against transubstantiation, though they themselves disagreed on the exact nature of the Eucharist. Although there are many different Protestant theologies of the Eucharist, all Protestant groups agree in their denial that the Eucharist makes the sacrifice of the cross present (which the Reformers said would crucify Him again and repeat His sacrifice, as if it were not sufficient) and their denial of transubstantiation. Luther held that Christ's body was substantially present alongside of the substance of the bread (consubstantiation), while Zwingli initiated the Swiss tradition that held that Jesus's body and blood were only symbolized by the bread and wine. Other denominations, particularly those related to the Radical Reformation movement, did not celebrate the Eucharist as worship but as an actual meal, known as the *agape* (drawing on ancient verbiage) that would embody the community's union and charity.

These heretical beliefs on the Eucharist did not simply change doctrine, as serious as that is. They constituted a change in the whole Christian vision of life. The modern period of theology has been marked by the need for ongoing apologetics against Protestant attacks, while pointing back to the sources in the early Church. By looking deep into history, Newman himself recognized the Church's continuity, leading him to enter the Catholic Church and to leave the rupture of the Reformation behind. The Council of Trent (1545–63) provided a strong affirmation of Catholic doctrine in light of the Reformation and sought to strengthen Catholic devotion. Many Eucharistic practices developed to bolster faith, such as stronger preaching, adoration, more engaging art, popular catechisms, and public processions. Nonetheless, the Church's faith in the Eucharist has become even more countercultural in the modern world. This has led to a conflict in the life of Catholics, trying to preserve faith in an individualistic culture that sees religious belief as private and relative. According to Pope Benedict XVI, the Church is even experiencing a "crisis of faith" from within.[24] The Eucharistic life of Catholics has worn thin. And

---

[24] Pope Benedict XVI, *Spe Salvi*, no. 17.

this crisis has manifested itself in a growing disbelief in the Real Presence.

The sacred has become eclipsed within modern culture, with life viewed only in horizontal and utilitarian terms. The Second Vatican Council (1962–65) attempted to bridge the divide between the Church and the world by communicating the faith more effectively, including in its reform of the liturgy, which it sought to adapt to the sensibilities of modern people. Above all, the council called for active participation in the liturgy, which led to the use of the vernacular language and greater simplicity in the rite of the Mass, as well as emphasizing clarity over mystery for catechetical purposes.[25] The Church in the West had preserved Latin as its sacred language until the promulgation of the new rite of the Mass by Paul VI in 1969, which initiated a vast project of inculturation aiming to express the liturgy through local language and culture. Critics held that the reforms broke the organic continuity of the development of the liturgy throughout history, resulting in the loss of a rich textual tradition of prayers and music, and decreasing the sense of reverence and mystery. Regardless, the new form of the Mass drastically changed the experience of prayer for Catholics, creating a uniquely modern liturgical expression, bearing many similarities to the liturgical traditions of the Reformation. The loss of the sacred in the modern world has been exasperated by an eclipse of an awareness of and reverence for the sacred by Catholics themselves.

---

[25] See Second Vatican Council, *Sacrosanctum Concilium*.

The Church is now calling us to enter into a new evangelization, calling non-practicing Christians to a renewal of faith, including, of course, a stronger faith in the Eucharistic presence of Jesus. To support this effort of evangelization, the ancient baptismal catechumenate has been restored by the Second Vatican Council as a means of providing more robust formation. The Church must also reengage in catechesis on the fundamentals of doctrine, which she has sought to do by giving us a new Catechism in 1992 to overcome a spirit of relativism and dissent that has plagued Catholics since the 1960s. Pope Benedict XVI prophetically pointed to the loss of a sense of the sacred in the contemporary Church and sought to restore it, especially in making the Traditional Latin Mass more accessible through his motu proprio *Summorum Pontificum* in 2007.[26] Traditional liturgy has appealed to many younger Catholics, who are drawn to its reverence and mystery, though not without controversy, as Pope Francis curtailed the celebration of the Latin Mass in 2021.

Despite efforts of renewal, Mass attendance plummeted from roughly 75 percent in the early 1960s to a little less than 40 percent today, accompanied by a clear breakdown in catechesis.[27] Many Catholics do not understand or believe in Jesus's presence in the Eucharist, as shown by a Pew survey in

---

[26] Two years later, in another bold move, he welcomed groups of Anglicans into the Catholic Church, and with them, a strand of the Protestant liturgical tradition entered in the Church with the Anglican Use Mass, drawing upon the Anglican Book of Common Prayer.

[27] Brandon Hodge, "The Pillar Survey on Religious Attitudes and Practice," November 29, 2021, https://www.pillarcatholic.com/p/special-report-the-pillar-survey?s=r.

2019 that reported that "nearly seven-in-ten Catholics (69%) say they personally believe that during Catholic Mass, the bread and wine used in Communion 'are symbols of the body and blood of Jesus Christ.' Just one-third of U.S. Catholics (31%) say they believe that 'during Catholic Mass, the bread and wine actually become the body and blood of Jesus.'"[28] This lack of belief points to a spiritual sickness within the Church and to the great need for a renewal of both faith and culture so that we can return the Eucharist to its central place in the Christian life. Disbelief in the Real Presence is a clear indication of how we worship: we do not act like Jesus is truly present in the Eucharist. We often do not observe a sacred silence in Church and can treat the Eucharist like an ordinary piece of bread.[29] Catholics must recover a sense of the sacred,

---

[28] Gregory A. Smith, "Just one-third of U.S. Catholics agree with their church that Eucharist is body, blood of Christ," *Pew Research Center*, August 5, 2019, https://www.pewresearch.org/fact-tank/2019/08/05/transubstantiation-eucharist-u-s-catholics/. It further pointed to a profound ignorance of the Church's teaching on the Eucharist: "Most Catholics who believe that the bread and wine are symbolic do not know that the church holds that transubstantiation occurs." The study did provide a somewhat more reassuring finding in that "about six-in-ten (63%) of the most observant Catholics—those who attend Mass at least once a week—accept the church's teaching about transubstantiation."

[29] Receiving Communion on the tongue, for instance, has been upheld by the Church for promoting greater reverence, even as indults have been granted to certain countries to permit receiving on the hand. Writing in 1969, the Sacred Congregation for Divine Worship offered the following reasons for preserving the practice of receiving Communion on the tongue: "This method of distributing holy communion must be retained, taking the present situation of the Church in the entire world into account, not merely because it has many centuries of-tradition behind it, but especially because it expresses the faithful's reverence for the Eucharist. The custom does not detract in any way from the personal dignity of those who approach this

approaching God's presence with reverence and awe, and, through a stronger faith, allowing Jesus's presence to enter into and transform their lives.

Eucharistic Holiness

The Eucharist is the vital pulse of the Church's life. More than simply a belief, it calls us to an incorporation into Christ that bestows a supernatural identity and should shape the way we live. If Catholics are dismayed by the current crisis within the Church or in culture, then we need to look to models for how to live out our Eucharistic faith more robustly. The saints provide the best examples of sanctity, demonstrating how faith can take flesh in the world. We have already seen a number of saints who have witnessed to the Christian belief in the Eucharist and have helped develop theology, but there are even more who have witnessed to the power of the Eucharist in their lives and the life of the Church.

Peter Paul Rubens captured this witness of the saints, those who have pointed us to the reality of the Eucharist and its power within the Church. In his painting *Defenders of the Eucharist*, he depicts how great saints from throughout history—Fathers of the Church, scholastic theologians, bishops, and religious—have spread the truth of the Eucharist,

---

great sacrament: it is part of that preparation that is needed for the most fruitful reception of the Body of the Lord. This reverence shows that it is not a sharing in 'ordinary bread and wine' that is involved, but in the Body and Blood of the Lord. . . . Further, the practice which must be considered traditional ensures, more effectively, that holy communion is distributed with the proper respect, decorum and dignity. It removes the danger of profanation of the sacred species." *Memoriale Domini*, Instruction on the Manner of Distributing Holy Communion, May 29, 1969.

including Saint Ambrose, Saint Augustine, Saint Gregory the Great, Saint Clare, Saint Thomas Aquinas, Saint Norbert, and Saint Jerome. The painting was a model within a large series of tapestries he designed, *The Triumph of the Eucharist*, commissioned in 1625 by the Infanta Clara Eugenia for the Descalzas Reales Monastery in Madrid.[30] Rubens's tapestry designs stand as one of the greatest triumphs of Eucharistic art, demonstrating the Eucharistic typology of the Old Testament, how the Eucharist triumphs over every difficulty, and how it leads to holiness in the Church. The design shown here provides portraits of those saints most connected to the Eucharist, who defended it, praised it, and allowed its power to flow through them.

Peter Paul Rubens, *The Defenders of the Eucharist*, 1625

---

[30] See Scribner, *The Triumph of the Eucharist*.

The following saints provide us a glimpse of how the Church honored the Eucharist through the centuries, showing us how to live a Eucharistic culture. They were icons of the Holy Eucharist, pointing all to the source of their holiness.

Saint John the Evangelist (c. 15–c. 100): The beloved disciple wrote the most theologically profound of the four Gospels. He laid upon the breast of Jesus during the Last Supper, modeling the heart-to-heart love of communion. He recorded the Bread of Life discourse and Jesus's high priestly prayer in the Last Supper discourse. In the Eucharist, Jesus calls each of us to lay our heads upon His breast and to become His beloved disciple.

Saint Ignatius of Antioch (d.c. 108): The bishop of Antioch, he wrote a series of letters to churches on his journey to Rome to face martyrdom in the Coliseum. In these letters, he spoke of Jesus's real presence in the Eucharist and of his impending martyrdom in Eucharistic terms, detailing his longing to be ground like wheat in the mouth of the lions. Ignatius models commitment to the Eucharist in his willingness to offer his life, which we can imitate by carrying our cross daily as a member of Christ's body.

Saint Tarcisius (263–75): Pope Damasus had an inscription carved on his tomb in the catacombs relating that he had died protecting the Eucharist. Tradition says that he was a young acolyte carrying the Eucharist to Christians in prison and was attacked by a young mob of boys who wanted to see what he was carrying. Pope Benedict XVI describes how when Tarcisius's body was recovered, "the consecrated Host which the little Martyr had defended with his life, had become flesh of his flesh thereby forming, together with his body, a single immaculate Host offered to God."[31] We should protect the integrity and dignity of the Eucharist with firmness and charity, especially in an age when attacks on the Holy Eucharist are becoming more frequent and intense.

Saint John Chrysostom (349–407): John was a priest from Syria and served in the great city of Antioch before becoming archbishop of the Greek city of Constantinople from 398–404. During those years, drawing upon his Syriac heritage, he composed the main texts for the Divine Liturgy, the form of the Mass still celebrated in Eastern Catholic and Orthodox churches today. Called the "golden-tongued," he was also known as an outstanding preacher, calling Christians to live their faith in the world. John's liturgy witnesses to the rich diversity of the Church's worship and calls us to experience God's transcendent glory.

Saint Gregory the Great (540–604): Pope Gregory I, a former prefect of Rome and monk, likewise compiled and advanced liturgical traditions, bringing the Roman rite to a stable form and perfecting its musical tradition, giving his name to Gregorian chant. He also advocated celebrating Masses for the souls in purgatory. One of his Masses occasioned a Eucharistic miracle and the depiction of the Mass of Saint Gregory, making the pope a witness to Christ's true presence. Through all of his efforts, he is rightly considered one of the fathers of Europe and a key creator of the culture of Christendom that grew up surrounding the Mass. He witnesses to the need for beauty in our celebration of the Mass.

---

[31] Pope Benedict XVI, "General Audience, August 4, 2010.

Blessed Lanfranc (1005–1098): This monk, abbot, teacher of the great Saint Anselm, and archbishop of Canterbury represents the height of monastic teaching. He wrote a treatise *On the Body and Blood of the Lord* to expound the teaching of transubstantiation, for the first time employing Aristotle's philosophy to do so. He bears witness to the need for us to grow in understanding and the defense of our faith.

Saint Norbert of Xanten (1075–1134): After a lax priesthood, Norbert's faith deepened after a close encounter with death. He embraced a life of penance and founded the Premonstratensian order of canons regular (known as the Norbertines). Through his preaching, he drew the entire town of Antwerp back to faith in the Eucharist after it had fallen into a heretical view of the sacrament. He would often celebrate Mass on the road as a traveling preacher, occasioning a number of miracles, including healing a blind woman by breathing on her after he received the Eucharist and remaining unharmed after consuming the Precious Blood when a poisonous spider had fallen into the chalice. Saint Norbert calls us to a greater Eucharistic zeal by overcoming our laxity and trusting in the Eucharist's power in our lives.

Saint Francis (1181–1226) and Saint Clare (1194–1253): Known for founding the Franciscan Friars and the Poor Clares, with a strong embrace of poverty, these two saints also fostered devotion to the Eucharist. Saint Francis, before he died, pressed his friars to embrace greater devotion to the Eucharist, including more solemnity and reverence in the Mass. Francis said that, in contrast to the life of the friars, there should be no poverty in the celebration of the Eucharist. Saint Clare showed great confidence in the Eucharist to protect her sisters when Saracens breached her convent walls in Assisi. Jesus spoke to her from the tabernacle, assuring His protection, and Clare was seen walking towards the enemy with a monstrance as the soldiers fled the other direction (as she is depicted in Rubens's painting). These two saints made the Eucharist the center of their lives, beckoning us to imitate their example.

Saint Hyacinth (1185–1257): Called the Apostle of the North, Hyacinth helped establish the Dominican Order in his native Poland. He rescued the Blessed Sacrament from Kiev during an invasion by the Mongol hordes. He stopped before the statue of Our Lady in church and apologized for not being able to lift it. According to legend, Our Lady replied, "If you had a little more faith and love for me, it would be easy for you to carry this burden." With the Eucharist in one hand and the statue of Our Lady in the other, Hyacinth crossed the Dnieper River, escaping the notice of the enemy forces. And the Eucharist can also strengthen us to do great things for Jesus if we trust in Him, for all things are possible with our Eucharistic Lord.

Saint Thomas Aquinas (1225–74): Aquinas is known for his unparalleled theology of the Eucharist, especially in his *Summa Theologiae*, as well as his Eucharistic hymns which the Church has adopted in the liturgy, written originally for the establishment of the Feast of Corpus Christi. These include the "Pange Lingua," sung on Holy Thursday, "Panis Angelicus," and the hymns used before and after Benediction. He would say Mass each morning and then attend another Mass in thanksgiving. He also composed prayers to be said before and after Mass. He provides a model of love and devotion for the Eucharist, guiding us in our prayer.

Saint Imelda Lambertini (1322–33): Patroness of first communicants, she was the daughter of a noble family from Bologna and was sent to a Dominican convent at age nine. She had a strong devotion to Jesus's real presence in the Eucharist and requested to receive her first Communion, though she was denied because of her young age. At age eleven, on the feast of the Ascension, a host appeared above her head, moving the priest to give her Communion. After receiving her first Holy Communion, which would also be her last, she died in ecstasy. She shows us that our desire for the Eucharist allows the sacrament to impact us more powerfully!

Saint Catherine of Siena (1347–80): Catherine, a Third Order Dominican, experienced many mystical graces through her reception of the Eucharist and lived for seven years solely on the sacrament. Her spiritual director, Blessed Raymond of Capua, described how "her fasting did not affect her energy, however. She maintained a highly active life during those seven years. In fact, most of her great accomplishments occurred during that period. Not only did her fasting not cause her to lose energy, but became a source of extraordinary strength." Through her prayer and devotion to the Eucharist, she received many mystical graces and sought to reform the Church, bringing the papacy out of its exile in Avignon. She manifests how the Eucharist provides the spiritual food most needed for our journey through life.

Saint Margaret Mary Alacoque (1647–90): This great visionary of the Sacred Heart, a Visitation nun in France, made known Christ's desire for greater devotion to His Heart in the Eucharist, through more fervent and frequent Communion and Eucharistic adoration. She also revealed the First Friday Devotion, in which Jesus asked for the reception of Communion on nine consecutive first Fridays of the month in reparation for sins against His Heart with the promise of assistance at the hour of death. The visions she received show the connection between the love of Jesus's Sacred Heart and His presence in the Blessed Sacrament. Margaret Mary shows us how we can love Jesus's heart during Communion and make reparation for sins committed against His Sacred and Eucharistic Heart.

Saint Alphonsus Liguori (1696–1787): This great Italian spiritual writer promoted the practice of spiritual communion and daily visits to the Blessed Sacrament. He founded the Congregation of the Most Holy Redeemer (Redemptorists) and also is known for promoting other devotions such as the Stations of the Cross. He wrote works such as *The Holy Eucharist* and *Visits to the Blessed Sacrament*. Alphonsus teaches us how to strengthen our Eucharistic devotion through spiritual reading and adoring Jesus's Real Presence.

Saint Peter Julian Eymard (1811–68): Founder of the Congregation of the Blessed Sacrament for men, and the Servants of the Blessed Sacrament for women, he was an apostle of devotion to Jesus's presence in the Eucharist, especially adoration. He wrote many works on the Eucharist, including *The Real Presence* and *Holy Communion*. He teaches us how to spread devotion to the Eucharist to others.

Saint Anthony Mary Claret (1807–70): Claret was a Spanish missionary to the Canary Islands and Cuba who had an extremely strong and miraculous devotion to the Eucharist. He reported that "the faith I have when I am in the presence of the Blessed Sacrament is so strong that I find it impossible to express what I feel. . . . When the time comes to leave I must force myself to overcome the inclination to prolong my stay with Jesus."[32] Jesus honored His desire and physically kept His Eucharistic presence within him until his next reception of Communion. He models the reality that we all become living tabernacles of Jesus's presence when we receive Him in the sacrament.

Saint John Neumann (1811–60): A missionary from Bohemia, he eventually became bishop of Philadelphia, where he actively promoted devotion to the Eucharist, including instituting the Forty Hours devotion of Eucharistic adoration in parishes. As founder of the first Catholic school system in the United States, he understood that devotion to the Eucharist must be taught and modeled at an early age. He shows us that our parishes and schools should express and spread devotion to the Eucharist.

Saint Pius X (1835–1914): Pius sought to promote more active participation at Mass, including the revitalization of the Church's tradition of Gregorian chant. He encouraged frequent reception of the Eucharist and lowered the age of first Communion for children to the age of reason. He understood the power of the Eucharist, especially for our children, provided we foster the right disposition of openness and preparedness to receive Jesus. He models zeal for

---

[32] "St. Anthony Mary Claret, a True Spiritual Master," *Catholic Insight*, October 24, 2021, https://catholicinsight.com/saint-anthony-mary-claret-a-true-spiritual-master/.

drawing others to Mass and Communion to experience their great spiritual depths.

Saint John Paul II (1920–2005): This great pope, with his strong devotion to quiet prayer before the Blessed Sacrament, sought to strengthen devotion to the Eucharist in the period of turmoil following the Second Vatican Council. He celebrated large Masses through the world, including some of the largest gatherings in human history at World Youth Day. He models how the Eucharist draws us together in unity and can change society, such as occurred during his Masses to Communist Poland. These Masses awakened the consciences of his fellow countrymen and show us that the Eucharist should be at the center of our work for justice and the renewal of civilization. Furthermore, he also loved to make visits to the Blessed Sacrament. No matter how busy he was, even during papal trips, he always found time to visit Christ.

PART II

The Summit: The Eucharistic Heart of the Christian Life

In the first section, we examined the key elements of culture: nature, people, practices, and belief. These chapters presented how the Eucharist is the *source* of the Christian life. In this second section, we now turn to how we can appropriate these elements in our lives through the Mass. The Eucharist is the *summit* of the Christian life because it is the highest good on earth, the true presence of the Son of God with us and in us. In this exploration of the Eucharistic renewal of our civilization, it is necessary to dwell at length upon the Mass as the means by which Jesus enters into our life to shape it from within. It is not an exaggeration to say that the Mass *is* Christian culture, its source and summit, giving rise to and perfecting the Christian life on earth. The other elements of Christian civilization translate and express the graces we receive at Mass into the rest of our lives.

This section focuses on our experience of the Eucharist. It explores what happens during the Mass and the gifts that it bestows on us, especially the presence of the Word incarnate. The Mass is not a static ceremony, a formality to remember a past event. Instead, it constitutes an invitation to participate in the actions of Jesus, a call to share in His own offering of Himself. In sacramental fashion, we need faith and devotion to penetrate beneath the surface of its ritual action to recognize its depth and participate in its hidden treasures. The acts of communion and adoration, in particular, offer us the most important ways of encountering Jesus and experiencing His true Eucharistic presence. This section also focuses on what needs to take place before and after Mass to fully experience its graces. Preparation, for instance, removes obstacles to experiencing the grace of the Eucharist, enabling it to penetrate and transform our lives more thoroughly.

The Mass is Catholic culture. As the center of the Christian way of life that can grow into a Christian civilization, it should lead to additional practices to surround it, both leading up to and flowing from it. Some of these are immediate, such as fasting before Mass or taking time in prayer. Some are more remote, such as penitential practices on Friday, the day of the Crucifixion, to prepare for Sunday, the day of the Resurrection. Either way, translating the Mass into culture means forming our lives around it and making it the center of all we do. In the Mass, we find our purpose in life, and from it, we are able to live the faith, drawing inner vitality from our communion with Christ. The Mass presents us with a call to which we must respond. Many miss it, because we have to try to enter it through prayer, to extend it through additional acts like adoration, and to dispose ourselves in how we live, removing obstacles and creating openness, such as through fasting and confession. We cannot take the Mass for granted; we should seek Jesus there, deepening our spiritual vision and finding in it the source and summit of an authentically Christian life.

The Mass is our plan of renewal. Although this book seeks to connect the Eucharist to the renewal of our civilization, a section on the interior life is not out of place. The Eucharist initiates a spiritual revolution that should spill out into the world if we allow it. For the Eucharist to change the world, however, it first has to change us. Entering into the spirit of the Mass, teaches us to put God first, to receive Him into our lives, to be transformed by His presence within us, and live in accord with it. This is the plan of the Mass: conforming ourselves to God through His presence there. God changes the world by changing people. He works in a personal way to change structures and nations by sending His disciples into the world to share His transforming presence with others. The renewal of our civilization requires a renewal of the soul, which can happen most powerfully through the Eucharist.

5

The Mass: Eternity Enters Time

When we look back to the foundations of Christian culture in the first part of this book, it is the Mass that makes them present, enabling us to enter into the whole story of salvation history. In the Mass, the central moment of the Incarnation begins to shape our own lives as we encounter Christ and live in communion with Him. It also provides the way in which Jesus remains present to His Church and His followers abide as members of His body. We first will look at the spiritual reality of the Mass that unites heaven and earth and how its mystical nature shapes its ritual expression. The Mass, like the Eucharist itself, uses physical means to make transcendent, spiritual realities tangible within the Church.

The Mass: The "Catholic Thing"

The Catholic faith could be defined, more than anything else, by the Mass. It is the heart of the Christian life because it provides us access to Jesus Himself through His continuing presence among us. Bishop Robert Barron speaks of the "Catholic thing," which he describes "as a keen sense of the prolongation of the Incarnation through space and time, an extension that is made possible through the mystery of the church."[1] The Word did not become flesh and then leave us to our own devices. He continues to become flesh primarily in the Mass but also in all the sacraments, as Barron describes how "Catholics see God's continued enfleshment in the oil, water, bread, imposed hands, wine, and salt of the sacraments; they appreciate it in the gestures, movements, incensations, and songs of the Liturgy."[2] Jesus continues to manifest Himself using physical means and tangible matter to make Himself present. The Church's ritual action in turn gives greater significance to the rest of Catholic culture. Catholics continue to see Christ's ongoing enfleshment as "they savor it in the texts, arguments, and debates of the theologians; they sense it in the graced governance of popes and bishops; they love it in the struggles and missions of the saints; they know it in the writings of Catholic poets and in the cathedrals crafted by Catholics architects, artists, and workers. In short, all of this discloses to the Catholic eye and mind the ongoing presence of the Word made flesh, namely Christ."[3] Through all these various expressions, the Mass stands at the center, the key expression of the "Catholic thing," the continuing Incarnation of Christ that shapes the whole of Catholic life and culture.

The Mass, or the Divine Liturgy as it is known in the East, forms the Church's worship, the commemoration of the Paschal Mystery—a ritual meal and a renewal of the covenant by partaking in the sacrifice of Christ. The Mass,

---

[1]   Barron, *Catholicism*, 3.
[2]   Barron, 3.
[3]   Barron, 3.

Sandro Botticelli, *Mystic Nativity*, 1500

by making Jesus present in the sacrament of His body and blood, is the chief way that we experience the gift of His Eucharistic presence. It constitutes the supreme act of Christian worship of God by sharing in Christ's own loving honor of the Father and the sacrifice He made of Himself for us. His Eucharistic presence enables the believer to encounter Him in a regular way and to abide in Him by entering into communion with Him. The union of Christ's actions, those of the priest, and also the congregation all converge in the celebration, as we see in the painting *The Mass of John of Matha*, which is related to the founding of the Trinitarian Order. An arc rises from the congregation that reaches its pinnacle in the host raised by the priest, which in turn creates an opening that rises directly to the Trinity and the heavenly worship above. The Mass is truly the work of Christ, a ritual enacted by the priest, and the moment of highest worship for all those who attend. The Church speaks of it in many ways to show its richness and the many ways in which we enter into its work. It is important, therefore, to walk through these various expressions and how they all help us to understand the Mass from different perspectives.

The word "Mass" (*Missa* in Latin) comes from the sending forth with which it concludes. *Ite missa est* means, "Go, it [the assembly] has been dismissed," or, more spiritually interpreted, "Go, it has been sent." It is somewhat surprising that the Church names its worship not from the Eucharist itself but from this sending forth. The name "Mass," therefore, implies that the worship and communion of the Church entails a mission to extend this experience of God into the world and the life of the believer.

The Eucharist originates from the command of Jesus at the Last Supper: "Do this in memory of me." It is an act of *obedience* to a clear instruction of Jesus to continue His actions at the Last Supper, tied to the offering of Himself on the cross, the gift of His body and blood offered to the Father for our salvation. The *memory* to which Jesus calls His Church does not simply entail looking to something in the past but constitutes a call to make Him present through the action of the Eucharist. When you remember something, you recall it and make it present to your mind. When you remember sacramentally, the saving action of God becomes present in its spiritual reality at that moment.

We refer to the Mass, along with Jesus's body and blood present to us through it, as the "Eucharist," literally *thanksgiving*. The prayers of the Mass express the Church's thanksgiving addressed to the Father, thanking Him for the gift of His Son and the gift of salvation. The Passover itself served as a thanksgiving meal for deliverance from Egypt, and Jesus gave thanks to the Father during the Last Supper. The Eucharist demonstrates how Christian worship responds with gratitude to the gift of God's grace and the friendship He offers.

The Eucharist also constitutes a *sacrifice*, making Jesus's one sacrifice of Himself on the cross present in an unbloody manner. Jesus wants to make the grace of His cross and resurrection vividly present in His Church, though without repeating His violent suffering. The priest offers the one sacrifice of Christ to the Father, opening this source of grace and life to those present at the sacrifice. Christ uses the matter and then the continued appearance and accidents of bread and wine to make His body and blood present in the Mass, which enable the Eucharist to become a sacrificial *meal*, like the Passover. Jesus is the great high priest who offers the sacrifice, but also the victim who offers Himself as the new Passover lamb, giving His flesh to eat and His blood to drink. This priestly action seals the new covenant of salvation in a sacred meal and also provides the food which gives life to the soul by incorporating into the Body of Christ, the Church, by consuming His Body.

We also refer to the reception of the Eucharist as *Communion* (*com* and *unus* in the Latin, meaning "with oneness"), in becoming one with Christ. This Communion can be understood as a marital union between the believer and Christ, as the two become one flesh in the reception of Christ's Body into the body of the communicant. The two also share one spirit in the Holy Spirit, the breath and life of God, who enters the soul and makes the body of the believer into His Temple. The common eating of the Church also creates the bond of unity in which all are united in the eating of this Body and spiritual unity within it.

The Mass is also the *liturgy*, literally the work on behalf of the people, the work of praise and glory offered to God. It is work offered to God by giving Him the justice of prayer owed to Him in return for His goodness and generosity to us. The whole Mass constitutes this work of glory given to God, even the readings, which appear more focused on the congregation. It is also a public work done for the good of the people, the congregation, who receive the grace bestowed in this divine worship.

Finally, we can see the Mass as a *dialogue*, a conversation of love. We could describe it as a dialogue with the Father, the one to whom all the prayers of the Mass are addressed. As we conform to the Body of Christ, Jesus draws us into His own relationship with the Father and speaks to the Father on our behalf through the prayers of the Mass. The

Mass teaches us how to pray and enter into greater intimacy with God in prayer.

Unveiling of Heaven

Underlying these different ways of speaking about the Mass stands the all-important reality of Jesus's presence. The Church's worship manifests the Kingdom of God on earth—the reign of God through His chosen king, the Christ (or Messiah), Jesus. The Mass draws the believer into His heavenly court, where Christ reigns over His Church and the entire world in glory, forever seated at the right hand of the Father. This entrance into Christ's court opens heaven to us, the place of perfect communion with God through Jesus. The Mass offers a foretaste of the eternal and perfect union with God in heaven. Jesus is the bridge who unites heaven and earth in Himself and, when He arrives at Mass through the Eucharist, heaven has arrived. He does not just present Himself at Mass so that we can be near Him, but He actually enters our bodies and souls, creating a union of love that is the essence of heaven.

Even in the Old Testament, the ritual of Israel arose in imitation of the pattern of heaven, a pattern shown to Moses on Mt. Sinai. Jewish worship created a place of meeting in the tent and temple that involved sacrifice, vestments, food and drink, light, and incense—all of which symbolized realities in heaven (see Heb 8:5). Christian worship perfects the signs of the Old Covenant and more perfectly anticipates our future perfection because of the communion with God that occurs through its ritual. The book of Revelation reveals or pulls the veil back on this pattern, revealing the tent "not made with hands" (Heb 9:11), and gives us a glimpse of the perfect worship of heaven. The Mass makes this heavenly worship present through its sacramental symbolism. Every believer, "full of the Holy Spirit," should be able to say with Stephen at the moment of his death, "Behold, I see the heavens opened, and the Son of man standing at the right hand of God" (Acts 7:56).

Jesus rules from the right hand of the Father to lead His Church, calling the faithful to His heavenly table. He wants to open the door to the heavenly banquet to us. In the book of Revelation, Jesus speaks to the church of Laodicea: "Behold, I stand at the door and knock; if any one hears my voice and opens the door, I will come in to him and eat with him, and he with me" (Rv 3:20). Jesus invites His followers to eat with Him even now on earth as a preparation for the heavenly worship. The next chapter helps us to see what happens when we respond and knock: "Lo, in heaven an open door!" (Rv 4:1). What the visionary, John, sees through this door provides a number of powerful images that show us how the worship of the Mass corresponds with that of heaven.

First, John sees a throne, indicating that in our worship, we enter into the court of God, addressing the Father. Gathered round the throne are twenty-four elders, using the Greek word for priest (*presbyteros*), who wear crowns, indicating that they share in the rule of the one seated on the throne.[4] Around the throne we see seven torches, akin

---

[4] In 1 Chronicles 24, we see twenty-four courses of the priesthood, but the number twenty-four seems to correspond to a fullness, drawing together the twelve tribes of Israel and the twelve apostles, representing the Church.

to our candles, representing the life of the spirit, as well as the angelic spirits in the form of a lion, ox, man, and eagle, indicating the proclamation of the Gospel and who sing "holy, holy, holy."[5] The elders also demonstrate the posture of worship as they fall down and prostrate themselves before the throne, the presence of God. Then, the lamb who was slain appears before the elders, the one who reveals the plan of God for salvation, contained in the scroll with the seven seals. The elders respond to the lamb with the music of harps and bowls of incense, presenting the prayers of the saints to him while prostrate in worship.[6] All of the angels of heaven join in the worship of the elders/priests, and all creation echoes their song: "And I heard every creature in heaven and on earth and under the earth and in the sea, and all therein, saying, 'To him who sits upon the throne and to the Lamb be blessing and honor and glory and might for ever and ever!' And the four living creatures said, 'Amen!' and the elders fell down and worshiped" (Rv 5:13–14).[7] Every creature should echo the praise given to the lamb in heaven.

Jan van Eyck captures this heavenly scene beautifully in the central panel of his famous Ghent altarpiece, *The Adoration of the Mystic Lamb*. Above the panel, God the Father is seated upon a throne, and in the panel (pictured here), we see not just the elders but all the saints of heaven gathered

---

[5] The Jewish menorah has seven candles, and it is traditional to have six candles on the altar with the Eucharist in the center as the main light.

[6] The elders also represent intercessory prayer here.

[7] We see this prayer evoked in the preface before the Eucharistic prayer: "And so, with Angels and Archangels, with Thrones and Dominions, and with all the hosts and Powers of heaven, we sing the hymn of your glory, as without end we acclaim: Holy, Holy, Holy . . ."

around the lamb. The scene is clearly Eucharistic, with a cup catching the lamb's blood as he stands upon an altar, intending to show us how our own worship unites to the heavenly one. The instruments of the Passion are next to the altar, the cross and the pillar on which He was scourged, with the angles singing and incensing the altar. The beautiful landscape represents the renewal of creation and the towers portray the new and heavenly Jerusalem where God will be worshipped eternally, with the Holy Spirit at the top center providing the light for the city as if He were the sun. Van Eyck depicts the whole Church in glory, completing the pilgrimage through life by reaching the perfect worship at the altar of heaven.

Jan van Eyck, *The Adoration of the Mystic Lamb*, 1432

The central elements of Christian ritual clearly emerge from Revelation 4–5 in the worship of the new Paschal Lamb. Surrounding Him are priests, the proclamation of God's revelation, flames, incense, singing, and praying the words "holy, holy, holy," "Amen," and "Alleluia," accompanied by kneeling in prayer. The Church does not simply invent these actions, because they perfect the worship of the Old Covenant and participate in the perfect worship to come. Already we share in the singing of the saints and angels in heaven. Our actions are not simply human and earthly actions; they directly participate in and find their ultimate power as flowing from the worship of heaven. Jesus related that just as His Father appointed Him a kingdom, so He promised: "you may eat and drink at my table in my kingdom" (Lk 22:30). The eating of the New Passover begins now and is completed in the banquet that is coming in heaven. The two actions are not separate. Our worship draw us into our final goal of union with God, making it present to us here and now.

Catholic culture is not simply a natural reality, built up by our own collective creativity and action. It is supernatural and heavenly, animated by an open door to heaven— the Mass. Through the Mass, eternity breaks into time; the end and goal of human life becomes present to us. Our own lives become supernatural in the heavenly encounter with the lamb that we experience there. Christian worship is truly cosmic by entering into the worship of the angels and singing the music of eternity with them. The Mass enlivens the whole of creation, awakening the cosmic tabernacle by allowing the world to render the Creator the worship for which it was created. Enlivened with eternal and everlasting significance, it should be clear why praying the Mass is the most important thing we can do in this life.

The Importance of Ritual

Every culture, which until now had religion at its center, expressed its deepest convictions through religious ritual. Ritual gave concrete expression to beliefs, commemorated the seasons and important festivals, and marked the major moments of passage, such as birth, coming of age, marriage, and death. This ritual enacted an opening to an unseen spiritual world and enabled believers to enter into a sacred realm. Ritual is a distinct kind of action, standing apart from the mundane and imparting meaning through solemnity and sacred symbolism. Christian worship, likewise, employs ritual in its sacramental action, enabling believers to enter into the life and saving action of Christ. This ritual gives shape to the Christian life and opens a sacred realm to believers.

Although Christian worship participates in heavenly realities, it does so by using tangible, earthly signs. This may seem unfitting, but thinking back to the creation of human beings as sacramental creatures—as body-soul unities—and the way that God established liturgy in the Old Covenant, the use of these signs makes sense. Jesus took up the ritual of the Old Law and used it to establish the memorial of the Eucharist, commanding His disciples to continue this liturgical action. From the Acts of the Apostles, we see that Christians gathered on the "first day of the week" to "break bread," already indicating the establishment of the Sunday Eucharist worship (Acts 2:42, 20:7). The Mass continued the Passover celebrated by Jesus, now in its realization and fulfillment through the cross and Resurrection. The new Christian Passover also had some similarities to the synagogue service in terms of reading from the Scripture, accompanied by an instruction and the singing of the psalms.

Across the ancient world—despite distances of geography and language—the Church developed the core elements of her ritual to express the heavenly worship. Key elements of this ritual can be traced back to the earliest accounts of the Mass: Invoking the Lord's name through the Sign of the Cross, using the prayer "the Lord be with you," praying with the psalms, asking for mercy (*Kyrie eleison*), glorifying God (*Gloria in excelsis*), having an opening prayer or collect, reading from the Old and New Testament, offering bread and wine, singing "holy, holy, holy," praying a prayer of thanksgiving called the anaphora and invoking God to transform the bread and wine (epiclesis), praying the Our Father, offering peace to another originally through a holy kiss, receiving the Eucharist in communion, and closing with prayer and a blessing. Saint Justin Martyr's account of the Mass, quoted in chapter four, gives clear testimony to this outline.

Language presents another crucial element of ritual. Although some Fathers spoke of the priority of the languages of the cross—those used on Pilate's notice hung on the cross, namely Hebrew, Greek, and Latin—the language of the first Christian community was Aramaic, a Semitic language (closely related to Hebrew), the one spoken by Jesus and His disciples. As the Church grew, it embraced Greek as the primary language of the communities that Paul founded and even the Church in Rome. When the Church spread to the northeast through Persia and central Asia, however, it maintained a closer connection to the Church's first language through Syriac, an Aramaic dialect. Eventually, Latin followed in the Western part of the Roman Empire, and as the Church spread, other liturgical languages emerged, such as Armenian and Coptic. Although the Catholic Church has seven liturgical rites today, distinct ways of celebrating the liturgy and sacraments, all of them trace back to the traditions of the first centuries and languages of Greek, Syriac, Latin, Coptic, and Armenian.[8] Across many different cultures, it became customary to maintain sacred languages distinct from the vernacular to demonstrate a greater solemnity, formality, and unity for the ritual of the Mass. Praying in a sacred language indicates that ordinary speech is not adequate to express the transcendent mystery of the Church's ritual.

The Roman Canon, the main Eucharistic prayer used in the West, arose in the fourth century, drawing upon earlier prayers, and Pope Saint Gregory I (pope from 590 to 604) solidified the Roman rite and chants that continue to this day. Although distinctive rites emerged in Western Europe, such as the Ambrosian in Milan and the various Gallican rites in Western Europe, the Roman rite has been the predominant expression of worship for the Latin Church of Western Europe, promoted by Charlemagne throughout his empire and propped up by the Council of Trent for greater unity following the Reformation. To the East, the liturgy continued to expand into other cultural contexts, with the Syrians bringing their rite into the Far East, including India, and the Copts of Egypt into Nubia and Ethiopia. Cyril and Methodius translated the Byzantine/Greek Rite

---

[8]   The Catholic Church has twenty-four distinct *sui juris*, or self-governing, Churches that use one of these seven liturgical rites: Latin, Byzantine, East Syriac, West Syriac, Coptic, Armenian, and Maronite.

into Slavonic in the nineth century. The stability of the Church's rites provides clarity and unity of worship so that the experience of the Mass does not depend upon the single personality of the priest. Ritual action in the Mass, rather, represents the action of Christ as expressed in the prayer of His bride, the Church. Although the Church's ritual develops throughout time, it is not subject to fashions and whims, and it maintains stability in its general structure and most solemn prayers throughout the centuries.

Ritual should express beauty, sacredness, and mystery. A great historical example of the liturgy's transcendent power comes from the Slavic tradition. Legend relates how Prince Vladimir of Kiev sent delegates to explore the traditions of both Western and Eastern Christianity, as well as Judaism and Islam, in order to strengthen his kingdom. The *Russian Primary Chronicle* describes the delegates reaction as they were received in Constantinople and entered into the grand church of Hagia Sophia:

> The Russes were astonished, and in their wonder praised the Greek ceremonial. . . . "We went to Greece and the Greeks led us to the edifices where they worship their God, and we knew not whether we were in heaven or on earth. For on earth there is no such splendor and beauty, and we are at a loss how to describe it. We only know that God dwells there among men, and their service is fairer than the ceremonies of other nations. For we cannot forget that beauty. Every man, after tasting something

sweet, is afterward unwilling to accept that which is bitter, and therefore, we cannot dwell longer here."[9]

Although the Ukrainian delegates experienced this beauty
in the East, all liturgy aims to make present to the senses the
great mystery of the sacred. Another example can be found
in the reaction to Guillaume Du Fay's polyphonic music performed at the dedication of the Duomo in Florence in 1436:
"The senses of all began to be uplifted. . . . But at the elevation of the Most Sacred Host the whole space of the temple
was filled with such choruses of harmony, and such a concert
of diverse instruments, that it seemed (not without reason)
as though the symphonies and songs of the angels and of
divine paradise had been sent forth from Heaven to whisper
in our ears an unbelievable celestial sweetness. Wherefore in
that moment I was so possessed by ecstasy that I seemed to
enjoy the life of the blessed here on earth."[10]

Giorgio Vasari's sixteenth-century frescos within the
cupola of the Florence Duomo reinforce that effect, leading
the believer to see the manifestation of heaven right within
the church. The music and decoration of the church accompany the ritual action to enhance the symbolism and to help
the believer to participate in them. The liturgy heightens
the sacramental nature of creation, drawing upon signs of
beauty to manifest God's presence in the world.

---

[9]   "The Conversion of Vladimir of Kiev," in Coakley, *Readings in World
Christian History*.
[10]   Quoted in Michael De Sapio, "The Eucharist and the Imagination,"
The Imaginative Conservative, https://theimaginativeconservative.
org/2019/06/eucharist-imagination-michael-de-sapio.html.

Cupola of the Florence Duomo with Vasari's frescoes.

The liturgy bears witness to our need as sacramental beings for outward, ritual expression. As sensory beings, tangible signs manifest the divine presence to us. These signs enliven the senses, imagination, emotions, and intellect to provide entry points into the sacred realities themselves. Human creativity is not enough to make the signs actually reach these realities. It was God who established a tabernacle for Israel to manifest His presence, and churches build upon this design by establishing a sanctuary, a place of assembly for the people, and an entry space, using architecture to show the presence of heaven. Jesus Himself established the sacramental system by which to encounter Him and receive

His grace. The ritual developed by the Church makes the sacraments accessible to us—helping us to understand them and to approach them with the proper disposition. The vestments, sacred vessels, music, gestures, and prayers not only symbolize the sacred but serve as vehicles for the encounter with God. Like the ritual of the feasts of Israel, the liturgy of the sacraments enables people to enter in the New Covenant, beginning with Baptism and Confirmation and renewed regularly through participation in the Eucharist.

Beauty plays an essential role in portraying mysteries which cannot be captured perfectly by words or a single image. The sacred actions and instruments, music, and architecture together seek to create an experience of transcendence that inspires reverence and a contemplative encounter with the true God. God is beauty itself, and in His infinity, no sign could capture His grandeur, but we should do our best to conform our worship to His greatness and majesty. The signs of the liturgy and ritual need to communicate clearly on their true aim: to give God glory and to draw us into His life. Although it may employ imperfect signs, the beauty of the liturgy points to the enduring beauty of the heavenly liturgy and enables a glimpse into it already here on earth.

6

Praying the Mass: Union
with Christ's Sacrifice

It is one thing for the Mass to stand at the center of Catholic culture and another to serve as the center of our own spiritual lives. This requires some effort and an active spiritual participation in the Mass, particularly Christ's own actions within it. The Church, as the Body of Christ, finds the deepest source of its existence in the Eucharist. Believers enter into a mystical union with Christ by receiving His Body and becoming one flesh with Him. Christ acts in His Church by offering His Body and Blood in the Mass through the ministry of the priest, which draws all of His members into His offering of love to the Father. This chapter focuses on our participation in the Mass, exploring how Christ acts in the Mass and how we can unite ourselves more fruitfully to His actions in prayer.

Recognizing the Hidden Lord

The Eucharist has primary importance in the Christian life because, while the other sacraments lead to Him, Jesus *is* the sacrament of the Eucharist. During the Mass, eternity enters into time and space as God Himself stoops down to us in His Eucharistic presence in the greatest expression of humility. And this presence opens up the key characteristic of the Christian life itself, enabling His faithful to encounter Him and to enter into communion with Him. To do so, however, we have to approach the sacrament with a renewed mind and heart. To receive what Jesus wants to give us, and to live in communion with Him, we need to see reality differently.

The first thing needed to participate properly in the Mass is to see what occurs there with the eyes of faith. If we look at the Mass with normal eyes, we would not necessarily see very much—a gathering of people that might seem somewhat mundane or perhaps even boring. To recognize the deeper reality there, we need a sacramental vision that sees the physical acts and material elements as the means of entering into spiritual realities. Jesus speaks to us and makes Himself present through efficacious words and signs that, through the ministry of the priest, make Him present. Faith opens to us to another world that surrounds us in our seemingly mundane gathering—the angels and saints surround us, and the true God visits us through these humble means. Imagine entering into a Catholic church and seeing what Raphael saw and portrayed in his *Disputation on the Eucharist*, the Church's contemplation of the Eucharist throughout time and space, portrayed majestically in the Vatican apartments. Although you might see only what looks like bread on the altar, a great celestial gathering surrounds Jesus's presence. He Himself is there as head of the body, although on the altar we see only the accidents of bread. The angels and saints see Him clearly and point us to Him, although we know their presence only by faith. Raphael helps us to see the truth of the Eucharist, what we can only recognize through the eyes of the spirit.

Raphael, *The Disputation on the Eucharist*

Faith discerns Jesus's presence hidden behind the appearance of bread and wine. Like all the figures in Raphael's painting, who contemplated and debated the Eucharist, we can still ask, "How is He present?" Jesus becomes present in the Eucharist in a unique and mysterious way, related to but distinct from His presence in heaven and in our souls. Jesus's glorified body is present physically in heaven, where He sits at the right hand of the Father. His presence can also be discerned in every soul in a state of grace, where the most Holy Trinity dwells as His temple. The same kind of presence can be discerned in Jesus's mystical Body, the Church, where He said He would be present when "two or three are gathered in my name" (Mt 18:20). In the Eucharist, however, Jesus has a unique sacramental presence that strengthens His presence in the soul and the Church by making His body and blood present in a supernatural and substantial way, while maintaining the accidents of bread and wine to support this presence.

Jesus's Eucharistic presence is one of the greatest of miracles. All the sacraments employ material things and use them as efficacious signs that make spiritual realties present to convey God's grace and life. In the Eucharist, the matter of bread and wine are offered to the Father in obedience to Jesus's own command, and when the words of institution from the Last Supper are spoken, the bread and wine cease to exist and, in their place, Jesus's own body and blood become present. We call this transubstantiation: the changing of one thing into another. The accidents—the physical appearance and characteristics—of the bread and wine remain, but their reality as bread and wine does not. The reality or substantial presence of Jesus's body and blood are made present at Mass through the accidents of the bread and wine.

Even though it is Christ's body and blood in particular that become present in the Eucharist, we receive the whole Christ during Communion. When the substance of the bread becomes the substance of Christ's body and the substance of the wine becomes the substance of Christ's blood, the entire person of Christ is made present by virtue of what Aquinas called concomitance. The body and blood of Christ cannot be separated from the whole substance and reality of Christ's existence. When we receive either one of them, we receive Christ in His body, blood, soul, and divinity.

In doing so, we do not chew upon the physical accidents of Christ's body. He presents the substance of His body to us through the accidents of the bread for a reason, making all the physical accidents of His body present in a spiritual rather than a material way. Most importantly, in receiving the substance of Christ's human body and blood, we also receive His divine nature, which is the nature of the Trinity: Father, Son, and Holy Spirit. Communion with Christ draws us into the life of God.

We can also see more deeply into the meaning of the physical signs that Jesus used to institute the sacrament, strengthening our sacramental vision. Jesus gave us the Eucharist as a sacrificial meal, drawing upon the signs of the Exodus and the worship of the Temple. It entails a sacrifice of bread and wine, liberation from the slavery of sin so that death passes over us, and the manifestation of God through a bread of His presence (of His face). The symbolism of sacrifice becomes even deeper as He offers His flesh as bread and blood as wine. When sacrifice was offered in the Old Covenant, the blood of the victim was drained and the body and blood were offered separately, with the flesh consumed but the blood, seen as the life, poured out. The offering of the body and blood of Christ separately continues to manifest how His blood was drained on the cross in sacrifice as the new Passover lamb. This offering also makes present the Resurrection because Christ is dead no more. The body and blood at the Mass, even though offered separately, are the presence of the Risen Christ, making His new life accessible to us by being consumed within us. Reading this symbolism strengthens our participation in the realities they symbolize, uniting us to the Paschal mystery.

Jesus also communicates to us in words so that in the Mass we can offer what Saint Paul calls a "reasonable" or "logical" worship (Rom 12:1). Jesus, the Word of God (the *Logos*), makes Himself present in both word and sacrament at the Mass, with word pointing to His truth and sacrament making this truth an efficacious sign. The Liturgy of the Word makes Christ present in speech, and hearing the Word of God draws the believer into His mind and the very essence of the truth. The word conforms us to Christ in faith to enable entrance into the sacrifice. The Liturgy of the Eucharist completes the Liturgy of the Word by making the same Word of God substantially present. The Mass does not consist of simply speaking to God, because the word leads us to an encounter Him in the flesh. In making Himself present in the Eucharist, Jesus continues to empty Himself, as the Son of God condescends to take flesh anew (cf. Phil 2:7). This service of love harkens back to the washing of the feet at the Last Supper, as the master comes to serve and wait upon His servants.

At Mass, Jesus calls us to dine with Him, drawing us together around food and drink, which is so central to any culture. Even though we are His servants, Jesus calls us, His followers, to become His friends as He pours Himself out for us in the sacrificial meal of the Eucharist. He sits down to serve us as we break from work to be refreshed by our maker and redeemer. Jesus offers this service as a consolation and reward to His disciples, one that we can experience at every Mass, anticipating the heavenly banquet: "Let your loins be girded and your lamps burning, and be like men who are waiting for their master to come home from the marriage feast, so that they may open to him at once when he comes and knocks. Blessed are those servants whom the master finds awake when he comes; truly, I say to you, he will gird himself and have them sit at table, and he will come and serve them" (Lk 12:35–37). Jesus is welcomed at each Mass with the words "blessed is he who comes," and He should be recognized as the master returning to His servants and friends. With the eyes of faith, we can approach this sacrificial meal and meet Christ within it.

Active Participation: Sharing in Christ's Sacrifice

The Mass is no ordinary meal. It is a sacrificial meal—making present to us the greatest of all sacrifices—the cross. The Protestant "reformers" were adamant, however, in arguing that the Mass was not a sacrifice. A sacrifice literally means to make something holy by offering it to God. The cross was a sacrifice because Jesus offered His life as a loving offering to the Father. The Mass certainly presents something to God to be made holy in offering bread and wine to God that becomes Christ's body and blood, making Christ's own sacrifice present. It can also become our sacrifice, as we unite ourselves to Jesus's own love and obedience and offer our lives with His.

At its core, the Mass consists of the action of Jesus. Within it, He addresses the Father and expresses His love for Him. Jesus, the great high priest, both priest and victim, offers the sacrifice of His own life to atone for sin and to draw others into this love. The Eucharist makes the sacrifice of Jesus present not simply in presenting His body and blood to Father but particularly by making His prayer of love and obedience to the Father accessible to us so that we can take on Jesus's own prayer. The Mass bridges past, present, and future, enabling us to stand at the foot of the cross and simultaneously drawing us into Christ's eternal prayer in heaven. Jesus, as high priest, acts as the mediator and bridge that draws us into the life of the Father.

The Mass can be misunderstood as a new sacrifice. Despite critiques stemming from the Reformation, Catholics do not believe that the sacrifice of the Mass puts Christ to death again: "For we know that Christ being raised from the dead will never die again; death no longer has dominion over him" (Rom 6:9). Christ does not die again. Rather, Christians are drawn into His death and resurrection: "For if we have been united with him in a death like his, we shall certainly be united with him in a resurrection like his" (Rom 6:5). The sacrifice of His body and blood, offered once on the cross, becomes present in the Mass as the Church offers this one sacrifice to the Father. This re-presentation occurs precisely to enable participation in the realty of the Paschal Mystery of Christ's death and resurrection. Jesus has already won salvation and grace for all of humanity, although these gifts must be communicated to the faithful. Faith in the reality of Christ's presence and prayer united to His draws the believer into the effects of salvation—the forgiveness of sins by the cross and a transformation of life by the Resurrection.

Jesus draws us into the mediation of His priesthood through the Mass. The Letter to the Hebrews explains the nature of Jesus's perfect sacrifice and the need to enter into the grace it offers: "Since then we have a great high priest who has passed through the heavens, Jesus, the Son of God, let us hold fast our confession. . . . Let us then with confidence draw near to the throne of grace, that we may receive mercy and find grace to help in time of need" (Heb 4:14,16). Jesus offered the sacrifice "once for all when he offered up himself," and "consequently he is able for all time to save those who draw near to God through him, since he always lives to make intercession for them" (Heb 7:27, 25). Jesus's priestly action does not end with the one sacrifice on the cross. Hebrews makes it clear that He continues to mediate in heaven, in the true Temple: "We have such a high priest, one who is seated at the right hand of the throne of the Majesty in heaven, a minister in the sanctuary and the true tent which is set up not by man but by the Lord" (Heb 8:1). The Mass makes the eternal priesthood of Christ present in the world, uniting to His one sacrifice and His ongoing mediation in heaven.

Matthias Grünewald's vivid and moving depiction of the crucifixion in his Isenheim altarpiece is best known for its realistic portrayal of Christ's agony. The altarpiece, meant as a backdrop for the celebration of the Mass, also points to our participation in a few important ways. John the Baptist points to Jesus as the lamb of God, as the priest repeats his own words at Mass, "Behold the lamb of God." It provides a call for us to recognize the sacrifice of Jesus and to participate in it like the figures to the left of Jesus—Our Lady, John, and Mary Magdalen. They are suffering with Jesus and sharing in His self-offering in a way that we should imitate in our own prayer. Grünewald painted the altarpiece for a hospital that treated those suffering of skin diseases. When you look at the details of Jesus's skin, you see that He took on that suffering in His own flesh, as He did for all of us, taking on our weakness and sin and overcoming them through His death. At Mass, we bring those burdens with us and unite them to the cross so that Jesus can overcome them as we join with Him in prayer.

Matthias Grünewald, Isenheim Altarpiece, 1512–16

There is another way of perceiving the action of Christ in the liturgy. Even though the faithful all share in the sacrifice of Christ, the Mass depends particularly upon the continuing action of Christ through His ordained priests. They do not have a priesthood or sacrifice separate from Christ's. In sacramental fashion, they make His priesthood and prayer present to us. Looking at the New Testament, it is clear that Jesus gave authority to His apostles and commanded them to perform the sacraments through that authority: "Baptizing . . . in the name of the Father, and of the Son, and of the Holy Spirit," "whoever sins you forgive are forgiven," and "do this in memory of me." The priest acts *in persona Christi* (in the person of Christ) when administering the sacraments. By virtue of receiving the sacrament of Holy Orders, the priest has been set apart by God to act on His behalf. Pope Pius XII describes how Christ acts through His priests: "It is the same priest, Christ Jesus, whose sacred person his minister truly represents. Now the minister, by reason of the sacerdotal consecration which he has received, is truly made like to the high priest and possesses the authority to act in the power and place of the person of Christ himself."[11]

In the Mass, Jesus acts through the words and actions of His priest. This does not entail a mere memory or commemoration of the saving actions of the past; it flows from the living and direct action of Christ that communicates these realities anew. Christ's grace does not flow from the worthiness of the priest—his personality, ability, or holiness—but from the sacramental conformity of the priest to Christ, making him an instrument of grace. Just as the body and blood of Christ appear in the Mass under the species of bread and wine, so Christ's priesthood is present sacramentally through the personhood and manhood of the priest. Although Christ is the perfect high priest who has no sin, His priests on earth serve

---

[11] Pope Pius XII, *Mediator Dei*, no. 39.

within their fallen humanity. This may give rise to scandal because of the discrepancy between the perfection of Christ and the imperfection of His ministers. This disparity relates, however, to Christ's own emptying of Himself in the Incarnation to take on the weakness of human flesh, His desire to establish a community of His followers to be His body on earth, and His decision to transmit His grace through the agency of human beings and material signs. All of these realities require faith to recognize Christ and His action despite the limits of the signs and instruments. The scandal of the cross continues in the Church, with God emptying Himself out to the world through the weakness of His Body on earth.

During Mass, the head (represented by the priest) and body (the congregation) pray together as the mystical body of Christ to offer the sacrifice. Although only the priest can consecrate the Eucharist, nonetheless, together the head and body enter into Christ's dialogue with Father. All the baptized share in the priestly action of Christ by uniting their prayers to His. The *Catechism* teaches that "incorporated into the Church by Baptism, the faithful have received the sacramental character that consecrates them for Christian religious worship. The baptismal seal enables and commits Christians to serve God by a vital participation in the holy liturgy of the Church and to exercise their baptismal priesthood by the witness of holy lives and practical charity."[12] This provides the true meaning of the "active participation" to which the Second Vatican Council have called the faithful. The Church as the body of Christ finds its true identity

---

[12] *CCC* 1273.

in sharing in the offering of this body during the Mass and thereby becoming one with the sacrifice. As members of the faithful, we should actively share in this offering and realize the call of our baptism to act as priest through our prayer.

How to Pray at Mass

The Mass invites us to join the prayer of Christ. Sacrifice, once again, makes holy, and the Mass opens a channel of grace to make our lives and culture to become holy. In fact, it is the greatest source of transformation and strength available to us, although many of us may not avail ourselves of it. The invitation of the Mass is to make our lives a sacrifice in union with Jesus's. Knowing that we pray with Jesus gives us courage through a "confidence to enter the sanctuary by the blood of Jesus" (Heb 10:19). Because Jesus has covered us with His blood and conformed us to Him, we can confidently approach the Father. We share in offering the Father the perfect act of justice, giving to God a divine gift of the Son's life, which the Liturgy of Saint John Chrysostom expresses with the words, "We offer to you yours of your own." Only Christ can offer the Father an infinite sacrifice that gives Him what He is due, and to atone for the infinite offenses we have committed against Him. Hence the Mass enables us to unite ourselves with the perfect sacrifice, Christ Himself, to the Father.

This spirituality of the Mass, however, may seem remote from the more mundane reality of attending church each Sunday. It can be hard to focus on the deeper spiritual realities transmitted by the outward actions. The architecture, music, and, of course, the words we pray should all direct our minds to the spiritual realities occurring during the Mass. Jose Gallegos y Arnosa captures a moment of prayer realistically blended with the details of the moment. We bring all the distractions of life into church with us, symbolized by the umbrella leaning against the kneeler, although we must look beyond them. The *Interior of the Seville Cathedral* portrays not so much the vast interior of the structure but the interior of the temple of the human person within it, seeking to concentrate the faculty of attention in a movement of prayer.

Jose Gallegos y Arnosa, *Interior of the Seville Cathedral*, c. 1889

Understanding the meaning of the outward movements and gestures, however, will enable these signs to lead us more deeply into Christ's sacrifice. When we first enter the Church, we bless ourselves with holy water to recount the salvation that came to us at Baptism. This Sign of the Cross, along with the one that opens worship, serves as an initial act of faith in the Trinity and the cross. We also genuflect to recognize Christ's real presence in the tabernacle. We stand at attention and fold our hands as the liturgy begins to show that something important and different from our ordinary experience has begun, keeping our body in receptive attention. We strike our breast to ask forgiveness for our sins to remove obstacles to prayer. We listen attentively to God's word, allowing Him to speak directly to us through His Word and make three additional crosses on our forehead, lips, and heart to show how we want them to be shaped by this Word. We bring our prayers and needs before the altar as we prepare the altar for the sacrifice.

In one of the Mass's most characteristic postures, we kneel to express the sacredness of the actions taking place, humbling ourselves before these sacred mysteries. Our voices echo the choirs of angels and saints of heaven, joining in one beautiful chorus of praise. When the priest elevates the host and the chalice during the consecration, we enter into the holiest moment of the Mass and a crucial time of prayer. To join in Christ's prayer at this moment, we must recognize the reality of Christ's sacrifice and choose to enter into it. We offer our lives, along with all those to whom we are united in prayer, with Christ to the Father. We can make a profession of faith during the elevation of the host and the chalice, repeating the words of the doubting Thomas, "my Lord and my God." After uniting to Christ's supreme offering, it is then possible to pray "Our Father" with Christ, sharing in His union with the Father and the peace that flows from it. After recognizing Christ as the lamb of God who takes away sin, there is a final prayer beseeching Christ to help us to make a worthy communion. Finally, having communed with Christ, we are sent forth into the world to share the fruits of the Mass.

All the actions in the Mass become clearer when prayer becomes aligned to its true goal. We go to Mass for God, to give Him the glory, thanks, and honor He deserves as Creator and Redeemer. The Mass has the same goal as human life—God's glory and human happiness by sharing in this glory—although it is the most direct and intense expression of it on earth. Hence the focus of the Mass is God, not us. We do benefit by going, of course, because through the Mass, God draws us into His own life, which is our true happiness. Every Mass provides an opportunity to enter into God's life and to give Him the most perfect praise, while at the same time receiving healing and strength in this encounter.

A traditional prayer recited before Mass captures the essence of the sacred liturgy:

> Eternal Father, I unite myself with the intentions and affections of our Lady of Sorrows on Calvary, and I offer Thee the sacrifice which Thy beloved Son Jesus made of Himself on the Cross, and now renews on this holy altar: To *adore* Thee and give Thee the honor which is due to Thee, confessing Thy supreme dominion over

all things, and the absolute dependence of everything upon Thee, Who art our one and last end. To *thank* Thee for innumerable benefits received. To *appease* Thy justice, irritated against us by so many sins, and to make satisfaction for them. To *implore* grace and mercy for myself, for [any special intentions], for all afflicted and sorrowing, for poor sinners, for all the world, and for the holy souls in purgatory. Amen.

This prayer also reminds us that our focus at Mass must be on God's glory. The Mass is not about what I can get out of it but what I offer to God in worship. It is through staying God-focused that the fruits of the Mass come to us. Saint Cajetan encourages this God-centered focus even in the act of Holy Communion. Writing in a letter to Elisabeth Porto, he says, "Do not receive Christ in the Blessed Sacrament so that you may use him as you judge best, but give yourself to him and let him receive you in this Sacrament, so that he himself, God your savior, may do to you and through you whatever he wills."[13] Mass exists for worship and communion, and only offers catechesis or instruction in a secondary sense, and it should stay focused on the dialogue of prayer that occurs with the Father. Everything that occurs at Mass does not need to be simplistic and straightforward, as this dialogue enters into God's mysterious transcendence. If the Mass inspires awe, it will communicate its eternal power more strongly than simple communication. The sublimity of the Mass, which should come through its solemnness and beauty, calls the worshipper beyond self and into God's transcendence.

---

[13] Kelly-Gangi, *365 Days with the Saints*, 154.

7

Divine Intimacy:
Communion and Adoration

If everything this book has related about the Eucharist thus far is true, the sacrament should be amazingly transformational in our lives. Why do we not see a greater impact and more fruit after going to Mass each week? Jesus wants to feed our souls, although we have to do our part to cooperate. This cooperation provides the opening that enables Jesus to shape our way of life. Jesus spoke clearly of what He intended in instituting the Eucharist. In John 6, Jesus says that He gives His flesh to eat so that those who believe in Him might "not hunger" and, after nourishing us, that He might raise us up on the last day (see Jn 6:35–40). He speaks of Himself as a new manna from heaven given to us so that we may abide in Him and have His everlasting life. The Eucharist, therefore, offers the spiritual food that strengthens the soul and keeps it on the right path. It is the supernatural sustenance that brings eternal life, drawing heaven down within us through the presence of Jesus. This divine food should completely transform us on our earthly pilgrimage to heaven! This chapter will examine how we can receive Communion fruitfully and worthily, entering into a loving union with Jesus and continuing to abide in this communion through adoration.

Forming the Right Disposition to Encounter Christ

If the Eucharist forms the heart of Catholic culture, as declared throughout this work, then it should guide how we live, perhaps imperceptibly at first, and then growing within us until it begins to shape things around us. Even though culture may seem primarily external—the customs and practices that shape daily life—it is animated by interior conviction and spiritual strength. Even with its seemingly external focus, culture itself, in attempting to form a shared way of life with others, expresses a deeply spiritual truth that we are made for communion. We can only find happiness with and through others, even on a human level, though especially in relation to God. In the Eucharist, God draws us into communion with Himself and gives us the deepest source of unity with others. It truly provides the animating principle of the Christian life.

For the Eucharist to shape our lives, we have to grow in receptivity to its grace. How we approach the sacrifice of the Mass impacts how much we get out of it. The more we focus our attention, unite our hearts to the sacrifice, and approach all the actions of the Mass with faith, the stronger the fruits that will arise from our prayer. The Bible presents models of different ways of relating to Jesus's sacrifice simply by looking to the foot of cross. First, we can see the negative reactions of some: the outright rejection of the Jewish leaders, the mockery of the Roman soldiers, and the indifference of so many who followed the crowds. On the other hand, we see the conversion of one solider, who learned to see Jesus truly, recognizing him as "the Son of God." The strongest models of love can be found in the repentant Saint Mary Magdalene, the faithful friendship of Saint John, and the shared sacrifice of Our Lady, who united herself most perfectly to Jesus in His suffering. In the end, everyone has a choice, two paths that are exemplified by the two thieves. We can refuse the Lord's mercy or confess our need for forgiveness, as Titian so beautifully depicts in the good thief's reaching out toward Christ. Reflecting on these possible dispositions can help us to avoid falling into distraction and apathy and can urge us on to imitate the loving union of Jesus's disciples. Like the thief, we can turn from our sin and seek the Savior's mercy.

Titian, *Christ and the Good Thief*, 1563

To foster a proper disposition for Mass, it is important to arrive early, which enables us to better remove distractions and thus achieve greater union with God. This preparation can even begin with added prayer the day before, as Saturday traditionally served as a day of preparation for the Lord's Day. This spirit of readiness not only frees our Sunday but turns our attention toward the Mass. On the day we attend Mass, it can also help to avoid those things that pull our minds and hearts away from giving ourselves completely to Christ in the Holy Eucharist, such as distracting entertainment. Taking extra time for prayer and avoiding things that turn our attention away from God increases our desire. It is amazing what a stronger desire can do for making a more fruitful Communion. It builds up our anticipation and increases our eagerness to participate, leading to greater focus and love—putting Jesus before other things. This is true love, as Saint Maximus the Confessor explains: "Love for God is this: to choose Him rather than the world," overcoming a love for self that remains stuck in the passions.[14] Putting God first shows that we truly desire communion with Him and prioritize it over other things. This desire pleases God and disposes us to His movement in our souls.

Increased preparation and desire for communion with Jesus leads us to make a deliberate choice to receive the Eucharist. Unfortunately, it has become increasingly routine to receive the Eucharist every time we go to Mass, to the point that we may be taking this great grace for granted.

---

[14] St. Maximus the Confessor, *Four Hundred Chapters on Love*, https://orthodoxchurchfathers.com/fathers/philokalia/st-maximos-the-confessor-four-hundred-texts-on-love.html.

Although frequent Communion was practiced in some places in the early Church, it became the ordinary practice in the Middle Ages to receive Communion only three times a year (at Christmas, Easter, and Pentecost), giving everyone ample time to prepare and anticipate these major occasions. More recently, the pendulum has swung in the other direction, with the reception of Communion seen as necessary at every Mass. With this regularity can come the possibility of making the Eucharist routine in a way that does not require deliberate thought and choice. If we receive the Eucharist frequently, then we should make each occasion a big deal, making a conscious choice to accept Jesus's gift of Himself.

Making a prayerful intention at each Mass can express our deliberate choice to receive Communion. This moment of prayer before Mass immediately breaks us out of a routine reception. A simple prayer can create greater openness to the grace of the sacrament, such as: "Lord, allow me to receive You this day. Help me to enter into communion with You today." A formal example of making an intention can be found in Saint Thomas Aquinas's prayer before Holy Communion, which begins, "Almighty and Eternal God, behold I come to the sacrament of Your only-begotten Son, our Lord Jesus Christ. As one sick I come to the Physician of life; unclean, to the Fountain of mercy; blind, to the Light of eternal splendor; poor and needy to the Lord of heaven and earth." There are many other beautiful prayers written to help in the preparation to receive the Eucharist and to pray well at Mass, such as those written by Saint Ambrose and Venerable Fulton Sheen that are included in many prayer books (see appendix II). Many sacristies have a sign reminding priests how to approach the Mass: "Priest of Jesus Christ celebrate this Holy Mass as if it were your first Mass, your last Mass, your only Mass." This same sentiment is important for the lay faithful to break us out of indifference and routine. Each time we receive Jesus, we receive an eternal gift, one not to be taken for granted

How often should we receive Communion? Many saints have upheld the benefits of frequent Communion as essential to the pursuit of holiness. Pope Saint Pius X, for instance, championed a more regular reception of Communion, issuing *Sacra Tridentina* to encourage it in 1905. Even as he preaches the great benefit of frequent Communion, he also reinforces the importance of having the proper disposition: "A right intention consists in this: that he who approaches the Holy Table should do so, not out of routine, or vain glory, or human respect, but that he wish to please God, to be more closely united with Him by charity, and to have recourse to this divine remedy for his weakness and defects." Pius gives some practical advice on preparation: "Since, however, the Sacraments of the New Law, though they produce their effect *ex opere operato*, nevertheless, produce a great effect in proportion as the dispositions of the recipient are better, therefore, one should take care that Holy Communion be preceded by careful preparation, and followed by an appropriate thanksgiving, according to each one's strength, circumstances and duties." We can greatly benefit from receiving the Eucharist regularly if we approach Jesus for the right reason and with the right disposition.

In addition to this guidance from Saint Pius, there are some other dispositions that help in approaching the Eucharist worthily and well. First, it is important to remember that we attend Mass primarily to honor God and to give Him glory. While there is an obligation to attend Mass each Sunday, we are required to receive Communion only once a year. This weekly duty calls us to stay God-centered rather than self-centered. The Mass is not about us, to make us feel good or provide entertainment. We could approach Mass as a consumer, seeking only what serves one's own sensibilities and comfort rather than moving out of oneself in receptivity and obedience to God. The Mass is about God and His glory, not our own self-satisfaction.

Second, to eat the supernatural food of the Eucharist, we need a supernatural approach, guided by the theological virtues of faith, hope, and love. With faith, we have the eyes to perceive the spiritual realities of the Mass and to approach them with reverence and devotion. Denying Jesus's true presence in the Eucharist in an act of disbelief, on the other hand, creates a serious obstacle that prevents one from receiving its grace. Receiving the Eucharist without faith, therefore, constitutes a sin of sacrilege, treating the sacrament as ordinary objects—bread and wine—rather than the true body and blood of the Savior. Hope, expressing our trust in God, also plays a crucial role in receiving Communion, inspiring us to confess our sins and to accept the mercy of God in order to approach the sacrament without fear. Receiving the Eucharist with a penitential attitude, asking forgiveness for venial sin and making reparation for past sins out of love constitutes a true attitude of hope.[15] The Eucharist strengthens our

---

[15] Those who commit serious or mortal sins should not approach the Holy Eucharist without first going to the sacrament of Penance. This will be addressed in the next chapter.

hope in God, giving us confidence that He will draw us to heaven. Charity expresses a Eucharistic attitude more than any other virtue, however, because it enables us to experience union with Jesus, uniting our minds and heart to Him out of love. The Eucharist should inspire us to love God more than ourselves or any created thing, as God gives Himself to us through it, the supreme good we could possess.

Third, communion should express gratitude, remembering that the word "Eucharist" stems from Jesus's own thanksgiving to the Father. Within her new Passover meal, the Church commemorates liberation from slavery and the new life won for us in the eternal promised land. In the moment of communion, when heart speaks to heart, gratitude for the Jesus's gift springs up naturally, reflecting on the eternal gift of Himself. This gratitude expresses joy for all that Jesus has done for us—giving us life, winning our salvation, providing for our every present and future need, and helping us to overcome difficulties. Gratitude provides a necessary disposition to welcome Jesus into our hearts in the great thanksgiving of the Eucharist.

Fourth, we can deepen our desire to receive Jesus. Saint Ambrose, drawing upon the Song of Songs, speaks of a yearning or longing for ever deeper intimacy with God through the sacraments: "You see how, delighted with the gifts of grace, she longs to attain to the innermost mysteries, and to consecrate all her affections to Christ. She still seeks, she still stirs up His love, and asks of the daughters of Jerusalem to stir it up for her, and desires that by their beauty, which is that of faithful souls, her spouse may be incited to ever richer love for her."[16] Desire, more often than anything else, can free us from complacency and routine receptions of the Holy Eucharist, as it looks to God in expectation, opening the soul to His gifts. Without this desire and proper preparation, it may be better at times to wait to receive the Eucharist at a future time, particularly as it may increase our spiritual appetite for the divine gift.

The Prayer of Saint John Chrysostom, which Byzantine Catholics pray before Communion, embodies many of these dispositions. Saying this prayer, or another like it, will assist in approaching the Eucharist with a proper spirit. Here are some selections from it (see the full prayer in appendix II):

> O Lord, I believe and profess that you are truly the Christ, the Son of the living God, who came into the world to save sinners, of whom I am the first. Accept me as a partaker of your mystical supper, O Lord. . . . May the partaking of your heavenly mysteries, O Lord, be not for my judgment nor condemnation, but for the healing of soul and body. I also believe and profess that this is truly Your most precious Body and life giving precious Blood, which I pray, make me worthy to receive, for the remission of all my sin and for life everlasting. Amen.[17]

The prayer both recognizes the reality of the sacrament and asks that we may be made worthy to receive the Holy Eucharist so that it can bear its intended fruit in us.

---

[16] St. Ambrose, "On the Mysteries," ch. 7.
[17] "Prayers and Devotions," *Byzantine Catholic Eparchy of Parma*, https://parma.org/prayer.

Union with Jesus in the Eucharist

Culture fosters communion through a communal striving after life's goal and purpose. Jesus offers us the greatest communion possible on earth by inviting us to become one with Him in the Eucharist. The very foundation of society stems from the family, providing its most stable foundation as a place of life and growth in love. In the Eucharist, a great sacrament of love, Jesus draws together God's family in the foundation of a supernatural culture. He gives us His entire self, anticipating the eternal marital union that God destined for us in heaven. Saint Paul describes how the man and woman become one flesh in marriage, no longer belonging simply to oneself (see 1 Cor 7:4; Eph 5:31). We speak of the Church both as the bride and body of Christ, and it is in the Eucharist where both of these realities become most fully present to us. Jesus offers us His own body and invites us to make a gift of self in return to become one flesh with Him.

As sacramental beings, Jesus does not offer the divine life in any abstract sense, beyond our comprehension or touch. Rather, He gives us His divinity to eat, offering us access to His whole self—His body, mind, soul, and heart—and His union with the Father and Holy Spirit. We have seen already the foundational role that food also plays in culture. Eating, therefore, provides another perspective for understanding the Eucharist as the source of life and growth. Saint Augustine related, writing in the voice of Jesus, how the sacrament feeds and nourishes us supernaturally: "I am the food of grown men; grow, and you shall feed upon me; nor shall you change me, like the food of your flesh, into yourself, but you

shall be changed into me."[18] Jesus feeds us eternal food in
order to draw us into His own eternal life, and by consuming His flesh, we become "partakers of the divine nature" (2
Pt 1:4). Through the Eucharist, Jesus conforms us to Himself, to His human virtues, and even to His divine life.

In our pursuit of life's goal and purpose, Jesus does not
leave us alone. He stoops down to us and gives us another
foundational good of human life—friendship. Communion
literally means to be made as one, and receiving Jesus in
this way creates a union of two hearts. Friendship entails
sharing good things in common, and in the Eucharist, Jesus
shows the extent of His friendship as He literally withholds
nothing from us, not even His communion with the Father
and the Spirit. He leads us into the bosom of the Father to
share in His own sonship, enabling us to share in His love
for the Father through His Spirit living in us. In the Eucharist, we can say that we no longer live alone. With Saint
Paul, we can say: "It is no longer I who live, but Christ who
lives in me" (Gal 2:20). In everything that we do, we can
live and love like Jesus by extending the communion that
He gives us to others—especially in being willing to sacrifice and suffer for them. This sacrifice forms the foundation
for any truly Christian civilization, born from Jesus's own
Eucharistic gift.

The Eucharist leads us into an abiding communion that
should last more than just a few minutes at Mass. We are
drawn into Jesus's life so that we ourselves can become a
Eucharistic communion. Saint Ignatius of Antioch describes

---

[18] Augustine, *Confessions*, book VII, 10, 16.

this best as he prays that through his impending martyr-dom, he would be "ground" up in order to become the "pure bread of God."[19] In our communion with Jesus, He wants to transform us and make us holy. The Eucharist, therefore, offers us the most important path to become saints. The transformation in us will happen when we give God regular access to our souls, to live within it and fashion it into His temple. Over time, He removes things that should not be there—our vices, attachments, and imperfections—and begins to perfect us more and more, building up the virtues, grace, and His own presence in us.

Many today doubt or overlook the Holy Eucharist's power, believing rather in a false narrative that they can change themselves or save themselves without God's help. Jesus can overcome this false narrative through the living power of His sacramental presence. As He once related in a private revela-tion to the Benedictine mystic, Saint Mechtilde of Hacken-born (1240–98): "The more often a soul communicates, the purer it becomes, as we become cleaner if we wash often. The more often a soul communicates, the more I operate in it; and the more it works with Me, its actions become more holy. The more often a soul communicates, the more profoundly does it dwell in Me; and the more it penetrates into the abyss of My divinity, the more is that soul dilated and capable of contain-ing the divinity. In the same way water falling on a certain spot of stone at length wears a cavity to fill."[20]

---

[19] Saint Ignatius wrote to the Romans, "I am the wheat of God, and let me be ground by the teeth of the wild beasts, that I may be found the pure bread of Christ." St. Ignatius, "Letter to the Romans," ch. 4.

[20] Saint Mechtilde of Hackenborn, *The Love of the Sacred Heart*, 160.

The moment of communion ought to be the greatest moment of our lives, for it is of the highest importance for our souls. God descends from heaven and through a real and physical presence, enters into us. Saint Mechtilde spoke of the Sacred Heart becoming "an open treasury from which we may take all we need," because "then our Lord not only gives graces, but Himself; and He gives Himself that He may be everything to the soul."[21]

Saints like Mechtilde manifest the true power of the Eucharist. They embraced its grace and overcame the obstacles that impede it, such as indifference, distraction, attachment to earthly goods, and a lack of fervor. They show a true appreciation for this divine gift, teaching us how to make up for "the neglect to which the majority of men have abandoned him," as Saint Peter Julian Eymard put it.[22] Just as there can be no Holy Eucharist without the priesthood, so there could be no saints without the Holy Eucharist. Saint Teresa of Avila, for instance, would go into ecstasy after receiving the Lord in the sacrament. Angelo Graf von Courten's painting *Holy Communion* gives us a glimpse of the hidden, spiritual power that comes to us in the Eucharist, reminding us not to take this moment for granted. At the moment we receive the Eucharist, we can ascend Jacob's

---

[21] Saint Mechtilde of Hackenborn, 155, 167.

[22] St. Peter Julian Eymard, *How to Get More Out of Holy Communion*. St. Faustina also spoke of a special day each month to pray in reparation for sacrilege against the Eucharist: "The crusade day, which is the fifth of the month, happened to fall on the First Friday of the month. This was my day for keeping watch before the Lord Jesus. It was my duty to make amends to the Lord for all offenses and acts of disrespect and to pray that, on this day, no sacrilege be committed." *Diary: Divine Mercy in My Soul*, no 160.

ladder to reach the hidden mysteries, sharing in the movement of angels from heaven to earth, ultimately leading us into God's own life. The Eucharist will change us if we approach Jesus in love and devotion.

Angelo Graf von Courten, *Holy Communion*

The power of union with Jesus during Communion can be extended by making a good thanksgiving. A thanksgiving prayer refers to the time after Communion when we remain in Jesus's Eucharistic presence for quiet prayer. Jesus remains present in the Eucharistic species so long as the accidents of bread and wine remain, which averages about ten to fifteen minutes for the species of the bread. It is important to remain in prayer for this duration and not to leave Mass beforehand, as Jesus's sacramental presence in us should be honored and respected (unlike Judas, who left the Last Supper immediately after receiving Jesus's gift). This practice shows Jesus the attention of hospitality during His visit into our body and soul. Padre Pio's prayer after Communion expresses this sentiment of asking Jesus to remain dwelling in us: "Stay with me, Lord, for I desire to love You ever more, and to be always in Your company. Stay with me, Lord, if You wish me to be always faithful to You. Stay with me, Lord, for as poor as my soul is, I wish it to be a place of consolation for You, a dwelling of Your love." This prayer, along with other beautiful ones, can help us to make a good thanksgiving (see appendix II).

Adoring Christ Always

"Stay with us" (Lk 24:29). Jesus listened to the request of the two disciples journeying to Emmaus and broke bread with them, manifesting Himself to them. Even after receiving the great gift of communion with Jesus, this can be our prayer too: "Jesus, do not leave me after this time together, but stay with me this week until I receive you again." Leaving Mass should not end our communion with Jesus but rather anchor

it. We are called to a life centered on the Eucharist, not ourselves. And our society is called to the same standard: a life
centered on God and others. Communion provides a foundation for the entire Christian life, guiding everything that
we do, which, in turn, should lead us back to this encounter
each Sunday as our inner life, finding constant refreshment
in an abiding communion with Jesus.

We abide in Lord's presence through prayer, strengthening our ongoing communion. Making a visit to the Blessed
Sacrament during the week extends our communion with
Jesus. The *Catechism* describes the prayer of adoration as
"the first attitude of man acknowledging that he is a creature before his Creator. It exalts the greatness of the Lord
who made us and the almighty power of the Savior who sets
us free from evil. Adoration is homage of the spirit to the
'King of Glory,' respectful silence in the presence of the 'ever
greater' God."[23] A few elements stand out from this definition. We need continually to recognize God's presence,
greatness, and our great need for Him that teaches us always
to rely on Him. We need to cultivate silence in order to abide
with our Eucharistic King. Adoration, in this sense, is a continual disposition of honor and respect toward Jesus, one
that leads us to seek Him out to spend time with Him. This
time opens the door to Jesus's lordship over our lives. Ingres's

---

[23] *CCC* 2628. Saint Peter Julian Peter Eymard described adoration of the
Blessed Sacrament in this way: "To adore Jesus Christ in the Most Blessed
Sacrament is to offer Him the sovereign homage of our entire being: of
our body by the profoundest respect, of our mind by faith, of our heart by
love, or our will by obedience, of all our senses by a worship of the deepest
reverence." *Eucharistic Handbook*, IV, article 1.

Virgin Adoring the Host depicts the Blessed Mother in prayer to demonstrate this disposition of adoration in relation to Jesus's Eucharistic presence. This strikingly beautiful and delicate painting captures the silence, dignity, and serenity that flows from approaching the King of Glory in His humble sacramental presence. It becomes the stability of our lives that sustains us each day and helps us to take up our crosses.

Jean Auguste Dominique Ingres, *Virgin Adoring the Host*, 1854

Adoration and the Mass are intertwined with each other. According to Pope Benedict XVI, "Eucharistic adoration is simply the natural consequence of the Eucharistic

celebration, which is itself the Church's supreme act of adoration. . . . The act of adoration outside Mass prolongs and
intensifies all that takes place during the liturgical celebration itself."[24] The practice of adoration follows naturally
from intimacy with Jesus in communion. When we grow
in friendship and love with Him, we seek Him out to spend
more time with Him. The Church reserves the Blessed Sacrament of the Eucharist in the tabernacle in church precisely
for this reason, as a place of refuge where we can find Jesus
at any time. The Council of Trent affirmed the practice of
reserving the sacrament in church as "a very ancient observance of the Catholic Church."[25] What began for the purpose of keeping Jesus's Eucharistic presence available for the
sick grew into a deeper devotion of coming to church specifically for prayer before the Blessed Sacrament.

In a Catholic culture, communal devotion becomes a
way of uniting the community around its central belief in
God's tangible presence within it. Belief in the true presence
marked the culture of medieval Christendom, stimulating
art, architecture, and personal devotion. Just as there are
developments in doctrine, so the Church's devotion developed as she sought to draw more people into an encounter
with Jesus in the Eucharist. Public acts of veneration and
processions began around the year 1000, and exposition of

---

[24] Pope Benedict XVI, *Sacramentum Caritatis*, no. 66. In an earlier
work, he explained, "Communion only reaches its true depth when it
is supported and surrounded by adoration." Ratzinger, *The Spirit of the
Liturgy*, 90.
[25] The Council of Trent, Session XIII, October 2, 1551, "Decree on the
Most Holy Eucharist."

the Blessed Sacrament in a monstrance[26] probably began during the thirteenth century. The first documented instance of perpetual adoration (which continues without ceasing in a particular chapel) comes from 1226 in the city of Avignon. Religious orders have also adopted this practice as their charism, the first being the Order of the Benedictine Nuns of Perpetual Adoration founded by Mother Mechtilde de Bar in Paris in 1654. The practice also arose of blessing people with the monstrance by making the Sign of the Cross, called Benediction, which is now generally prayed with Eucharist hymns composed by Saint Thomas Aquinas (*O Salutaris* and *Tauntum Ergo*) and by reciting the Divine Praises (a series of invocations that begins "Blessed be God").

Outward actions strengthen faith, including Eucharistic devotion. British sociologist Stephen Bullivant notes that intense public devotion to the Eucharist, such as Forty Hours, provides credibility to the faith, as Catholics make public sacrifices to manifest their devotion.[27] At a time when Jesus's Eucharistic presence was questioned by Protestantism, a number of saints began promoting forty hours of continuous Eucharistic adoration in parishes. The number forty originally arose to match the time Christ spent in the tomb and then became a time of penance during the extravagance of Carnival. Many saints have promoted this practice, including Saint Anthony Maria Zaccaria, Saint

---

[26] The monstrance is a gold vessel with a base, a shaft where it can be held, and sunburst at the top with a glass opening in the center for veneration and metal rays and a cross extending from there.

[27] Bullivant, *Mass Exodus*, 102. Bullivant describes these Eucharistic practices as Credibility Enhancing Displays (CREDS).

Charles Borromeo, Saint Philip Neri, and Saint Francis de Sales during the Counterreformation. Pope Clement VIII arranged for it to be practiced by Roman churches in succession so Jesus would always be adored in the city. Forty Hours was first encouraged in the United States by the immigrant bishop of Philadelphia Saint John Neumann, a practice confirmed and spread by the Plenary Council of Baltimore in 1866. Benedict XVI asked for the Church to return to the devotion in his exhortation on the Eucharist, *Sacramentum Caritatis*. No matter how adoration occurs—before the tabernacle, with Jesus exposed in a monstrance, at Forty Hours, or a special event like a Eucharistic Congress—it entails a powerful practice of prayer and contemplation, intensified by the sacramental presence of Jesus.

Adoration gazes upon the face of Jesus in the Eucharist, even if hidden by the accidents of bread, in order to become like Him. Silent adoration maintains a simplicity of prayer, taking time to kneel before Jesus and just to be with Him. Saint John Vianney observed this in one of his parishioners who stopped in church twice each day. When the saint asked what he said to Jesus during these visits, he replied, "Eh, Monsieur le Curé I say nothing to him, I look at him and he looks at me!"[28] Adoration beckons us away from the noise and distraction of daily life into a sanctuary of peace and grace. The papal preacher Father Raniero Cantalamessa points out that adoration should be "done, as far as possible, in a state of outer and inner silence."[29] "It is by staying in

---

[28] *CCC* 2751.
[29] Cantalamessa, *The Eucharist*, 61.

silence," he urges us, "and possibly for long periods, before Jesus in the Blessed Sacrament, that we perceive what he wants from us, put aside our own plans to make way for his, and let God's light gradually penetrate the heart and heal it."[30] When you think about it that way, how could our life not be enriched from spending more time with Jesus?

In order to strengthen His Church, Jesus calls all of us, both laity and clergy, to return to the practice of adoration in order to make reparation for sin and to obtain an out-pouring of holiness for our renewal. The solutions to our problems—personal, ecclesial, and societal—are hidden in the Blessed Sacrament. Simply by making a visit to Jesus in church or in adoration each day or each week, a transforma-tion will occur in us. Adoration gives Jesus more time to act in our souls, to bless us, and through us to give renewed life to our family, our parishes, and to the Church. Silent prayer before the Blessed Sacrament will transform our lives and bring about many graces. It can guide and direct our lives so that we live with, in, and through our communion with Jesus each day.

---

[30] Cantalamessa, 61.

8

Eucharistic Practices:
Fasting and Confession

Culture arises when exterior practices give shape to the most fundamental beliefs about human life. More than simply survival, culture strives after the highest things, guided by ritual and festivity. The interior elements of human life take precedence—what we believe, our virtue and character, for instance—but they only arise and endure by regular external practice. The Eucharist becomes culture through regular practices that lead to it and live out its grace. This chapter will explore some of the most important practices that surround the Eucharist and enculturate it in our lives—namely, preparation, fasting, and confession.

Why Preparation Matters

We spend a lot of time preparing for the most important things in life. Think of all the hours spent studying to earn a degree or land a job. As Catholics, we are accustomed to lengthy preparations to receive the sacraments, requiring months for marriage preparation and almost an entire year to get ready for first Communion. We also take time to recollect our sins before confession. The Eucharist is the most important sacrament, but due to how frequently we receive it, it is easy to limit our preparation. It is not a once and done sacrament, as the communion it engenders is meant to endure in a way akin to marriage. Just like in marriage, there is a need to continue to develop the relationship so that it does not grow lukewarm or lose its romance. The most significant moment of our lives, our communion with God, requires significant preparation.

A Eucharistic life requires great preparation not only to receive but also savor the fruits of our encounter with Jesus in the sacrament. Jesus Himself warned us about approaching the feast of His kingdom without the right disposition. In a somewhat shocking parable, Jesus evokes the festive nature of the Church's celebration of the Mass with a "king who gave a marriage feast for his son, and sent his servants to call those who were invited to the marriage feast" (Mt 22:2–3). When those invited first do not arrive, the king's servants fill the wedding hall with anyone they could find, good and bad. As we see in Vincent Malo's depiction of the parable, the new guests receive scrutiny: "But when the king came in to look at the guests, he saw there a man who had no wedding garment; and he said to him, 'Friend, how did you get in here without a wedding garment?' And he was speechless. Then the king said to the attendants, 'Bind him hand and foot, and cast him into the outer darkness; there men will weep and gnash their teeth.' For many are called, but few are chosen" (vv. 11–14). We have been so blessed to receive an invitation to the feast, yet we have to do our part and make ourselves ready to enter it. Looking at Malo's painting, we could ask, "Why bring the man in only to scrutinize him?" He can be judged, however, based on the fact that he did not put forth effort to come prepared to the feast, thinking that his dingy dress would be appropriate. On one level, God has given us the robe we need in the sacrament of Baptism, although He calls us to keep our robe clean (see Rv 22:14). No one may celebrate the feast of the lamb without proper preparation.

Vincent Malo, *Guest without Wedding Attire*, 1631

The Eucharist requires ongoing conversion, an openness to God's grace that enables us to receive the sacrament worthily. Jesus invites everyone to come to His feast, although as seen in the parable, "both the bad and good" attend the wedding feast. Saint Thomas Aquinas, in his hymn "Lauda Sion," describes how this point relates to the Eucharist: "Both the wicked and the good / eat of this celestial Food: / but with ends how opposite! / With this most substantial Bread, / unto life or death they're fed, / in a difference infinite."[31] As Aquinas explains, the wicked consume the Eucharist to their spiritual death. They have not kept their wedding garment clean, and coming to the Eucharist unprepared only makes their situation worse. Those separated from God in mortal sin do not approach the sacrament in the friendship and love necessary for genuine communion.

Receiving the Eucharist without the proper disposition and preparation harms the soul. Saint Paul describes the spiritual and even physical harm that comes from approaching the Eucharist unworthily: "Whoever, therefore, eats the bread or drinks the cup of the Lord in an unworthy manner will be guilty of profaning the body and blood of the Lord. Let a man examine himself, and so eat of the bread and drink of the cup. For any one who eats and drinks without discerning the body eats and drinks judgment upon himself. That is why many of you are weak and ill, and some have died" (1 Cor 11:27–30). Paul speaks of being worthy, doing an examination, and discerning Christ's body. He points to the need for faith along with the right state of soul to avoid a sacrilegious Communion. This brings us back to the need

---

[31] Likewise, a fifteenth-century English poet, the Franciscan Friar James Ryman, spoke of the Eucharist as a source of life: "Eat ye this bread, eat ye this bread / And eat it so ye be not dead. / This bread from heaven did descend / From all ills us to defend / And to give us life without end. / In Virgin Mary this bread was baked / When Christ, of her, manhood did take / Free of all sin mankind to make."

for deliberation and making a conscious choice to receive the sacrament only when we are ready.

The greatest preparation comes from ongoing conversion, literally a "turning toward" the Lord and turning from what leads us away from Him. We may have had a dramatic conversion moment in our lives, although conversion needs to endure as a continual striving to align our lives to Christ. In *Introduction to the Devout Life*, Saint Francis de Sales gives practical advice on this point: "We cannot be fed by that Living Flesh and hold to the affections of death," otherwise there will be contradiction in our souls. Saint Francis continues, "Those who communicate weekly must be free from mortal sin, and also from any attachment to venial sin, and they should feel a great desire for Communion; but for daily Communion people should furthermore have conquered most of their inclinations to evil, and no one should practice it without the advice of their spiritual Guide."[32] Approaching the Eucharist in serious sin or even with an attachment to sin (wanting to sin and not trying to stop) impedes its grace from bearing fruit. Deeper and prolonged preparation, on the other hand, creates a greater receptivity to its grace.

We need to ask, "Are we impeding the great graces that Jesus gives us in the Eucharist? Are we in a state of spiritual sickness or death that comes from receiving the Eucharist without discernment?" Father Jacques Philippe raises this challenging question from another perspective, asking "why, for instance, are so many people who receive Communion

---

[32] Saint Francis de Sales, *Introduction to the Devout Life*, 106–7.

frequently not more holy?"[33] The problem is not on the side of the Eucharist, surely, so we need to think about how we can receive its grace and to live in it more fully. Our lives certainly cannot contradict Jesus's presence and truth. Receiving Communion, rather, must accompany a life turned toward God in prayer and one turned away from sin. Living a life centered on Jesus and His Eucharistic presence in prayer, virtue, and charity removes obstacles and unlocks its power in our lives—keeping the door of our hearts open to Him to act. Jesus will begin to sort things out in our life, conforming us to Himself more and more, if we take time for prayer and do our best to remove those things that lead us away from Him. The Eucharist truly is the greatest source of grace to transform our lives.

The Necessity of Fasting and Penance

Even if interior conversion forms the strongest preparation, exterior acts reinforce our interior state. There is one exterior form of preparation that the Church insists upon. It mandates a period of fasting before receiving the Eucharist. Jesus Himself makes the connection between fasting and His presence, pointing to the festive nature of communion with Him. In response to a challenge from the Pharisees that John's disciples fast while His do not, Jesus answers, "Can you make wedding guests fast while the bridegroom is with them? The days will come, when the bridegroom is taken away from them, and then they will fast in those days" (Lk 5:34–35). As he continues to explain, Jesus, the bridegroom,

---

[33] Philippe, *Time for God*, 24.

wants to offer us a new wine that requires letting go of the old, for "new wine must be put into fresh wineskins" (Lk 5:38). The old wine, speaking on one level of the practices of the old covenant, also speaks universally to letting go of an earthly way of thinking and living. Fasting helps us to turn away from the "old man," our old ways of thinking and living, so that we can enter the wedding feast of the lamb with a new mind and heart.

We fast to prepare to meet the bridegroom so that we can feast with Him at Mass. The Church's fasting requirement points to the need to pause from our normal way of doing things for at least a short time in order to switch gears. To eat the bread of life, we stop eating ordinary food so that we can distinguish between them. This fast of no food or drink (other than water and medicine) one hour prior to Communion constitutes at least a small break from the attachments that hold us back from a deeper encounter with Jesus in the Eucharist. [34] Exterior actions have an influence on our interior disposition. Fasting fosters the disposition and demeanor needed to receive the flesh of Christ. The *Catechism* teaches that "to prepare for worthy reception of this sacrament, the faithful should observe the fast required in their Church. Bodily demeanor (gestures, clothing) ought to convey the respect, solemnity, and joy of this moment when Christ becomes our guest."[35] Fasting accompanies

---

[34] Traditionally the fast began at midnight the prior night, although Pope Pius XII changed it to three hours before Communion and then Pope Paul VI to one hour following the Second Vatican Council.

[35] *CCC* 1387.

bodily movements of respect, reverence, and even clothing to complete the wedding garment needed for the feast.

Fasting detaches us from earthly cares in order to receive supernatural goods. More than a formulaic requirement, fasting frees us from material attachments before receiving the Eucharist. Attachments come from loving earthly things or comforts too much, in a way that keeps us from desiring and pursuing spiritual things. Saint John of the Cross said that not only the chains of sin keep us from flying but even a simple thread can keep us bound to the earth: "For it comes to the same thing whether a bird be held by a slender cord or by a stout one; since, even if it be slender, the bird will be well held as though it were stout, for so long as it breaks it not and flies not away."[36] Even if not always sinful, attachments impede our full participation in the liturgy. For instance, the Liturgy of Saint John Chrysostom calls attendees to cast aside all worldly matters when approaching the altar: "Let us who mystically represent the Cherubim and sing the thrice holy hymn to the life creating Trinity, now set aside all earthly cares." Saint Dominic, as depicted by the renowned Greek artist El Greco, provides a model for approaching prayer without the burden of our earthly cares. Despite the dark clouds swirling around the saint, Dominic remains focused on the cross. His fixed gaze and posture reveal his intense efforts to concentrate his entire being on God. The simplicity of the composition and starkness of color points to the absence of distraction as he enters prayer.

---

[36] Saint John of the Cross, *The Ascent of Mt. Carmel*, Bk. 1, ch. 11, no. 4.

El Greco, *Saint Dominic in Prayer*, 1605

We need times of fasting to order our lives rightly, pointing us to the true source of our nourishment. By overcoming our ordinary hunger and bodily demands, fasting creates hunger for the things that satisfy our deeper needs. Without stopping the ordinary flow of meeting material needs, we can miss the demands of the soul and stay focused on passing things. By fasting before Mass along with designated days throughout the year, including abstaining from meat, the Church points to fasting as a necessary means of spiritual growth. Saint Francis de Sales, for example, recommends regular fasting:

> If you are able to fast, you will do well to observe some days beyond what are ordered by the Church, for besides the ordinary effect of fasting in raising the mind, subduing the flesh, confirming goodness, and obtaining a heavenly reward, it is also a great matter to be able to control greediness, and to keep the sensual appetites and the whole body subject to the law of the Spirit; and although we may be able to do but little, the enemy nevertheless stands more in awe of those whom he knows can fast. The early Christians selected Wednesday, Friday and Saturday as days of abstinence.[37]

The bond between fasting and the Eucharist is so strong that the Church calls for penance by abstaining from meat every Friday in order to prepare for the Sunday Eucharist. Thus, every Friday unites us to Good Friday in order to enter into the joy of the Resurrection on the Lord's Day. Friday presents a day of spiritual preparation for Sunday, to create the disposition to receive the Eucharist more worthily. Currently, the Code of Canon Law mandates that every Friday and all of Lent are considered days of penance: "All Fridays through the year and the time of Lent are penitential days" (Can. 1250) and "abstinence from eating meat or another food according to the prescriptions of the conference of bishops is to be observed on Fridays throughout the year unless they are solemnities; abstinence and fast are to be observed on Ash Wednesday and

---

[37] Saint John of the Cross, 182–83.

on the Friday of the Passion and Death of Our Lord Jesus Christ" (Can. 1251). Meatless Fridays are the default penance for the universal Church, although the United States bishops allow for the substitution of another penance in its place.[38]

Living in a post-Christian era, with ever greater challenges and temptations, the need for penance has increased greatly. Penance provides an essential and even obligatory part of the Christian life, one that Jesus Himself practiced and commended to His disciples. Penance has played a significant role in the Christian life, primarily through reparation and meritorious suffering, although this centrality of penance has been eclipsed in our time as the Church has relaxed its requirements. Fasting and penance carry an internal link to the Eucharist because they seek participation in Christ's offering of His body on the cross. As Saint Thomas Aquinas says, "In order to secure the effects of Christ's Passion, we must be likened unto Him."[39] Saint Paul puts it more mysteriously: "Now I rejoice in my sufferings for your sake, and in my flesh I complete what is lacking in Christ's afflictions for the sake of his body, that is, the church" (Col 1:24). The only thing lacking in Christ's suffering is our participation in them, a participation which conforms us to Christ who offered Himself out of love. Paul also tells us: "Present your bodies as a living sacrifice, holy and acceptable to God" (Rom 12:1). In penance, the Christian offers self in love, sharing in Christ's sacrifice of His body, the very heart of the Eucharist.

---

[38] See National Conference of Catholic Bishops, "Pastoral Statement on Penance and Abstinence," November 18, 1966, http://www.usccb.org/prayer-and-worship/liturgical-year/lent/us-bishops-pastoral-statement-on-penance-and-abstinence.cfm.

[39] St. Thomas Aquinas, *Summa Theologiae* III, q. 49, a. 3, ad 2

Modern culture has become self-centered. Rather than dying to self, our culture affirms all of our desires as good and pushes us to pursue them at whatever cost. Living a Christian way of life, however, requires that we die to ourselves, confess our sins, and make amends. In this ongoing conversion, fasting and penance play a key role, pointing us beyond ourselves. Penance also reminds us that "here we have no lasting city, but we seek the city which is to come" (Heb 13:14). The Church requires penance after confession to make up for the temporal consequences of sin, and the Christian life should always remain penitential. Fasting and penance seek continual union with the cross within a life in imitation of Jesus in His simplicity, poverty, and gift of self. They call us to eat less and not as extravagantly, to step back from the dominance of technology and entertainment, and to focus more on prayer. In this sense, the penitential nature of the Christian life points back to the Eucharist through focusing more on being filled by its sustenance than on anything else. And building a Eucharistic civilization points us to the world without end, heaven, where our true citizenship lies.

The Necessity of Confession

Jesus gives us the wedding garment we need to attend His banquet at Baptism. He entrusts this garment to us to keep clean, although He also gives us a way of washing it in His blood—by confessing our sins in the sacrament of Penance (also called confession or the sacrament of Reconciliation). In Baptism, we become His beloved children. Although when we sin, we set out from His house and leave Him behind for earthly pleasures, like the prodigal son. In confession, the Father welcomes us back into His love and mercy and invites us to feast on the fatted calf, a sign of the sacrificial banquet of the Mass. Jan Steen makes the connection clear between the tender forgiveness and the celebratory banquet in His painting of the moment when the father welcomes his son back home, particularly through the prominence of the calf in the lower left corner. You can see how the garment given to the son has become tattered, and so a new robe has been prepared in the hand of the person in the doorway. The father will restore his son, clothing him, and leading him into the celebration of his restored life.

Jan Steen, *The Return of the Prodigal Son*, 1668–70

Cultivating a Eucharistic life requires continual openness to God's grace and mercy. Jesus clearly linked worship to the state of our souls, teaching us the need for reconciliation before worship: "So if you are offering your gift at the altar, and there remember that your brother has something against you, leave your gift there before the altar and go; first be reconciled to your brother, and then come and offer your gift" (Mt 5:23–24). If we need to reconcile with our brother, how much more so with God? Psalm 51 addresses this need: "The sacrifice acceptable to God is a broken spirit; a broken and contrite heart, O God, thou wilt not despise" (v. 17). Entering into the sacrifice of the Mass requires not only an exterior conformity of body through fasting but also an interior conformity of a life in union with the sacrifice of the Mass. The interior life must be brought into line with the sacrifice of Christ to share in its fruits.

The Church has always recognized the need for reconciliation to receive the Eucharist. Saint Paul directed the church in Corinth to cast a public sinner out of the community until he repented (1 Cor 5). The very first catechetical document of the Church, the *Didache* from the first century, spoke of the need for confession and reconciliation before celebrating the Eucharist: "But every Lord's day gather yourselves together, and break bread, and give thanksgiving after having confessed your transgressions, that your sacrifice may be pure. But let no one that is at variance with his fellow come together with you, until they be reconciled, that your sacrifice may not be profaned."[40] Even if the practice of confession has developed

---

[40] *The Didache*, ch. 14.

over time—moving from a public to a private setting—the Church has remained consistent in teaching the need to confess serious sin before receiving Communion.

Because sin constitutes a rebellion against God and ruptures our relationship with Him, we must remove the obstacle of sin before receiving Communion. To approach the sacrament, we must be in a state of grace, having confessed any serious sin. Otherwise, we will commit another mortal sin, the sin of sacrilege against the Eucharist. Saint Paul wrote of this to the Corinthians as well: "Whoever, therefore, eats the bread or drinks the cup of the Lord in an unworthy manner will be guilty of profaning the body and blood of the Lord" (1 Cor 11:27). Saint Cyprian, in his treatise on "The Lapsed," speaks of examples of those who approached the Eucharist without confessing and reconciling with God and the Church, with disastrous consequences:

> And another woman, when she tried with unworthy hands to open her box, in which was the holy (body) of the Lord, was deterred by fire rising from it from daring to touch it. And when one, who himself was defiled, dared with the rest to receive secretly a part of the sacrifice celebrated by the priest; he could not eat nor handle the holy of the Lord, but found in his hands when opened that he had a cinder. Thus by the experience of one it was shown that the Lord withdraws when He is denied; nor does that which is received benefit the undeserving for salvation, since saving grace is changed by the departure of the sanctity into a cinder.[41]

---

[41] St. Cyprian, "Treatise 3, On the Lapsed," no. 26.

Those who receive the Eucharist with serious sin on their soul do not receive the grace of the Eucharist. Instead, they sin against this grace, receiving the equivalent of this burnt cinder rather than the treasure Christ wants to impart.

The Eucharist does not stand alone but flows from and leads to the other sacraments.[42] In this light, we see the interdependence of the Eucharist and confession. The Church requires attendance at Mass every Sunday, the reception of the Eucharist once a year, and the confession of sin also once a year. These three requirements have an intrinsic connection: the Eucharist makes the Risen Lord present each Sunday, and confession enables the reception of the Eucharist in good conscience. Catholics face many obstacles that require the healing grace of Reconciliation. We owe everything to God and the obligation to attend Mass on Sunday honors this debt. Deliberately skipping Mass constitutes a mortal sin because of its refusal to give God what we owe Him. Unfortunately, only a minority of Catholics attend Mass faithfully each week, and

---

[42] The Eucharist draws us into communion with God and fellow believers and forms the Church as the Body of Christ. Baptism begins initiation into the Church of Christ, though its grace is strengthened and completed by Confirmation, which provides spiritual maturity. The Eucharist completes initiation into the Church, making union that is the goal of all the sacraments. The sacraments of Baptism and Confirmation make a permanent impress on the soul, conforming it to Christ, enabling one to enter into the worship of the Father and to defend the faith (respectively). The Eucharist not only completes initiation but also leads one to abide in the other sacraments. Msgr. Nicola Bux describes how "there is interdependence between the Eucharist and the other sacraments: one would with that the faithful be inculcated with the knowledge that they flow forth from the Eucharist and flow together back into it as to their source: in fact the sacrifice of Christ is the paradigm of the life and death of man, and it accompanies every sacrament." Bux, *No Trifling Matter*, 86.

as we have seen, many Catholics do not believe in Jesus's true presence in the Eucharist.[43] Objectively speaking (as we cannot judge the state of anyone's soul), most Catholics are not in the right state to receive the Eucharist fruitfully and need the grace of confession to do so.

Can we see tangible effects of skipping Mass and confession in the Church? Saint Paul spoke of serious consequences of receiving the Eucharist unworthily, including sickness and death (see 1 Cor 11:30). We are languishing without the proper reception of these sacraments. To overcome the general crisis regarding the Eucharist today—lack of faithful Mass attendance, decline in faith, and infrequent confession—Pope Benedict XVI called for a "reinvigorated catechesis on the conversion born of the Eucharist, and of encouraging frequent confession among the faithful."[44] To address this spiritual starvation, the Church must teach the truth of Jesus's presence in the Eucharist, call the faithful to a proper preparation, lead them through how to make an examination of conscience, and make confession accessible regularly. Offering more frequent opportunities for confession reinforces the need for the sacrament, including offering it on Sunday when people are already at church.[45] One

---

[43] CARA, "Frequently Requested Church Statistics," http://cara.georgetown.edu/frequently-requested-church-statistics/; https://cara.georgetown.edu/realpres.jpg, accessed 11/09/2019.

[44] Pope Benedict XVI, *Sacramentum Caritatis*, co. 21.

[45] The Congregation for Divine Worship and Discipline of Sacraments affirmed the legitimacy of hearing Confessions during Mass. See *Adoremus*, "Reply to Hearing Confessions During Mass," https://adoremus.org/2007/12/31/Reply-to-a-question-about-hearing-confessions-during-Mass/, 12/31/2007.

hour a week, or even a few, does not suffice for large parishes with thousands of parishioners and cannot address the spiritual problem that arises from a lack of confession.

Preparing for the Eucharist begins by acknowledging our need for forgiveness. Denying the reality of sin—along with its painful effects and its offense to God—prevents us from seeking forgiveness. A report from CARA, Georgetown's Center for Applied Research in the Apostolate, conducted almost a decade ago, shows that "three-quarters of Catholics report that they never participate in the sacrament of Reconciliation or that they do so less than once a year."[46] Catholics no longer recognize the need to reconcile with God and others before coming to the altar. Sin has been conceived in private terms today (as in, I am not hurting anyone else), but because we are all members of the same Body, there is a need for reconciliation with the other members of the Church as well. Dostoyevsky describes this reality in his novel *Demons* through the character Stepan Trofimovich: "In sinning, each man sins against all, and each man is at least partly guilty for another's sin. There is no isolated sin."[47] We wound the body of Christ through sin, contributing to the spiritual crisis of the Church. The congregation, therefore, confesses its sins to one another at the beginning of every Mass, asking for each other's prayers during the *Confiteor*, and acknowledges its unworthiness before Communion, asking for forgiveness, "Lord, I am not worthy that you should enter under my roof, but only

---

[46] CARA, "The Sacrament of Reconciliation," https://cara.georgetown. edu/reconciliation.pdf, accessed 11/09/2019.

[47] Fyodor Dostoyevsky, *Demons*, trans. Robert Maguire (New York: Penguin Classics, 2008), 781.

say the word and my soul shall be healed," echoing the words of the centurion to Jesus. The Mass itself points to the need for the forgiveness of sins before receiving the Eucharist, and the sacrament of confession provides the grace needed to overcome the obstacle of sin and to make a worthy Communion.

Confession is a great blessing for Catholics, not the burden that our culture would make it out to be. Catholics are often presented as guilt-laden and obsessed with commandments. Catholics, rather, can face up to their sins and receive consolation from the confidence that God forgives us when we sincerely ask His pardon in the sacrament.[48] This consolation overflows into our reception of Communion, enabling us to receive the Eucharist with an unburdened conscience and a heart at one with God. We have to allow God to remove the spiritual obstacles that keep us from fruitful communion with Him. Our sin puts up blocks, and if we refuse to confess them, they compound over time, turning us away from God and impacting others. To live a genuine Eucharistic culture, therefore, we need the regular practice of confession, aiding our general preparation, constant conversion of heart, and fasting so that we can reap the fruit of our spiritual eating.

---

[48] For the sacrament of confession to be valid, we must have contrition—a true sorrow for our sins, which includes a firm resolution not to sin again— we must confess our sins, and express a willingness to perform penance.

PART III

The Christian Life: Building a Eucharistic Civilization

The Eucharist, as we have seen, is the source and summit of the Christian life. After exploring the source of Christian culture in part I and its summit in the Mass in part II, we now turn to talking more directly about how it shapes the Christian life. This section explores details of what a Eucharistic life looks like. Faith in the Eucharist needs to become a culture, giving rise to a way of life centered on and flowing from Jesus's true presence in the sacrament. If we truly encounter Jesus and enter into communion with Him at Mass, this should change everything in our lives. Jesus does not give us His body and blood in the Eucharist only for one hour a week. Through it, He wants to transform our whole lives. He wants us to put our faith into action, allowing it to take flesh in how we live, giving rise to a Christ-centered culture.

The Church has always understood that the way we pray is bound up with what we believe and how we live. As the *Catechism* explains, "the Church believes as she prays."[1]

---

[1] *CCC* 1124.

Likewise, how we pray and what we believe shapes the way in which we live. Traditionally, the interlocking nature of prayer, belief, and life has been expressed as *"lex orandi, lex credendi, lex vivendi,"* that the law of prayer leads to the law of belief and the law of life. In fact, it is a perfect expression of how Catholic culture develops, originating in our encounter with God, giving rise to how we think about life, and culminating in a life infused by this prayer and belief. More recently, the sociologist Stephen Bullivant has expressed this same reality. He describes how the "ways in which human beings pray, worship, and participate in religious rituals, individually and collectively, have concrete effects on people's moral, social and cultural lives, as they also do upon their beliefs and identities. *How* we worship matters."[2] There is nothing more important than our worship, as it brings us into a relationship with our maker and savior, the one who leads us to our true fulfillment.

This final section explores the relationship of the Eucharist to culture and how, over time, a renewal of culture can restore a Christian civilization. First, it looks at this relationship in itself, analyzing how the Eucharist shapes our life, leads to festivity, and shapes our imaginative vision of the world. Second, it explains the importance of making time for prayer, as it shapes each day, week, and year. Third, it describes how the Eucharist shapes space, the building dedicated to its celebration, of course, but also how these places influence the world while renewing our faith. Next, it looks at the Eucharist in light of our relationships and mission.

---

[2]   Bullivant, *Mass Exodus*, 256.

The Eucharist is the sacrament of love, inspiring us to transform the world for Christ by serving others, especially the poor. Charity will help build a Eucharistic civilization, for the love of Christ is the cornerstone of any true Christian society. Living a Eucharistic life allows the Lord to shape our own lives, influence others, and lay the foundation for broader societal renewal—as explained in the final chapter.

9

Living a Eucharistic Life:
The Heart of Catholic Culture

Catholic culture is a way of life that grows out of and is centered on faith. Catholic culture makes our faith come alive and take flesh in the world, giving supernatural life to all the elements of our mundane world. Jesus does not intend for the reception of the Eucharist at Mass to stand as an isolated act. It should serve, rather, as the source and summit of the entire Christian life. Contrasting with how His followers should live, He says simply in the Sermon on the Mount, "Do not be like them" (Mt 6:8). Referring to the Gentiles, He distinguishes their life from the natural life of the world. The Eucharist contains a revolution within itself as God takes on flesh anew in the life of His faithful. A Catholic, therefore, cannot worship God on Sunday and live the rest of the week as if He did not exist. The faithful live as the friends and stewards of the great high priest and King of heaven and have been tasked with spreading the kingdom on earth. The Eucharist should lead to a way of life centered on an abiding communion with God in prayer, the gift of self in service of neighbor, and a social life that incarnates faith.

The Eucharist: The Heart of Culture

What is Christian culture? John Senior, the great educator who inspired many converts while teaching at the University of Kansas, answers simply, "It is essentially the Mass."[3] In the *Restoration of Christian Culture*, he explains how the Eucharist gave shape to Western culture as a whole:

> Christendom, what secularists call Western Civilization, is the Mass and the paraphernalia which protect and facilitate it. All architecture, art, political and social forms, economics, the way people live and feel and think, music, literature—all these things when they are right, are ways of fostering and protecting the Holy Sacrifice of the Mass. To enact a sacrifice, there must be an altar, an altar has to have a roof over it in case it rains; to reserve the Blessed Sacrament, we build a little House of God and over it a Tower of Ivory with a bell and a garden round about it with roses and lilies of purity. . . . And around the church and garden, where we bury the faithful dead, the caretakers live, the priests and religious whose work is prayer, who keep the Mystery of Faith in its tabernacle of music and words in the Office of the Church; and around them, the faithful who gather to worship and divide the other work that must be done in order to make the perpetuation of the Sacrifice possible—to raise food and make the clothes and build and keep the peace so that generations to

---

[3]   For an overview of his life and thought, as well as the impact of the Integrated Humanities Program at the University of Kansas, see Bethel, *John Senior and the Restoration of Realism*.

come may live for Him, so that the Sacrifice goes on even unto the consummation of the world.[4]

Senior's claim could seem like an exaggeration, although it is simply a fact that the medieval city arose around the monastery and cathedral. Schools and then universities grew out of these churches, and artisans gathered around to enlarge and decorate them. Western music took shape out of the church's tradition of chant and polyphony. The Mass plainly and simply provided the great stimulant that grew the culture of Christendom and led to great achievements in learning, the arts, and the general cultivation needed to support the Christian life.

The Mass as the heart of culture can be seen in the city of Florence. Its cathedral, Il Duomo, not only served as the mother church of the city, literally where all of its citizens were baptized into the faith, but also provided the great stimulant for the Renaissance. All the greatest artists endeavored to beautify it as a symbol of the city itself, with the Eucharist at the center. Giotto, Ghiberti, Donatello, and Michelangelo are only a few of the renowned artists who helped build and adorn it. Rosselli's fifteenth-century cityscape shows the Duomo at the center of the city. Brunelleschi's dome, one of the greatest architectural achievements in history, dominates the skyline, a copula serving as giant baldachin for the Mass, giving the church its central prominence over the whole city.

---

[4]   Senior, *The Restoration of Christian Culture* (IHS Press), 17.

Francesco Rosselli, Florence, 1470

Cardinal Robert Sarah also points to the Mass as the source of Christian culture: "All of Christian civilization is born from the altar as from its source. . . . The altar is the heart of our cities. Literally, our towns are built around the altar, huddled around the church that protects them. The loss of the sense of God's grandeur is a dreadful regression toward savagery. The sense of the sacred is indeed the heart of all human civilization."[5] The Mass provides soil for the Christian life in the world, which should give life, as an oasis in the desert of the secular world. This hearkens back to Ezekiel's vision of water flowing from the temple in heaven (see chapter 47), giving life to the world. From the Mass, Christ's precious blood is spilled over every land and every people, renewing and saving our fallen race. From the center of the Mass, we see how faith should order all of life. Sarah argues, "The loss of the sense of God is the origin of all crises," because "the primacy of God ought to mean the centrality of God in our lives, our actions, and our thoughts."[6]

---

[5]   Sarah, *The Day Is Now Far Spent*, 44.
[6]   Sarah, 36; 37.

The transubstantiation of bread into Christ's body is only the first step of the transformation God intends. We are the next step, as Christ takes on flesh in us.

If the Eucharist truly constitutes the source and summit of the Christian life, then it should provide the grace needed for our interior life to blossom and bear fruit in the rest of our lives. Pope Saint John Paul II affirms that "the Church lives from the Eucharist."[7] Like a spring of water, the divine life springs up in us from it, irrigating and enlivening everything from this source. With this living water, the ordinary becomes extraordinary, flowing from God's presence within us. The trivial things of our life take on a supernatural character when we eat supernatural food. Therefore, Pope Benedict XVI calls for a Eucharistic culture that "embraces the whole of life."[8] Receiving the Lord's body can remain an isolated moment in life—meaningful, but not central to one's identity or daily life. God does not give us the Eucharist for our salvation alone but "for the life of the world" (Jn 6:51). And therefore, the Eucharist must not remain restricted to Mass or some secret devotion for our interior life. Rather, the Eucharist ought to inspire a Christian culture, a communal and social way of life that enables faith to take on flesh, not just in us but also in the world.

Christ has given us a mission in the world, one that goes beyond our own personal salvation (as some Christians might want to reduce it). When Jesus said to go out into every nation and make disciples (see Mt 28), He said that we must baptize

---

[7] Pope John Paul II, *Ecclesia de Eucharistia*, no. 1.
[8] Pope Benedict XVI, *Sacramentum Caritatis*, no. 77.

them and teach them to observe all that He commanded us. This centrally involves His command, "do this in memory of me," meaning that we as Catholics have a sacred obligation not to hold onto this treasure of Christ's Eucharistic presence simply for ourselves. Jesus wants us to share this presence with the world in order to sanctify it so that all may eat of His body for eternal life. In fact, gathering around the Lord's presence provides the true lifeblood for Christian community, feeding us with God's own life and drawing us into true communion with one another. Christian culture is not an individual affair, pointing to the fact that our salvation necessarily entails our bodily and social life.

Christian culture, from its source in the Eucharist, consists in a shared way of life that expresses and instantiates faith. Just as the Word became flesh, so faith must take on flesh within the life of each Christian. Even though Jesus said that His kingdom is not of this world, Christians must still live in the world, though in a way that seeks the true citizenship of heaven. Christians live in two worlds, seeking to shape this life through faith while looking ultimately to the next. The liturgy bridges the gap between these two worlds and grounds the shared way of life of Christians, giving them the supernatural power to transform the natural world. A Christian culture, therefore, exists as a way of life that draws its source in the Eucharist and finds its fulfillment in a life transformed by a holiness that shapes everything.

Bringing the Eucharist into the world gives shape to a liturgy of life that makes every act in the world an offering to God, seeking to give Him honor and glory. Putting God first in one's life enables the right ordering of everything else.

The liturgy of the Mass should touch not only the soul but extend its fruits into family life, work, and leisure. Christian culture itself becomes sacramental, an expression of the divine penetration of creation, extending the power of God's own entrance into the world. In the Eucharist, God enters the world again, renews creation as spirit transforms matter, and enables His creation to offer back to Himself a perfect work of prayer and sacrifice, a gift of infinite value. God thus draws human work into His sacrifice, sanctifying life and culture. By transforming the soul and making God present anew in the world, the Eucharist gives the spiritual power to shape human life and the world, transforming human culture and giving rise to a way of life centered on faith

We might think of culture as a supplement to faith, but, in fact, the Eucharist actually depends upon culture. It does not stand on its own, apart from a community or the material elements of culture. Faith does not exist in a vacuum; it leads us to form practices and to live what we believe. As John Paul II taught often, "faith must become culture," translating belief into stable and consistent action.[9] Robert Louis Wilken contends even further that "the Church is a culture in its own right. Christ does not simply infiltrate a culture; Christ creates culture."[10] Christians are not a group

---

[9]   Pope John Paul's press secretary, Joaquin Navarro-Valls, reports that the pontiff repeated the phrase often. Joaquin Navarro-Valls, "Faith Must Become Culture: John Paul's Legacy to Intellectuals and Scientists," *Interdisciplinary Encyclopedia of Religion and Science*, 2011, https://inters. org/faith-must-become-culture.

[10]   Robert Louis Wilken, "The Church as Culture," *First Things,* April 2004, https://www.firstthings.com/article/2004/04/the-church-as-culture.

of isolated believers as Christ established a Church through which they would live in the world. Their life is an extension of His life so that "the form taken by the community's life *is* Christ within society."[11] Could we imagine the celebration of the Eucharist without the essential elements of culture, which Wilken describes as "the pattern of inherited meanings and sensibilities encoded in rituals, law, language, practices, and stories that can order, inspire, and guide the behavior, thoughts, and affections of a Christian people"?[12] As Christians, we need culture to provide fertile ground from which our worship rises up and takes shape.

The *Catechism* also describes the Eucharist's dependence on culture, explaining how the sacraments weave together the goods of nature, culture, and salvation history:

> A sacramental celebration is woven from signs and symbols. In keeping with the divine pedagogy of salvation, their meaning is rooted in the work of creation and in human culture, specified by the events of the Old Covenant and fully revealed in the person and work of Christ. In human life, signs and symbols occupy an important place. As a being at once body and spirit, man expresses and perceives spiritual realities through physical signs and symbols. As a social being, man needs signs and symbols to communicate with others, through language, gestures, and actions. The same holds true for his relationship with God.[13]

---

[11] Wilken.

[12] Wilken.

[13] *CCC* 1145–46.

Just as grace builds upon and perfects nature, so the Eucharist draws upon the elements of human culture and transforms them into a means of His divine presence. Bread and wine, two of the most fundamental works of culture, do not arise naturally out of the earth but from human intelligence, which forms them from the fruits of the earth. The celebration of Eucharist requires these works of culture, as its matter cannot consist in simple wheat and grapes. The sacrament transforms these works of culture into acts of cult (worship), making them supernatural and divine. The worship of the Mass becomes the highest expression of culture as the work of man finds its highest affirmation in God's divine action, which builds upon it to do what man cannot—to bring heaven down to earth. We could think of it as an ongoing revolution that brings the supernatural into the world to change it one person at a time.

A Life of Festivity

We underestimate the power of a meal. In our frenetic culture, we often do not prioritize eating together as a family, preferring fast food instead. A meal should, however, slow us down and become a kind of sacrament of human life and communion. "Babette's Feast," a short story by Isak Dinesen (1958), turned into a beautiful film by Gabriel Axel (1987), presents a parable of the way in which even the extravagance of a meal can break the bonds of daily life. Dinesen's story portrays the austere life of members of a Lutheran sect in their small Norwegian village: "Its members renounced all the pleasures of this world, for the earth and all that it held to them was but a kind of illusion, and the true reality was the New Jerusalem toward which they were longing."[14] Their renouncing of the pleasures of this life was unexpectedly interrupted by a feast prepared by a French, Catholic woman, Babette, who provides the occasion for the guests to realize that "grace is infinite."[15] Yet, this infinity pours itself upon the characters in and through their finiteness, offering them a glimpse of "the universe as it really is."[16] Through the outpouring of grace, they experience the realization of what was surrendered, lost, or unachievable in time, occasioned by the sacramental embodiment of this grace in the context of a meal—the pleasures of food and drink, not as focused on themselves but signs of something beyond. "Time itself had merged into eternity," as the meal provided a sacramental encounter with reality that opened the minds, imaginations, and hearts of the banqueters, creating an opening to God's love and grace.[17] Christians can see the deepest meaning in the good things of earth, with grace transforming them into openings to the divine.

Although many in today's world find Christianity boring, it is, in fact, our secular culture that fits its own accusation, as it descends into boredom and blandness. We have lost a sense of purpose and have become fixated on passing distractions and pleasures that leave us completely unsatisfied. Unmoored from deeper meaning, even the pleasures

---

[14]   Robert Louis Wilken, "The Church as Culture," 23.

[15]   Wilken, 60.

[16]   Wilken, 62.

[17]   Dinesen, "Babette's Feast," 61.

of life lead people to depression. Christians, however, have an inner impulse to celebrate the good things that God has done for them! Faith, on the other hand, may not offer immediate sensual pleasures, but it does provide a true and lasting joy and gives us a reason to celebrate. Although the Mass itself may seem boring on the outside without the eyes of faith, it is the greatest moment of praise, thanks, and celebration as a response to the salvation that God has won for us. We have greater cause for rejoicing than anyone. The more we think about everything God has given us, the more joyful, thankful, and ready to celebrate we should be. Going to Mass begins the Christian celebration, although we should continue it in culture. Festivity is the celebration of holy days outside of Mass, feasting and engaging in wholesome fun to show the joy we have in our life and faith.

Our culture may have holidays, days off for recreation, yet it lacks festivity. It is not that we should oppose holidays, as the word itself points to the root of holy days, when people stop the ordinary course of things to focus on what is most important. What is needed is to recover the holy root of these days and deepen the meaning of our communal celebrations. We need to rediscover how to celebrate our faith in a cultural way, which is public, communal, and festive. The Old Covenant actually required the Israelites to celebrate three feasts a year in Jerusalem to commemorate God's saving actions. These times required not only pilgrimage and prayer but also eating and drinking. Wine was recognized as so essential that it even was given to the poor so that no one

would be without it for the Passover.[18] It was on that feast
that Jesus inaugurated the Mass as a new festive celebration
of the salvation He offered the world. Saint Paul described
the festive joy of salvation when he told the Corinthians,
"For Christ, our paschal lamb, has been sacrificed. Let us,
therefore, celebrate the festival" (1 Cor 5:7–8). Every time we
come to Mass, we celebrate our salvation and should rejoice
in the Lord's feast! The Mass gives God praise through worship in a direct way, while festivity expresses this praise indi-
rectly by celebrating in a cultural way.

The Old Testament demonstrates many of the key characteristics of festivity. For instance, for the festival of trumpets,
the Lord directs: "You shall have a holy convocation; you shall
do no laborious work" (Nm 29:1). And for another feast in
Jerusalem, we see the combination of prayer and celebration:
"And the people of Israel that were present at Jerusalem kept
the feast of unleavened bread seven days with great gladness;
and the Levites and the priests praised the LORD day by day,
singing with all their might to the LORD. . . . So the people
ate the food of the festival for seven days, sacrificing peace
offerings and giving thanks to the LORD the God of their
fathers" (2 Chr 30:21–22). And after coming back from
Exile, Nehemiah, Ezra, and the Levites had to reeducate the
people on how to celebrate a holy feast: "'This day is holy to
the LORD your God; do not mourn or weep.' For all the people wept when they heard the words of the law. Then he said
to them, 'Go your way, eat the fat and drink sweet wine and
send portions to him for whom nothing is prepared; for this

---

[18] Pitre, *Jesus and the Jewish Roots of the Eucharist*, 151.

day is holy to our Lord; and do not be grieved, for the joy of the LORD is your strength. . . . And all the people went their way to eat and drink and to send portions and to make great rejoicing'" (Neh 8:9–10, 12). God wants us to experience His joy in a holistic way, combining prayer with feasting.

The new covenant does not abandon the tradition of feasting, though it transforms it through the Church's sacramental life. Every Mass constitutes a covenantal feast of salvation that enables the Christian to rejoice in the Lord, expressing joy and hope amid the drudgery of daily life. This festive character of the Christian life shaped the Church's counting of time, as we use the word *feria* to describe a normal weekday Mass. *Feria*, the word used for the festival days of ancient Rome, expresses the reality that with the coming of Christ there are no ordinary days any longer. With the daily celebration of Mass, every day became a feast, although the Church still celebrates particular feast days and solemnities to commemorate the major mysteries of salvation and the saints. In the Middle Ages, these feasts also stopped the normal course of work and were occasions for communal and public feasting. They also marked the changing of the seasons and days of the harvest, such as the blessing of plows following Epiphany, processions in the fields for the feast of Saint Mark, and the harvest festival at Martinmas on November 11.

Festivity involves a break from ordinary life to engage in worship, singing, rejoicing, eating, and drinking, along with helping the poor and receiving instruction in the Lord's teachings. Most fundamentally, this religious feasting responds to something good—remembering God's promises manifested in a saving event. The community rejoices in God's goodness and expresses this joy through celebration. Festivity transcends a mere party or entertaining distraction, as it entails more solemn merriment. Solemn occasions call for prayer, as well as its extension into a continuing celebration in the family and community. God even makes celebration a religious duty through the command to keep the feasts and the cessation of work every Sabbath. Festivity also gives shape to the liturgy of life by finding concrete ways to express the joy, gratitude, and happiness received from God. It also creates a shared way of life, gathering the community together to praise God through fellowship, feasting, music, and prayer.

Pieter Brueghel the Younger conveys the nature of festivity in his depiction of a village festival honoring Saints Hubert and Anthony. The saints make a solemn entrance on the right side of the painting, carried in a procession, and while the church bells ring, a man kneels to confess his sins. Others do not seem to notice the procession and focus instead on the earthier side of the celebration, with large cauldrons of food, music, and dancing. Brueghel also captures how this small town's spiritual traditions created an atmosphere of communal joy. We tend to think of the religious and secular as discreet spheres, although everything in Christendom's culture was ordered toward God. Spiritual practices and recreation blend seamlessly together in Brueghel's painting, as both express the community's celebration of its patron saints, albeit in different ways.

Pieter Brueghel the Younger, *A Village Fair*,
late 16th–early 17th century

Festivity extends the celebration of the Mass into culture,
prolonging the liturgical celebration and translating it into
social life. The foundation for Christian festivity stems from
Acts of the Apostles: "And day by day, attending the temple
together and breaking bread in their homes, they partook
of food with glad and generous hearts, praising God and
having favor with all the people" (Acts 2:46–47). Liturgy
enlivens the feast, as the celebratory meal following Mass
becomes itself a reflection of the Eucharist, praising God
with food, drink, and fellowship. The music, singing, and
dancing continue the praise of prayer and, when rightly
ordered, express the overwhelming joy of life made visible
through the body. The toast, as a kind of blessing, provides
the clearest expression of the affirmation of the goodness of

life as everyone raises a glass to honor one another, and the many blessings received from God.[19]

Feasting can capture a glimpse of heaven, a sign of that angelic "festal gathering" in the life to come (see Heb 12:22). Looking toward the ultimate goal of life enlivens festivity by increasing joy in the goodness of God's creation and His arrival in this world to sanctify it. Josef Pieper, the great philosopher of festivity, affirms that "to celebrate a festival means: to live out, for some special occasion and in an uncommon manner, the universal assent to the world as a whole."[20] This assent to the world, in a moment of leisure, entails a breaking out of the mundane ritual that confines the everyday. It opens one up to the transcendent so that "in celebrating festivals festively, man passes beyond the barriers of this present life on earth."[21] The joy of the festival, drawing together the memory of both earthly and divine blessings, points to the eternal joy of heaven by giving us a small, imperfect glimpse of the eternal feast. In fact, Saint Thérèse of Lisieux loved Sundays so much that she didn't want them to end. She once declared, "I longed for the eternal repose of heaven, that never-ending *Sunday* of the *Fatherland*."[22]

Rediscovering festivity beckons to us as an urgent necessity for building a Eucharistic culture. Secular culture removes faith from public life and attempts to keep its expression

---

[19] The Latin toast, "Prosit," which became the German "prost," affirms the goodness of life, while the romance languages bless one another wishing for health, through their "salute," "santé," and "salud."

[20] Pieper, *In Tune with the World*, 30.

[21] Pieper, 43.

[22] St. Thérèse of Lisieux, *Story of a Soul*, 42.

within the confines of church. Festivity tears apart this dichotomy by gathering Christians together for communal celebrations of faith. Many Catholic parishes have festivals that are open to the entire community, thus inviting all people to discover the richness of the Faith. This also provides an essential witness of hope that there is something worth celebrating and a reason for joy. Without real reasons to celebrate, our culture falls into fake festivals dominated by consumerism that offer only passing distractions. Partying has no purpose, and its pleasures fade quickly into regrets. For Christians who live with a clear purpose, the Lord's Day and the great feasts of the year manifest the glory of God giving them a reason to stop work: genuine celebration points to the unending feast of heaven.

A Eucharistic Imagination

The Eucharist needs culture as it intrinsically builds upon the cultivation of nature. We can see humanity's contribution to God's continued enfleshment not only in the making of bread and wine but also in the signs and symbols used to beautify the celebration. The Eucharist, therefore, gave birth to Christian art, which arose surrounding the Mass to support its celebration. Art points to the transcendent reality of the Mass, helping the believer to see the importance and majesty of the sacramental action. If Bishop Barron is right that the Incarnation is the Catholic thing, this certainly includes the Eucharist—the ongoing Incarnation in the life of the Church: "Catholicism is a matter of the body and the senses as much as it is as much as it is a matter of the mind and the soul, precisely because the Word became flesh."[23] Therefore, it is necessary for us "to look and listen" to perceive God's presence within the Church.[24]

Although words have a central place in the Christian tradition, the Catholic faith is a religion of the Word made flesh. In addition to words, therefore, we need places, images, and sounds to understand the power of the Eucharist in the Christian life. We certainly would be aided by reading Aquinas's theology, although Mozart also indicates the movements of sacramental worship. Classical music arose out of the Church's tradition of chant, while also incorporating European dance styles, such as the minuet, gavotte, passacaglia, and allemande. Similar rhythms entered into the Mass settings of the great composers, whose compositions bring ecstatic joy and exuberance into the liturgy. After all, the Mass is festive, a kind of divine dance (and I do not mean liturgical dance), where our physical gestures express our movement toward our divine lover. The same can be said of the visual arts, focusing our gaze onto our beloved. Although we might be used to admiring a Caravaggio in the isolation of a museum, most of his paintings were meant to be viewed above the altar, where the gestures of his figures and dramatic lighting take on different significance, calling our attention to the sacred action.

The Church needs art to express what words cannot. For this reason, Pope Benedict XVI taught that "everything related to the Eucharist should be marked by beauty" in order

---

[23] Barron, *Catholicism*, 4.
[24] Barron, 4.

to "foster awe for the mystery of God . . . and strengthen devotion."[25] Some churches are more conducive for meditation than others, especially those where beauty permeates the entire Church from the tabernacle to the stained glass windows to the holy water fonts. God is beauty itself and sacred spaces, art, and music should reflect His splendor. Benedict also related something that we all know from experience, that "we cannot say that one song is as good as another" for Mass.[26] Some hymns help us to pray, particularly the Church's own sacred chant, while other pieces that have drawn inspiration from Broadway and pop culture do not draw us into an encounter with God.

The church building guides our own understanding of the Church, both in its structure and purpose. The church provides a home for Christ, in which He dwells sacramentally and gathers His family together. Indeed, the first churches were homes, such as the house church in Dura Europos, Syria. Dating from the early third century, the expanded house contains some of the earliest art in Church history, with its symbolism pointing to what happens within the church. It contained stars on its ceiling and vines on the walls, both indicating a new creation or garden through the liturgy, with biblical images such as David and Goliath symbolizing the spiritual combat of Christians leaving a pagan culture behind, the healing of the paralytic representing Jesus's restorative grace, and the procession of the wise virgins to the wedding

---

[25] Pope Benedict XVI, *Sacramentum Caritatis*, no. 41.
[26] Pope Benedict XVI, no. 42.

feast calling Christians to imitate their approach of the bridegroom in the liturgy. The early frescoes of the catacombs depicted many Eucharistic motifs, such as vines, loaves and fishes, agape meals, and even the Last Supper. With the construction of larger churches, the first Christian architecture emerged by adapting Roman basilicas, the meeting halls of the emperor. Christians portrayed Christ in gold mosaics in the apses of these basilicas, showing Him to be the true Lord drawing His people together in assembly.

The liturgy's solemnity and joy naturally leads us to sing. Speaking does not suffice for words so important by which we praise and glorify God, so we extend and embellish our prayer in song. Saint Paul describes how the Spirit moves us to express our faith by singing, connecting it to our Eucharistic prayer of thanksgiving: "Be filled with the Spirit, addressing one another in psalms and hymns and spiritual songs, singing and making melody to the Lord with all your heart, always and for everything giving thanks in the name of our Lord Jesus Christ to God the Father" (Eph 5:18–20). Music is so essential to the Mass that the Church even created an entire form of music, Gregorian chant, specifically for the liturgy. Chant fits the liturgy in its ethereal quality, clearly spiritual and even otherworldly in nature, with its melody designed to draw us into contemplation of the text prayed. From its origin in the scholas of Rome, it grew increasingly complex at monasteries in the Middle Ages, leading to the creation of the first musical notation and scales to transmit it throughout the Church. Out of this chant grew the tradition of polyphony, singing with many voices in harmony, which in turn stimulated the development of classical music. Sacred music requires attention to the word, accentuating the meaning of Scripture and other liturgical texts, with a spiritual power removed for sensual and mundane melodies and rhythms, and a beauty that inspires peace and prayer.

Craftsmanship also embellishes our celebration, as we decorate the building, construct the altar, and fashion sacred vessels, vestments, candles, images, and furnishings. The dignity of these constructions points to the reality of Christ's sacrifice, with each article providing a little sign of the importance of the sacred action. The Eucharist inspires artisanship to communicate its supreme spiritual beauty, though one veiled by the accidents of the bread and wine. The splendor and solemnity of the Mass manifests what lies hidden within it. The Eucharist makes an encounter with beauty-incarnate possible, as the One who is beauty itself makes His infinite beauty accessible through the appearance of bread and wine. In fact, the Eucharist as the continuing Incarnation inspires artists, along with all Christians, to make Christ present in the world even further through the sacramentals, culture, and art that surround the Mass. The beauty of the Mass and the dignity of good art point to the reality of Christ's beauty made present within it. Art, therefore, forms an essential part of the experience of the Eucharist, shaping the mind, imagination, and sentiments by directing the soul toward God through what is true, honorable, just, pure, lovely, gracious, and excellent (cf. Phil 4:8).

Jesus, who is beauty itself, wants to beautify our lives through His gift of Himself. The word *Eucharist* contains the Greek word *charis*, not only meaning "thanks" and "grace" but also "delight" and "beauty." Though a hidden power, this beauty radiates its splendor within the tabernacle of the Christian life. Eating this beauty, medieval theologians asserted, will make the Christian also become beautiful. Ann Astell's book *Eating Beauty* gives one example: "Christ, crucified and risen, is for Bonaventure the source of the beauty of all the saints, whose beauty in turn mirrors and magnifies His."[27] His beauty, Bonaventure, claims, has "become the beauty of all."[28] Astell also comments on the German Renaissance cardinal Nicholas of Cusa, who said that eating Christ's glorified body draws us into an "'incomprehensible spiritual splendor'; the claritas or brightness of unchanging Beauty," which likewise will make our bodies and souls eternally "beautiful, well-formed, and radiant."[29] Christ's beauty, as our crucified Lord, goes beyond the ephemeral, taking root primarily through holiness, radiating in a life transformed by grace.

The art that surrounds the Eucharist—architecture, furnishing, vestments, sacred vessels, stained glass, painting, sculpture, and music—should manifest the presence of Christ, expressing the sacredness of the Mass and the joy of its celebration. The artist, therefore, plays a key role in teaching us how to pray and encounter Christ. When we walk into a beautiful church, it automatically invites us to

---

[27] Astell, *Eating Beauty*, 40.
[28] Astell, 39.
[29] Astell, 2–3.

pray because we are moved by the unique sacred beauty of the space. A noble vestment points to the fact that the priest acts not in an ordinary manner but in the person of Christ. Sacred music moves our hearts and itself becomes a prayer and means of encountering God. In this way, Christian art continues the Incarnation by tangibly manifesting the presence of Christ in the Church's sacramental life. Good Catholic art serves the Church by forming the imagination and memory through holy images and sounds, instructing through symbolism, and pointing us toward a beauty that surpasses this world.

Springing from Christ's incarnate presence in the Church, the Catholic faith has inspired the greatest art in history. It should not surprise us that God's Eucharistic presence would enliven the imagination, incarnate beauty, and manifest His presence. Canaletto, the great cityscape painter of Venice, captured the power of sacred art in his depiction of the interior of the cathedral basilica of San Marco. Stepping into the church truly transports the believer into a sacred realm, with the overpowering gold mosaics pointing to the presence of the angels and saints to accompany the prayer of the Mass. The space itself becomes a testimony to Christ's true presence in the Eucharist, facilitating the closest union with Christ on earth. Yes, like Moses before the burning bush, we too are standing on "holy ground" every time we enter a Catholic Church (see Ex 3:5). It only fitting that our Eucharistic King's dwelling on earth mirror His heavenly dwelling.

Canaletto, *The Nave of San Marco Looking East*, 1755–56

Along with San Marco, we could point to the unrivalled beauty of churches such as Saint Peter's Basilica in Rome, the great Hagia Sophia of Constantinople, and France's Chartres Cathedral. And many conversions have occurred simply by entering these magnificent dwellings because only God could have inspired their surpassing beauty. The greatest paintings in history have arisen to adorn these sacred sites, such as Giotto's Arena Chapel, Michelangelo's frescoes in the Sistine chapel, and Caravaggio's images of Saint

Matthew in the church of Saint Louis in Rome. Painting progressed in its realism and perfection in order to capture the reality of the Incarnation and its power in the life of the Church, inviting us to contemplate the realities of faith made present to us through them.

Art leads us through the story of salvation history, adorning the church and guiding our meditation. We could think of the sculptures of medieval artisans like Gislebertus in Burgundy, whose somewhat terrifying depiction of the Last Judgment at the Autun cathedral situates the believer in the great cosmic drama of salvation. Great Renaissances masters made a more personal appeal to the believer, such as the call to repentance found in Donatello's moving portrayal of Mary Magdalene for the Duomo in Florence. And then there are the dramatic creations of the Baroque, like Bernini's masterpieces, such as the ecstasy of Saint Teresa, that point to the power of the divine to break into our lives at any moment. The Mass also inspired some of the greatest music ever composed, especially the Mass settings of Palestrina, Bach, Mozart, and Haydn. Saint Thomas Aquinas, the greatest poet of the Eucharist, inspired the classic chant settings used for benediction, as well as César Franck's moving "Panis Angelicus." Another short prayer, the Ave Verum Corpus, "Hail, true body, born of the Virgin Mary," inspired Mozart's masterpiece, perhaps the greatest setting of a Eucharistic prayer.

Like the Church's theology, sacred art teaches all people—rich and poor, scholarly and uneducated, saints and sinners—about Jesus's true presence in the Eucharist. It bears witness to the power of the Eucharist to transform the mind and imagination, enabling faith to take on flesh in the world. It glorifies God, inspires us, magnifies our prayer, and draws others to recognize the truth of the Faith and the greatest miracle on earth. Art shows us how the Eucharist becomes culture, and it should inspire us, as God's own handiwork, to serve as an icon of Christ to others.

10

Keeping Eucharistic Time: Shaping the Rhythm of Life

Prayer forms Catholic culture more than anything else, especially when centered on the Eucharist. Encountering Christ daily in prayer enables the Eucharist's divine life to grow and transform everything else. Prayer should shape the rhythm of the Christian life by giving order to each day, providing time to celebrate each week, and drawing us deeper into salvation history through the liturgical year. Time manifests the lordship of Christ by bringing each day under His direction and seeking to conform all things to Him. Christ's kingdom does not belong to this world, even as it gives shape to the world. Abiding in prayer allows the kingdom of heaven to shape earthly life, drawing the duties, cares, joys, and hardships of this life under its guidance. Prayer bridges the divide between heaven and earth, strengthening Christ's Eucharistic presence within the soul of the disciple.

Daily Prayer

Daily prayer provides the necessary foundation for a Eucharistic life. Specifically, personal daily prayer extends the presence of Jesus within the soul, allowing His life to guide ours in an abiding state of communion. Encountering Jesus in the Eucharist initiates a call to remain close to Him and to live out His teaching and commandments. "Abide in me, and I in you. . . . If you abide in me, and my words abide in you, ask whatever you will, and it shall be done for you. By this my Father is glorified, that you bear much fruit, and so prove to be my disciples. As the Father has loved me, so have I loved you; abide in my love. If you keep my commandments, you will abide in my love, just as I have kept my Father's commandments and abide in his love (Jn 15:4, 7–10). Although we begin to abide with Jesus through the Eucharist, He teaches us that this communion requires our continued action to follow Him and remain faithful to His commands. Our life cannot contradict the union He offers us; rather, it should reinforce it by following Jesus the rest of the week. Prayer and right living together open our hearts for Jesus to enter in and abide there.

Prayer creates the continual space for Jesus to act in our lives. We are literally not alone when we pray, because through it we come close to Jesus, giving us strength and comfort. The evangelist Luke relates how Jesus told His disciples that "they ought always to pray and not lose heart" (Lk 18:1). When Paul exhorts the Thessalonians to do the same, he urges them always to give thanks, the word for the Eucharist, showing that we should maintain the disposition of prayer at Mass continually: "Rejoice always, pray constantly, give thanks in all circumstances; for this is the will of God in Christ Jesus for you" (1 Thes 5:16–18). Every moment is an opportunity for praise and thanks. Paul also tells the Ephesians to redeem, or ransom (*exagorazo*), the time, an intriguing image calling us to draw each moment to Christ, redeeming it from the influence of the enemy (see Eph 5:16). The redemption of Jesus should extend to how we spend our time, living under the kingship of Christ and not the prince of this world, the devil.

Jesus continually offers us Himself to us in the Eucharist at daily Mass, the clearest way to abide with Him. Being a daily communicant feeds the soul each day with Christ's body and blood, enabling a deeper transformation of life and conformity to Him. Pope Benedict XVI describes how "the Eucharist, since it embraces the concrete, everyday existence of the believer, makes possible, day by day, the progressive transfiguration of all those called by grace . . . [and] tends by its nature to permeate every aspect of our existence."[30] Receiving the Eucharist often, with the right disposition, creates a path to holiness, with its grace animating our prayer, work, home, and leisure. Eucharistic communion teaches us how to pray, which at its heart consists of an encounter, expression of love, and conversation with God. The intense encounter with Christ in the Eucharist should overflow into a daily renewal to strengthen the friendship and unity found at Mass.

How we spend our time shows our true priorities. If we value communion with Jesus, we will seek to spend time

---

[30] Pope Benedict XVI, *Sacramentum Caritatis*, no. 71.

with Him. Jesus awaits us every day, hidden in the Eucharist, and invites us into deeper friendship with Him. Francisco de Zurbaran's painting *The Eucharist* shows the continual adoration that Jesus's Eucharistic presence receives from the angels. This presence is a continual invitation to join in this ongoing adoration as an anchor to our life, giving us spiritual stability. We can take our place next to the angels, gazing at Jesus's hidden presence and allowing it to soak into us, making us more like Him.

Francisco de Zurbaran, *The Eucharist*, 17th century

For those not able to attend daily Mass, the saints have recommended the practice of making a spiritual communion. Saint Alphonsus Liguori strongly advocates making spiritual communions often during the day to ask Jesus continually to strengthen the grace of union with Him. He wrote the following spiritual communion prayer: "My Jesus, I believe that Thou art truly present in the Most Blessed Sacrament. I love Thee above all things, and I desire to possess Thee within my soul. Since I am unable now to receive Thee sacramentally, come at least spiritually into my heart. I embrace Thee as being already there, and unite myself wholly to Thee; never permit me to be separated from Thee."[31] This desire for Communion can truly strengthen Christ's presence within us. Saint Juliana Falconieri, for instance, could not receive the Eucharist before her death due to digestive problems, and so she asked simply to look upon the host. As it was brought before her, it disappeared, and after her death, the image of the host was found inscribed over her heart. This shows us the true power of making a spiritual communion. An important tradition also exists of reciting short prayers throughout the day, reminding us of God's presence and directing our hearts to Him. Some examples include the following: "O Sacrament most holy, o sacrament divine, all praise and all thanksgiving be every moment thine," or "May the heart of Jesus in the most Blessed Sacrament be praised, adored, and loved with grateful affection at every moment in all the tabernacles of the world, even until the end of time."

---

[31] Liguori, *Visits to the Blessed Sacrament*, 2–3.

Visiting a nearby church can help us to make a more impactful spiritual communion. If the church offers Eucharistic adoration, it also strengthens our prayer time because we can pray before Jesus's sacramental presence. Adoring the Eucharist outside of Mass manifests our love and friendship for Christ, ensuring His presence there will not be forgotten or abandoned. His constant, silent presence in church shows His great love and humility as He awaits our visit. Furthermore, the Eucharistic Heart of Jesus desires to give us more graces than we can receive. But we must make visiting Him a priority. Many saints have pointed to the need for daily mental prayer, consisting of at least fifteen minutes of quiet meditation and conversation with God. Others, such as Venerable Fulton Sheen, have recommended the practice of making a holy hour in front of the Blessed Sacrament as often as possible, but especially on Thursday evenings, in response to Jesus's question on Holy Thursday in the garden: "Could you not watch with me one hour?" (Mt 26:40). Our daily prayer throughout the week, in turn, will lead to a more fruitful Sunday Communion.

This watching with Jesus, staying alert and faithful in prayer, should happen each day. Jesus Himself exhorts us, as He did with His disciples, "Watch and pray that you may not enter into temptation; the spirit indeed is willing, but the flesh is weak'" (Mt 26:41). From the Church's beginning, the custom arose of marking the hours of the day in prayer. The Didache spoke of praying the Our Father three times a day, which grew into the practice of the Liturgy of the Hours, traditionally marking seven daytime hours and one night hour by praying the psalms (see Ps 119). From these many hours, the Church has pointed to Morning Prayer (Lauds) and Evening Prayer (Vespers) as the hinges of the day, the former offering the day to God and the latter as a time of thanksgiving, whereas Night Prayer (Compline) ends the day with an examination of conscience and offering of life to God before sleep. The Carmelite nun Saint Mary Magdalen de' Pazzi (1566–1607) spoke of these hinges in terms of living in friendship with Jesus: "A friend will visit a friend in the morning to wish him a good day, in the evening, a good night, taking also an opportunity to converse with him during the day. In like manner, make visits to Jesus Christ in the Blessed Sacrament, if your duties permit it. It is especially at the foot of the altar that one prays well."[32] Other devotions, such as the Rosary and Angelus, also provide opportunities to pray throughout the day while meditating upon the mysteries of salvation. Unceasing prayer invites Jesus to be with us in all that we do.

Celebrating the Lord's Day

Every week recapitulates the original seven days of creation, leading us through God's ordering of time that culminates in His Sabbath rest. In addition, the Church Fathers spoke of the eighth day, the day of the new creation, making Sunday not only the first day of creation but the day of Christ's work of redemption that inaugurates a new day of the resurrection that will never end. The Church celebrates Jesus's resurrection every Lord's Day, marking the culmination of our salvation in the new life that Jesus offers to believers.

---

[32] Hardon, *The History of Eucharistic Adoration*, 19.

Every week, therefore, contains a festival day when Christians celebrate their salvation, thanking God for the gift of life and looking forward to the new life that comes with eternal rest. The "rest" that we observe on this new Sabbath day (versus Saturday in the Old Covenant) reveals that God created man for more than the daily work, which man was entrusted on the sixth day of creation. God lovingly commands us to dedicate one day for worship and rest, pointing to His own eternal rest. In doing so, God wants us to experience a taste of heaven on earth—that is, His perfect life and happiness.

This weekly cycle of festivity impresses on us the constant need for memory, recalling God's saving action and honoring it.[33] The Lord's Day cannot be celebrated at Mass alone as it is a festive day, not a festive hour. Speaking of the Sabbath to Moses in Leviticus, God clearly linked the whole day to festivity, reaching into the home itself: "The appointed feasts of the Lord which you shall proclaim as holy convocations, my appointed feasts, are these. Six days shall work be done; but on the seventh day is a sabbath of solemn rest, a holy convocation; you shall do no work; it is a sabbath to the Lord in all your dwellings" (Lv 23:2–3). God frees us from the cycle of bondage to work so that we can experience His holiness breaking into and shaping time. According to Josef Pieper,

---

[33] The Lord's Day offers a glimpse into the meaning of each day when redeemed by Christ. Every day should point toward Sunday and find its fulfillment in it. There is a traditional devotion for each day of the week that keeps us focused on the Faith. For example, Saturday is the day of the Blessed Mother, Friday the Sacred Heart and the Passion, while Thursday is the day devoted to the Eucharist.

work exists for the sake of leisure, to create the conditions to enter into the higher things.[34] Work provides for the care of the body and its needs, serving the family and society, thus enabling the enjoyment of rest that comes from accomplishing these goals. Pieper pinpoints worship as the highest act of leisure, engaging in public ceremony to praise and thank God and affirm the goodness of the life He has given.

The chief and essential way to celebrate the Lord's Day, however, comes from attending Sunday Mass. This is how we enter into the festivity of Christ's resurrection, participating in it as a living reality made present to us in the liturgy. As the most important event of the week and of our lives, we ought to prioritize it above everything. This is why it is customary to wear one's Sunday best (our best clothes), dressing in a way that makes clear the importance and solemnity of the Mass. After Mass, the same importance can be shown to honor Jesus's presence within the home through hospitality, welcoming people into the domestic church for a festive meal, especially the needy. The celebration continues with additional expressions of leisure: eating meals with family and friends, enjoying the beauty and relaxation found in nature, playing games and activities, taking more time for prayer, and enjoying the arts. All of these activities manifest the reality of belief, giving witness to the fact that there is something worth taking time for and rejoicing. Sunday actually provides a source of great hope. By properly observing it, we show that we are living for heaven, not earth. Fulfilling the third commandment "to keep holy the sabbath

---

[34] See Pieper, *Leisure the Basis of Culture.*

day" also reveals that Christian life transcends busyness, the saturation of technology, and consumerism (Ex 20:8).

The Lord's Day is a day of the family. The home is the domestic church, the place where children learn to live and love the Faith. Hence, our devotion and love for the Eucharist should flow from the Mass to our home. Our Lord told Saint Margaret Mary, "I will bless every place in which an image of my Heart is exposed and honored."[35] In a mysterious way, when our homes are adorned with an image of the Sacred Heart, Our Lord's Eucharistic Heart is also exposed since the Sacred Heart and the Eucharist are one. Our homes become a school of love and piety, the training ground of virtue, under the gaze of the Sacred and Eucharistic Heart. For if we cannot love those who live with us, we will never be able to truly love. And if Christ's Sacred and Eucharistic Heart reigns in our homes, we can be assured of His promises to Saint Margaret Mary, "I will establish peace in their homes."[36] Yes, God wants the peace and joy of His Eucharistic Presence to permeate not only Sundays but every day so that our homes become a tiny sanctuary from the world's evils.

On Sundays, families should experience genuine freedom from outside constraints in order to have communion with each other. The Lord's Day is a gift from God, not a burden, enabling the family to be what it is called to be: the instantiation of Christ's love for His Church. Having fun together, especially by reducing personal technology, provides a huge step in recovering this gift. Because the home

---

[35] "12 Promises of the Sacred Heart," EWTN, www.ewtn.com/catholicism/library/12-promises-of-the-sacred-heart-13683.
[36] "12 Promises of the Sacred Heart."

should act as an extension of Jesus's Eucharistic presence, it should bear some sign of this presence, with holy images and a specific place for prayer. Taking time for prayer and for one another on Sunday begins to shape a way of life or culture in the family. Ultimately, it shows our children what we value the most. The painting *Evening Prayer* depicts how the home becomes a place where we learn the Christian life. Children often learn to pray from their parents' laps as the stepping-stone for their prayer at Mass.

Pierre Edouard Frère, *Evening Prayer* 1857

Despite the centrality of the Lord's Day, too often it is forgotten or overshadowed. Arriving in the United States from traditionally Catholic Austria, Maria von Trapp was surprised to discover it to be a "land without a Sunday."[37] For many today, Sunday has become no different from any other day. Even worse, it has now become a primary day for shopping. This stands in sharp contrast with the early Christians, who were willing to die for celebrating the Lord's Day. Early martyrs from North Africa, in about the year 303, were interrogated by a proconsul, who asked them, "Why have you received Christians in your home, transgressing the imperial dispositions?" A man named Emeritus answered, "*Sine dominico non possumus* (We cannot live without Sunday)."[38] Likewise, Saint Ignatius of Antioch spoke of "living in the observance of the Lord's Day," showing that there is a way of life that springs up from our weekly observance of the Resurrection.[39] Although celebrating Sunday may no longer cost one's life, it remains a battle against a secular and utilitarian culture. Stopping the normal course of time and business witnesses to the true meaning of life that surpasses these mundane things. The Lord's Day calls us to focus on the most important things of life, putting everything else in context. Work and practical matters should support the things that lead to ultimate meaning and purpose rather

---

[37]   von Trapp, "The Land without a Sunday."
[38]   See Pope Benedict XVI, "Homily for the Closing of the 24th International Eucharistic Congress in Bari, Italy," May 29, 2005, http://w2.vatican.va/content/benedict-xvi/en/homilies/2005/documents/hf_ben-xvi_hom_20050529_bari.html.
[39]   St. Ignatius of Antioch, "Letter to the Magnesiansch," 9.

than compromising them. Worship points to *the* most important thing, putting God first. This act of worship also offers liberation from the demands of passing things, including technology, echoing the Exodus of old and reconnecting us with family, friends, nature, and beauty.

Living the Liturgical Seasons

The weekly cycle of time progresses into a broader annual cycle also centered on the Resurrection as its holiest moment. Just as each Mass makes the Paschal Mystery present, so the celebration of the great feast days make present the mysteries they communicate. Throughout the Church's liturgical year, she instructs and bestows particular graces upon her sons and daughters regarding the great mysteries of our salvation. The celebrations of the Christian calendar lead us into the goal of each Mass: conformity to Christ. The great spiritual teacher Blessed Columba Marmion, abbot of Maredsous in Belgium, relates that "each one of His mysteries contains its own teaching, brings its special life; is for our souls the source of a particular grace, the object of which is to 'form Jesus in us.'"[40] We not only learn about Christ through His mysteries, but due to our conformity to Christ, they also mark the stages of our own spiritual journey.

The mysteries of Christ's life celebrated throughout the liturgical year provide the means by which we enter into God's very life. These mysteries involve the same memory of the Mass that makes these past events present, thus enabling our participation in them as living realities, not simply

---

[40] Marmion, *Christ in His Mysteries*, 12.

bound to the past. Blessed Columba Marmion also teaches us that "it is true that in their historical, material duration the mysteries of Christ's life on earth are now past; but *their power* remains, and the grace that allows us to share in them operates always."[41] The celebration of the mysteries within the liturgy do not just remember; they participate in the grace that emanates from them. Liturgy and the sacraments provide access to the mysteries of Christ and a mystical conformity to Him.

The liturgical year begins in Advent, which looks not only to Christ's coming at Christmas but also to Christ's two other comings—at the end of the world and also at every Mass in the Eucharist. Advent, a penitential season like Lent, creates a disposition of expectation and openness to all three of these comings. The solemnity of the Nativity on Christmas (Christ's Mass) celebrates the Word become flesh, the same reality made present at each Mass. At Christmas, the Church leads the faithful in rejoicing that God entered into His creation and came close to humanity as Emmanuel (God with us). The New Year marks another year from the Incarnation (counted as *Anno Domini*, year of the Lord), and the Epiphany honors the manifestation of Christ to the nations, as well as the light of His divinity that shone through His baptism and miracle at Cana. The celebration of Christmas traditionally stretches to the feast of the Presentation (also known as the Purification of Mary and Candlemas) in which candles are blessed for the year honoring Christ as

---

[41] Marmion, 20.

the light that has been revealed to the nations (quoting the Canticle of Simeon, recited as Night Prayer).

Lent originates from the period of intense preparation before the Easter Vigil when the elect, preparing for Baptism, would engage in lengthy periods of prayer and penance. The practice spread to the rest of the faithful and extended to its current length, helping everyone to renew the grace of their baptism. Originally, Christians fasted the entire day until evening and practiced abstinence from meat, animal products, oil, and wine throughout Lent, although the length of the daily fast gradually shortened in length throughout history. It has been the most important time to receive the sacrament of Penance as part of the renewal of the spiritual life, preparing for the reception of the Eucharist at Easter. Although generally passed over in modern culture, Easter, as the holiest time of year, should be celebrated with the greatest solemnity and festivity. The Triduum marks the most solemn liturgies of the year and the entire Easter octave of eight days of solemnities should mark a time of great rejoicing. The fifty days of Easter, longer than the forty days of penance, culminate in the coming of the Holy Spirit at Pentecost. Pentecost begins the time of the Church, punctuated by great feasts such as Trinity Sunday, Sacred Heart, Immaculate Heart, Saints Peter and Paul, the Nativity of John the Baptist, the Assumption, the Exultation of the Cross, and All Saints. This annual cycle—with its alternating times of penance and rejoicing—makes the story of salvation history come alive to us through the Mass and also shapes the rhythms of our family gatherings and celebrations.

Some feast days focus entirely on the Eucharist, such as the institution of the Eucharist on Holy Thursday, Corpus Christi, and the feast of the Most Precious Blood. Corpus Christi has become the central feast day for Eucharistic veneration in the liturgical year. The feast has a dramatic history, beginning with Saint Juliana of Liège (1193–1258), a Belgian canoness who received a vision urging the celebration of a feast in honor of the Eucharist. She advocated for this devotion successfully, leading to its first local celebration in her hometown in 1246. In 1264, Pope Urban IV, following the Eucharistic miracle at Bolsena the year before, established it as a universal feast for the Latin rite of the Church, taking place on the Thursday following Trinity Sunday (the Sunday after Pentecost). The miracle occurred when a Bohemian priest celebrated Mass in the parish of Bolsena on his way to Rome, although he doubted Jesus's true presence in the Eucharist. During the consecration, the host bled on to the white corporal (cloth) that was on the altar and even down unto the stones at the foot of the altar. The miracle was a sign for Urban, who commissioned Saint Thomas Aquinas to write the hymns for the new feast, which are now best known for their use on Holy Thursday ("Pange Lingua") and during Benediction of the Blessed Sacrament ("O Salutaris" and "Tantum Ergo"). Every year, the feast of Corpus Christi provides the best occasion to witness publicly to our belief in the Real Presence through processions, such as Walter Tyndale depicted in Viterbo, Italy, in the early 1900s. These processions are important moments to manifest faith in the Eucharist to society more broadly.

Walter Tyndale, *Corpus Domini en Viterbo*, 1912

All Souls Day, our day to pray for the dead, also has a strong connection to the Holy Eucharist, though in a more subtle way. On this feast, which occurs on November 2, the Church permits every priest to offer three Masses[42] for the holy souls in purgatory. The feast arose at the great Burgundian monastery of Cluny, particularly through the leadership of the Benedictine abbot Saint Odilo (962–1049). The practice was not novel, as the early Church gathered to pray at the tombs of the dead and the Roman canon, the ancient Eucharistic prayer of Rome asks: "Remember also, Lord,

---

[42] Canon 905 states: "A priest is not permitted to celebrate the Eucharist more than once a day except in cases where the law permits him to celebrate or concelebrate more than once on the same day. If there is a shortage of priests, the local ordinary can allow priests to celebrate twice a day for a just cause, or if pastoral necessity requires it, even three times on Sundays and holy days of obligation."

your servants N. and N., who have gone before us with the sign of faith and rest in the sleep of peace. Grant them, O Lord, we pray, and all who sleep in Christ, a place of refreshment, light and peace." Pope Saint Gregory the Great also initiated the practice in the sixth century of offering Masses specifically for the dead to assist them in purgatory (continued in the practice of Gregorian Masses, said for a departed soul on thirty consecutive days). The feasts of All Saints and All Souls demonstrate the communion of saints that is experienced at every Mass, placing the faithful in contact with the prayers of the saints in heaven and with those undergoing purification in purgatory. The Eucharist draws us into communion with all the faithful, whether on earth, purgatory, or in heaven, all joined in our shared union with Christ.

The liturgical year unfolds a narrative of salvation that opens up Christ's mysteries and grace to the faithful. Although these mysteries are present at every Mass, the great feasts of the Church teach us how to relate to them more deeply and to celebrate the splendid work of salvation. Robert Louis Wilken exhorts us that "we should not underestimate the cultural significance of the calendar and its indispensability for a mature spiritual life."[43] This is because we become holy in relation to the Eucharist as it is celebrated in the life of the Church, God's chosen people, making the great mysteries of salvation come alive to us. The Eucharist shapes the time of the Church and, in turn, creates a rhythm

---

[43] Robert Louis Wilken, "The Church as Culture," *First Things,* April 2004, https://www.firstthings.com/article/2004/04/the-church-as-culture.

of prayer and holiness in our own lives. Through prayer, our faith guides how we direct our time for building up God's kingdom. This shaping of time provides the ground for Catholic culture to take root in our lives, guiding each day, week, and year.

11

Making Space for Jesus:
The Tabernacle of the World

The Eucharist turns the faithful into tabernacles for their own sake and also to restore the earth itself as a temple. God created the earth for this purpose, with the Garden of Eden as a sign of God's intention to dwell peacefully with humanity. Church buildings restore this purpose by serving as public signs of Christ's incarnate presence in the world. From the church building, the faithful should radiate His presence back into the rest of the world. Processions extend God's presence beyond church walls and into the surrounding community. Pilgrimages also seek out and honor those places made holy throughout the world by the saints and other miracles. Some of these sites specifically honor places where Jesus manifested the reality of His presence through Eucharistic miracles. All churches and holy sites serve as public signs, pointing to the Eucharist's reality while providing opportunities to engage and sanctify the world.

Architecture as a Eucharistic Sign

Churches provide the most visible public image of the Eucharist, standing as a sign of Christ's presence to the world. In a secular culture, they remind us of the transcendent and invite an encounter with divine beauty. Their beauty provides a glimpse of heaven on earth and invites all who enter to a silent encounter with God. Sergei Bulgakov, an Orthodox theologian, reflects upon the power of his first visit to the great church of Hagia Sophia in Constantinople (modern day Istanbul): "An ocean of light explosively spreads from on high and dominates all this place, enclosed and yet free. The grace of the columns and the beauty of their marble embroideries, the royal dignity—not luxury but royalty—of the walls of gold and of their marvelous ornamentation: all this

Sandro Botticelli, *Mystic Nativity*, 1500

captivates, melts, subjects, and convinces the heart. There results from it a feeling of interior transparence."[44] Churches

---

[44] Quoted in Lemna, *The Apocalypse of Wisdom*, 231. Constructed by Emperor Justinian in 537, this was the largest Christian Church of the

manifest the divine, reminding us of God's presence and grandeur through the architecture and ornamentation.

The word *church* comes from the Greek word *kyriakos*, meaning "of the Lord." Although it is easy to take for granted that every Christian denomination builds churches, the structure itself arose specifically to gather for the Eucharist. The first Christian community immediately celebrated the Mass weekly, rather than annually like the Passover, and decided that it should not take place in the Temple or the synagogues. Luke describes the first Christians as "attending the temple together and breaking bread in their homes" (Acts 2:46). The Eucharist, as a sacrificial meal for God's new covenantal family, found a proper setting in the home. Wealthier families offered their homes for Christian worship, such as Saint Pudens and his daughters in Rome, who hosted Saint Peter in their home (and over which was later built the church of Saint Prudenziana). Even when larger structures took their place, churches continued to serve as the central familial gathering place for Christians—places where the major events of life would take place—baptism, the ongoing reception of the sacraments, marriage, and burial.

With the public tolerance of the Church, Christians built their first large-scale structures. Constantine patronized the construction of the first basilicas in Rome, modeled not on the style of pagan temples but the rectangular shaped meeting halls used by the emperors. Rather than the seat of the emperor, the apse contained mosaics of Christ the king with

---

Byzantine Empire, and one of the largest ever constructed. In 1453, after the fall of Constantinople to the Ottoman Empire, it became a mosque and later a museum. Today it has been reconverted to a mosque.

the chair (*cathedra*) of the bishop and altar in the sanctuary. This structure has remained mostly unchanged from the early 300s to today—a central space in the nave and two side aisles, a vestibule, and an atrium outside. Styles would continue to develop, of course, and from the Roman basilica would come forth the round domes of Constantinople, and the rebirth of architecture in the West through Romanesque churches, which attempted to recapture the glory lost with the fall of Rome. By the High Middle Ages, this style transitioned into the bright Gothic style with the verticality of the pointed arch, dazzling rose window, and gravity defying flying buttresses. The Renaissance sought a return to the simplicity and order of the classical style, though it gave way to the explosive exuberance of the Baroque. The Romantic era nostalgically restored and replicated the past glories of the medieval period, and the modernist style of the last century iconoclastically broke away from traditional styles.

Catholics build churches as a sign of their faith in Jesus's presence in the world, most especially in the Holy Eucharist. Father Jean Corbon asks, "What is a church, as a sacramental space, if not an icon of the body of Christ?"[45] As such, they are constructed to transition the worshiper from this world into the transcendent reality of faith, offering them as sign of their own identity as a tabernacle of Christ. The building communicates this purpose beginning with its design as a specifically sacred space dedicated to Christ. Its customary cruciform shape signifies how Christ and His sacrifice become instantiated there. Its ascending steps lead

---

[45] Corbon, *The Wellspring of Worship*, 192.

through a spiritual ascent, while entering through a portal and a large door represent the transition from the mundane and temporal into a sacred space. The vestibule provides a transitional space before entering into the main place of worship, the nave. Named for a ship (*navis* in Lain), the nave, the body of the church, represents the ark of the Church as a shelter in the midst of the world. The altar rail or communion rail found in many Churches separates the nave from the sanctuary, in a similar fashion to the Eastern iconostasis. It is a treasured spot for many Catholics, a gate to heaven where they are fed with the bread of angels. The sanctuary serves as the focal point of the church, with the ambo for the readings and preaching and the central altar as the place where the sacrifice of Christ is made present, the exact place where heaven touches earth. Christ's presence remains in the tabernacle (tent of presence), many times constructed as a miniature church, the holy of holies of the building, which makes the entire church a tabernacle of Christ in the world.

When someone enters the church, there is a transition from the ordinary world. Therefore, as Christopher Carstens explains, "the door of the parish church . . . is no ordinary entrance. It appears different [than an ordinary door] because it *is* different: it is a mark of God's house and a sign protecting those within, as at the first Passover. It is an entrance into the Great King's city and His Temple . . . where we touch God."[46] Entering the church enables us to enter mystically into our eternal homeland. The first churches did not meet in homes accidentally, as our parishes still serve as Christ's

---

[46] Carstens, *A Devotion Journey into the Mass*, 13–14.

home and the place where the members of His body should find their deepest home during the pilgrimage of life. The Church orientation itself should direct them toward their true home in heaven. From the earliest days of the Church, the altar was built so that priest and people could face east, toward the rising sun, as a sign of the Lord's resurrection, a sign of the eschatological order of worship leading toward the final resurrection. This liturgical direction, called *ad orientem* or "to the east," remains an important witness of the transcendent order of worship toward God, with the priest and people together facing the Lord rather than one another, keeping the Mass centered on God and not ourselves.[47]

Churches—including their art and furnishings—should communicate the sacredness of their function and provide a reflection of God's own beauty. Pope Benedict XVI related that "the beauty of the liturgy . . . is a sublime expression of God's glory and, in a certain sense, a glimpse of heaven on earth. The memorial of Jesus' redemptive sacrifice contains something of that beauty which Peter, James and John beheld when the Master, making his way to Jerusalem, was transfigured before their eyes (cf. Mk 9:2). Beauty, then, is not mere decoration, but rather an essential element of the liturgical action, since it is an attribute of God himself and

---

[47] The east provides a natural symbol for the Resurrection with the rising of the Son. Early Christians looked to the east in expectation, seeking the second coming. According to tradition, when Christ ascended to the Father, He ascended toward the east, and He will "return in the same way as you have seen him going into heaven" (Acts 1:11). In expectation of his coming again from the east, Catholics are even buried facing this direction.

his revelation."[48] Marble, gold leaf, beautiful craftsmanship, and stained glass all communicate the importance and holiness of the space and actions performed there. Height, light, color, and shape should enliven the senses and direct them toward meditation on the sacred realities of the Faith which become present in the Mass. The dome, for instance, in its circular shape, represents eternity and creates a sheltered space under its upward thrust that points the mind toward the higher things. Stained glass embodies the illumination and splendor that shine forth from the grace that enlivens the soul. Statuary and images of the angels and saints portray the mystical communion surrounding us during Mass.

Extending Worship through Procession and Pilgrimage

If churches serve as tabernacles of God's presence for all the world, they should enliven the surrounding community. Even though largely unseen, Christians uphold the entire world through their prayer, and the Mass and parishes sanctify their entire neighborhood. Processions, as sacred and liturgical movement, offer some sign of the sanctuary's extension into the world, temporarily reclaiming the cosmos as the original temple of the Lord and extending the Church's prayer for the world out into its domain. Outdoor processions embody the mission given at the end of Mass in the *ite missa est*, the sending forth into the world. Jesus's own procession into Jerusalem is commemorated each Mass during the Sanctus, as the congregation repeats: "Hosanna!

---

[48] Pope Benedict XVI, *Sacramentum Caritatis*, no. 35.

Blessed is he who comes in the name of the Lord!" (Mk 11:9). Christians process as a sign of Christ's kingship, manifesting the triumphal march of His Church, following the cross as the sign of victory in self-giving service.

Processions have been central to the Mass throughout the Church's history. Movement in the liturgy is not haphazard but is sacred and symbolic of entrances and proclamations. This includes the Introit, or entrance, to the altar and reading of the Gospel in the Western liturgy and the Little and Great Entrances in the Divine Liturgy of the East (processions of the Gospel book and gifts respectively). The blessing with holy water at the beginning of Mass gives a glimpse of larger procession that occurred each Sunday in the Middle Ages that blessed not only the faithful in church but also the surrounding land and cemetery. The Synod of Nantes, taking place about the year 655, describes how "every Sunday before Mass, each priest is to bless water in a vessel which is clean and suitable for so great a mystery, for the people to be sprinkled with when they enter the church, and let him make the round of the yard [atrium] of the said church with the [processional] crosses, sprinkling it with the holy water, and let him pray for the souls of them that rest therein."[49] This holy water would be taken home each week for the family to bless their house, showing how the procession with the holy water continued in the sanctification of the community.

Liturgical processions mark major feasts, such as the Presentation (with candles after they are blessed), Palm Sunday, Holy Thursday, Corpus Christi, and the Assumption.

---

[49] Thurston, "Processions."

Although now a rare occurrence, public outdoor processions occurred regularly in the past to bless plantings and harvests, as well as to avert calamities in times of disease, famine, and war, along with thanksgiving for answered prayers. Jules Breton captures this tradition so powerfully in his painting of the wheat blessing outside of Artois, France, as the priest carries the monstrance in the middle of the prayers of the people processing out into the fields. The most ancient of these outdoor processions (stretching back to the Roman Empire), the Rogation Days, sought God's blessing on the fields and to avert danger. They entailed a series of processions beginning with the major rogation on the feast of Saint Mark, April 25, and then the minor rogations on the three days before the Ascension. Processions of icons, statues, and relics marked the feast of saints and invoked their intercession for the community in times of trouble. The most famous processions of icons occurred along the city walls of the great city of Constantinople, with the patriarch carrying the great icon of Our Lady, the Panagia of the Akathist, and averted many sieges against the city.

Jules Breton, *The Blessing of Wheat in Artois*, 1857

The first public Eucharistic procession occurred in the eleventh century on Palm Sunday in commemoration of Christ's own procession into Jerusalem that day. The tradition of processions with the sacrament grew after the establishment of the feast of Corpus Christi, making it the largest annual procession of the Eucharist, with processions continuing throughout the feast's eight-day octave. Corpus Christi processions became a major civic moment, with the town doing its best to honor Jesus's presence. Pope Benedict XVI, thinking back to his Bavarian childhood, thought of Corpus Christi in light of the words of Saint Justin Martyr that the priest should offer prayers "as much as he is able," connecting it to his town's own efforts:

> This is what the entire community feels called to do at Corpus Christi: dare to do what you can. I can still smell those carpets of flowers and the freshness of the birch trees; I can see all the houses decorated, the banners, the singing; I can still hear the village band, which indeed sometimes dared more, on this occasion, than it was able! I remember the *joie de vivre* of the local lads, firing their gun salutes—which was their way of welcoming Christ as head of state, as *the* Head of State, the lord of the world, present on their streets and in their village.[50]

Abandoned in the 1960s by many parishes, Corpus Christi processions have made a comeback. In some traditionally

---

[50] Ratzinger, *The Feast of Faith*, 127.

Catholic places of Europe like Valencia, Spain, they continue to express their once central role in Catholic culture. Hence Robert Lewis Wilken challenges us to reinvigorate processions and other public demonstrations of faith to revitalize Christian culture: "If Christ is culture, let the sidewalks be lit with fire on Easter Eve, let traffic stop for a column of Christians waving palm branches on a spring morning, let streets be blocked off as the faithful gather for a Corpus Christi procession. Then will others know that there is another city in their midst, another commonwealth, one that has its face, like the faces of angels, turned toward the face of God."[51]

Such practices help form culture by uniting people in public expressions of faith, reinforcing one's own beliefs and providing a sign to others of a higher reality present even in our secular culture. Above all, these processions remind our world that God is *literally* with us, and that He is truly the King of heaven and earth, for His Kingship will never end (cf. Dn 7:14; Lk 1:33).

Eucharistic Congresses honor Jesus's presence more broadly in entire regions and nations at once, gathering large groups of people for communal adoration. The first congress occurred in Lille, France in 1881 through the inspiration of a laywoman, Emilie-Marie Tamisier, and they now gather pilgrims internationally every four years to honor the Blessed Sacrament. In 2024, the United States will hold its first national Eucharistic Congress since 1976

---

[51] Robert Louis Wilken, "The Church as Culture," *First Things,* April 2004, https://www.firstthings.com/article/2004/04/the-church-as-culture.

as part of a multi-year Eucharistic revival. Even though every parish celebrates Mass on the local level, Eucharistic congresses provide an example of embarking on a Eucharistic pilgrimage.

Every Mass consists of a spiritual pilgrimage that enters into the adoration of the Lamb in the new and heavenly Jerusalem. Nonetheless, setting out from home on a journey of faith can provide an opportunity for a renewed encounter with Christ in the Eucharist at a holy site or shrine. A pilgrimage sets out on a journey to seek God. It aims at a holy site or shrine to provide a powerful encounter with the realities of faith: the communion of saints, our Catholic heritage, and the sacraments. Pilgrimages provide time for spiritual renewal, a new encounter, and for a deeper experience of confession and the Mass. They usually involve hardship and can be arduous, and thus, they provide an image of life itself as a lifelong, difficult journey toward our true homeland.

Pilgrimages have been central to biblical faith from the beginning. Abraham set out to follow God and seek a new homeland, while Moses led the Israelites on a penitential journey through the desert. Jews came to Jerusalem three times a year, including the Feast of Booths to commemorate the wandering pilgrimage of the desert (and when booths were constructed to eat and sleep in), along with Passover and Pentecost. Jesus Himself traveled as a pilgrim to Jerusalem for these festivals. Visiting the great sites of Christendom and the Holy Land make the life of Jesus and the saints more accessible while reminding us of the Mass's sacred realities. Pilgrimages provide an encounter with God, inspiring us through beautiful, sacred spaces. Visiting shrines in groups will also renew Catholic culture by restoring contact with many lost treasures, as well as providing times of festivity and fellowship. These holy adventures, often requiring sacrifice and suffering, honor Jesus and lead to greater conversion and growth. Pilgrimages also stimulate culture by engaging participants in practices that make our faith come alive, giving us additional time for prayer while also experiencing the lost beauty of Catholic culture. Furthermore, these more extraordinary events can deepen our faith in the Eucharist so that upon returning home, we can pray at Mass with even greater devotion.

Eucharistic Miracles as Confirmation of Christ's Presence

As weak human beings, we need moments of renewal and outward signs to strengthen our faith. In seeking greater union with God, pilgrimages can draw us into the Eucharist and sacraments more deeply, providing more spiritual riches than any site or object. In fact, many pilgrimage sites provide opportunities to experience the real presence of Jesus in new ways. Catholic shrines preserve a number of relics related to the Eucharist and Jesus's passion. These include the chalice of Valencia (the purported cup of the Last Supper), a cloth of the Precious Blood at Bruges, the relics of the cross and nails discovered by Saint Helen at Santa Croce in Rome, and the Shroud of Turin (which one recent theory claims also as the tablecloth at the Last Supper in addition to Christ's burial cloth).[52] These relics

---

[52] Jackson *The Shroud of Turin*.

are not necessary to support faith, although they do spark devotion, pointing us back to the Eucharist and helping our intellect and imagination to perceive Jesus there. When visiting the Basilica of the Precious Blood at Bruges, a priest told me he was not interested in visiting the shrine because he drinks the "real thing" every day. While it is true that every Catholic can experience Jesus's Eucharistic presence at their own parish, pilgrimages to shrines that preserve Eucharistic miracles can strengthen our faith and renew our love for Christ.

Miracles have surrounded the Mass throughout the Church's history. We have already seen Saint Cyprian's account of fire preventing an unworthy communion and the apparition to Saint Gregory the Great as a sign in response to his prayer for a doubter. Other saints have had exterior manifestations to confirm their faith. Saint Edward the Confessor, the eleventh-century king of England, saw the Eucharistic host appear as the Christ child during the elevation at Mass. Likewise, Saint Faustina spoke of a similar vision in her diary: "During the Midnight Mass, I saw the Child Jesus in the Host, and my spirit was immersed in Him. Although He was a tiny Child, His majesty penetrated my soul. I was permeated to the depths of my being by this mystery, this great abasement on the part of God, this inconceivable emptying of Himself."[53] Miraculous Communions have also occurred, such as the young Saint Imelda being taken immediately to heaven at her first Communion, Saint Teresa of Avila's levitation after receiving Communion from Bishop

---

[53] St. Faustina Kowalska, *Diary*, no. 182.

Diego de Yepes, Saint Lucia Fillipini receiving a host miraculously from the altar, and the children of Fatima receiving
Communion from an angel.

Eucharistic miracles, in particular, often strengthen
faith in Jesus's real presence, and are given to help overcome
doubts, not prove the Faith. When asked why Jesus miraculously appeared as "flesh or a child" on several occasions,
Saint Thomas Aquinas shed light on this matter. In fact,
Jesus may appear inwardly to individuals or "by an appearance which really exists outwardly."[54] The interior vision is
given as a consolation or warning to an individual, while an
outward appearance provides a public sign. The presence of
genuine human flesh in Eucharistic miracles, for instance,
which has been confirmed by modern science, occurs
through a miracle distinct from the normal sacramental
presence. Aquinas holds that "there is a miraculous change
wrought in the other accidents, such as shape, color, and
the rest," with a new "species miraculously formed."[55] Like
the accidents of the bread and wine which remain after
transubstantiation, the human flesh created in the miracle
exist to make Christ's true body in heaven present for the
senses to perceive.

Many publicly visible Eucharistic miracles have occurred
throughout the world, so many, in fact, that a young man,
Blessed Carlo Acutis, who died at fifteen from leukemia, created
a website to compile them all. His site, www.miracolieucaristici.
org, accessible in seventeen languages, lists over one hundred

---

[54] St. Thomas Aquinas, *Summa Theologica*, III, q. 76, a. 8, corpus.
[55] Aquinas, corpus, ad 2.

miracles in twenty countries across every major continent. Each miracle has its own dedicated subpage with an explanation of its history. The most recently confirmed miracle occurred in Legnica, Poland in 2013, where a dropped host was placed in water to dissolve, but a fifth of it turned into a cross-striated muscle, consistent with a heart muscle in agony. In 2008, in another town in Poland, Sokolka, a similar instance occurred, with evidence of a myocardial, heart tissue of a living person nearing death, with this tissue completely intertwined with the accidents of the bread. Other recent miracles include a bleeding host in Tixtla, Mexico in 2006, which in 2010 continued to shed fresh blood, an image of Jesus appearing on a host during exposition in 2001 in Chirattakonam, India, and a distressed heart tissue appearing in another host in Buenos Aires in 1996. All of these cases have withstood scientific examination with no possible explanation.

There are four general patterns in Eucharistic miracles. First, the host turns into flesh; second, the host bleeds; third, images appear on the host; and fourth, hosts miraculously resist decomposition or destruction. The most famous of the first type occurred in Lanciano, Italy in 750, making it the first, major Eucharistic miracle in history. An Eastern monk saying Mass in the Latin rite had doubts about the doctrine of transubstantiation, and after saying the words of institution at the consecration, the sacred species became human flesh (also from the heart) and coagulated blood, without decomposition to this day. An example of the second type can be seen in Santarem, Portugal, where in 1247 a woman stole a host from Mass for use in sorcery, and when she arrived home, the host began to bleed. Not long after in Bolsena, Italy in 1263, as we have seen, another host bled during Mass in response to the doubts of another priest on pilgrimage to Rome (this was the miracle that prompted the papal approval of the feast of Corpus Christi), with the blood-stained corporal now on display in the cathedral of Orvieto. In Raphael's fresco depicting the miracle, you can see not only the miracle occurring on the left of the altar but also Pope Julius II on the right of the altar. Pope Julius II, who commissioned the painting for the Vatican's Apostolic Palace, can be seen honoring the Eucharistic miracle, accompanied by pilgrims, thus modeling how piety increases in response to these Eucharistic miracles.

Raphael, *The Mass of Bolsena*, 1511

Corresponding to the third type, in 1430, a lady purchased a monstrance in Monaco with the consecrated host still within. She used a knife to remove it. It then shed blood and an image of Jesus seated on a throne with instruments of the Passion surrounding Him was imprinted upon it. The host was moved to Dijon, where it remained until it was destroyed during the French Revolution.

Finally, a number of miracles have preserved the Eucharistic species from destruction and decay. In 1345 in Amsterdam, a host was preserved after being vomited by a dying man; it was then also preserved from being deposited in the fire. The host is still carried in procession through the city each year. In Avignon, the flashpoint of the Great Western Schism which ended not long before, a flood swept through the city in 1433 and some Franciscans abandoned a church with the Eucharist still exposed for adoration. When they came back by boat, they found the water miraculously had been kept away from the altar and a pathway to it opened through the water within the church. Finally, in Siena in 1730, the sacred vessels were stolen, and 351 consecrated hosts were stuffed into the poor box. After recovery, they were placed into a container to decompose, but they never have and can still be seen in the glass container.

These miracles, along with church buildings and processions, continue to manifest Jesus's continuous presence within our world. They invite Christians to reclaim the world for Christ, manifesting His presence through beauty, extending His presence into our streets, and pointing people to visible signs of His Eucharistic life. Churches are microcosms of what God wants for the world: for His presence to be recognized, accepted, and honored. The world exists to give God glory and to provide a place where we can enter into communion with God. As Catholics, we should not hide behind the walls of the church but carry our faith with us into the world, reclaiming it for its rightful king.

12

Fostering Eucharistic Encounters: Honoring Christ's Body in the World

The Eucharist is missionary in nature. By consuming Christ in the Eucharist, we become one with Him, and therefore, we must live like Him. In becoming one flesh with Him, Jesus calls His followers to love others as He does and to enter into His own mission. Pope Benedict XVI describes how "the Eucharist draws us into Jesus' act of self-oblation. More than just statically receiving the incarnate *Logos*, we enter into the very dynamic of his self-giving."[56] This conformity to Christ shapes our identity, leading us to recognize how our own body expresses and continues the gift of the Eucharist. Likewise, the Eucharist helps us to discern the presence of Jesus in others, especially the poor. Finally, it initiates us into Jesus's Eucharistic mission when we give of ourselves (our gifts, our love, or our time) to others.

---

[56] Pope Benedict XVI, *Sacramentum Caritatis*, no. 21.

The Body as Eucharistic Gift

Human beings are made in the image and likeness of God, Who bestows an innate dignity on all people. We are beings who can know and love, and we find our happiness in communion with others. The Incarnation deepens our dignity because the Son of God took our nature to Himself and called each person into a new birth "not of blood nor of the will of the flesh nor of the will of man, but of God" (Jn 1:13). The God made man, Jesus Christ, reveals the ultimate goal of human life: happiness through communion with the Trinity by entering into His divine life for eternity. The Eucharist is truly the one necessary thing that opens up the deepest meaning and purpose of our lives, teaching us how to love and to find light in the darkness.

And it was the greatest love of so many on earth, including J. R. R. Tolkien, who called it "the one great thing to love on earth: The Blessed Sacrament." As seen in the foreword, Tolkien said that you will find everything in the Holy Eucharist "romance, glory, honor, fidelity," and so much more.[57] Tolkien makes a bold claim, but one we can accept if we believe in the True Presence: the Eucharist contains the real drama of human life, giving us life by leading us into the death of self-sacrificial love. The Eucharist opens the path, the drama and romance, of our ultimate fulfillment even now, anticipating the true happiness of this complete communion. The gift of the Eucharist provides a model for life: finding happiness in a gift of self to others.

---

[57] Tolkien, *The Letters of J.R.R. Tolkien*, 53. See also Smith, *Lord of the Rings and the Eucharist*.

Pope Saint John Paul II's *Theology of the Body* sheds light on how God created the body as a means of entering into communion. The body serves as a sacrament of the soul, tangibly expressing it in the world and enabling communion as a means of presence, communication, and service. John Paul sees the reciprocal gift of self to the other in marriage as the deepest natural expression of the communion of persons for which human beings have been made. Christ elevated marriage, making it a sacramental means for overcoming sin and of entering more deeply into His own love for the Church. In Ephesians 5, John Paul sees the Eucharistic nature of Christ's gift of self to His beloved bride, the Church: "This would seem to be indicated by the following words about nourishing one's own body, which indeed every man nourishes and cherishes 'as Christ does the Church, because we are members of his body' (5:29–30). In fact, Christ nourishes the Church with His body precisely in the Eucharist."[58] John Paul recognizes in the Eucharist the fruit of Christ's own marital love for His bride, making it a sign also of the self-gift that should mark Christian marriage. These two realities—the Eucharist and marriage—will be drawn together in heaven, as we truly become one with God in the great wedding feast of the lamb (Rv 19:9). The early medieval manuscript presented here captures this great festivity that awaits us, with Our Lady representing the Church, the true bride of the lamb, and with all the faithful joining in: processing with music, food, and drink. Christ, the Lamb of

---

[58] Pope John Paul II, General Audience, October 27, 1982. Celibacy is a supernatural expression of the gift of self, participating even more directly in Christ's gift of Himself to the Church.

God, feeds us with Himself even now as a beginning of the more perfect joy of union that is to come.

Medieval Illumination of the Wedding Feast of the Lamb

The Eucharist is a sacrament of love that expresses Jesus's marital love for His Church, the complete gift of Himself to us. By drawing His bride into a union where the two become one, Jesus conforms the Church to Himself. His body is the source of life: "The bread which I shall give for the life of the world is my flesh" (Jn 6:51). If we eat this flesh and become one with Jesus, we become truly alive, living a life according to the Spirit, the very love of God. And the more this assimilation into Christ occurs, as members of His body, the more we then are able to show His divine love to others. This is the goal of the Eucharist: to draw us into a dynamic communion that overflows to others, bearing fruit for their lives as well. The Eucharist moves us to give of ourselves more generously to others, sacrificing our body to serve them in imitation of Christ. John Kane explains that "every fruitful

Holy Communion is a union not only with Christ, but also with our fellowmen. . . . The spirit of self-oblation by which Christ gives Himself to us must, by eliminating—or at least controlling—our natural selfishness, unite us in the bonds of charity with others."[59] The Eucharist would ignite a revolution of love if only we allowed it to take root in us. The love it offers can become contagious if our communion with Jesus expands to others.

Jesus is the true source of communion with others. He enables true friendship to blossom, helping us to pursue our true good with others. Sin, a selfish turning inward, conversely, wounds our communion with God and others, dividing the body of Christ. By pushing God and others away from us, sin causes scandal that can lead to discouragement and doubt, particularly when we give a counter example to the faith. People begin to wonder how the Faith could be true when the Eucharistic fruits of joy, faith, generosity, and charity are dormant, or even apparently absent. Following sin, we need reconciliation both with God and others to restore communion and renew a right relationship. The Eucharist, following from this reconciliation, enables us to live out this restoration in love, as Matthew Levering explains: "After original sin, however, the sacrificial offering, to restore justice, must be the free and loving offering of one's own bodily life, because only such sacrifice could reflect the returning to God of what human beings, in choosing the creature over the Creator, arrogated to themselves."[60] The

---

[59] Kane, *Transforming Your Life through the Eucharist*, 43.
[60] Levering, *Sacrifice and Community*, 175.

Eucharist renews from within, bringing about a conversion from living for oneself to living for others.

A Eucharistic life, however, meets a fundamental challenge in our self-centered and autonomous culture. In our culture, love is understood as a feeling that arises from one's own self-satisfaction. This notion contradicts the self-sacrificial gift of love that the Eucharist inspires. A necessary battle must occur in every Christian to sort out desires and reorder the body to higher goods. We must break free from the chains of slavery to our feelings and pleasures. This battle relates even to our own identity. Is the body a gift that we receive from God or something subject to our own self-creation and whims? Jesus gives us His body and His blood, in part so we may come to know ourselves better as His creatures and friends, and discover the purpose of our lives as incarnate beings. Christians have to live counterculturally—viewing the body as a gift to be given rather than a self-serving tool or burden.

Our secular and consumerist culture distorts the body's proper role with its fascination on exterior things—the flashy and immediately gratifying. William Cavanaugh relates the Eucharist to the problem of consumerism, which tempts us to find our identity in a never-ending process of purchasing, discarding, and repeating. It is an empty process that literally leaves us empty, ever grasping but never finding satisfaction. The Eucharist, however, turns "the act of consumption . . . inside out: instead of simply consuming the body of Christ, we are consumed by it."[61] When Christ

---

[61] Cavanaugh, *Being Consumed*, 54.

consumes us, we change from passive consumers to sharers of a gift, "for becoming the body of Christ also entails that we must become food for others."[62] Christians do not have the same restless search, because their hearts have found rest in the food that truly satisfies. They should be able to resist the allure of the newest product—the newest, largest, and fastest—and the constant distraction of media, because they can find in their heart the source of true peace.

Christians should serve as a sign of contradiction against modern autonomy and a witness to the joy of living for others. This witness upholds the dignity of the body and manifests its role in the gift of self. This includes even the way we present ourselves to others and how we communicate with our bodies. Jesus brings about an inward change in us first, for the right order of the soul is most important. Over time, if we are open to the Eucharistic graces, we should see a change, a growth in generosity, self-control, gentleness, humility, and charity. The inward change manifests itself exteriorly, including how we pray, with genuflections, folded hands, and kneeling in adoration, showing the body's own way of honoring God. It also includes the way that we dress, with our clothing manifesting our dignity and modesty, as well as expressing charity to others. Clothes can honor God and reinforce the fact that our bodies are temples of the Holy Spirit. When we dress for God, it should lead us away from anything that would demean ourselves or offend others.

The body's ultimate dignity comes from serving as a tabernacle of Christ for eternity. Jesus promised this very clearly

---

[62] Cavanaugh, 55.

in John 6: "He who eats my flesh and drinks my blood has eternal life, and I will raise him up at the last day" (v. 54). Saint Irenaeus reflects on how the body will be transformed gloriously in eternity, just as bread changes into the body of Christ. The Eucharist, he says, is that "by which our bodies live and grow. . . . our bodies, which have been nourished by the eucharist, will be buried in the earth and will decay, but they will rise again at the appointed time, for the Word of God will raise them up to the glory of God the Father."[63] We were made temples of God at our baptism, and each Holy Communion renews the Holy Trinity's presence within us, transforming our earthly vessels into the sacred dwelling place of the Most High. The Eucharist transforms death and suffering in love, making it redemptive for others. The sacramentality of human life will continue as God becomes all in all, perfecting the body, and the whole person, into the temple of His divine presence.

Discerning the Body of Christ in the World

Just as we need a spiritual vision to recognize Jesus's true presence at the Mass, so we also need the eyes of faith to see Him in the world. If we come close to Him in Communion, He also wants us to seek Him out, hidden in those most in need. Jesus told His followers very clearly, "Whatever you did for one of the least of my brothers and sisters, you did it to me" (Mt 25:40). He also gave an example at the Last Supper when He washed the feet of His disciples, exhorting

---

[63] Saint Irenaeus, *Against Heresies*, Bk. 5, ch. 2, quoted in Liturgy of the Hours, Office of Readings, Thursday of the third week of Easter.

them (and us): "A new commandment I give to you, that you love one another; even as I have loved you, that you also love one another" (Jn 13:34). At the very moment when He gave His body to the Church to eat, He also commanded His followers to give of themselves to one another, imitating His gift. The Eucharist is bound up essentially with charity.

The first Christian community recognized the link between the Eucharist and the poor. Even as they gathered to break bread in their homes, we also hear that "all who believed were together and had all things in common; and they sold their possessions and goods and distributed them to all, as any had need" (Acts 2:44–45). The communion with Jesus we receive in the Eucharist is meant to continue by communing with Him also in the poor. They must go together, for, as the *Catechism* teaches us, "the Eucharist commits us to the poor," stating further that "to receive in truth the Body and Blood of Christ given up for us, we must recognize Christ in the poorest, his brethren."[64] In making us more like Him, the Eucharist inspires generosity in us and impels us to love others like Jesus.

Jesus's words "this is my body" refer not only to the Eucharist but also to His presence in the poor. Saint Paul connected the two presences by telling the Corinthians not to neglect the poor in the meal surrounding the Mass. We must discern Christ's presence in the Eucharistic species and also in those in need, which the community was neglecting. He exhorts them to see the unity we have in the one Body of Christ: "For anyone who eats and drinks without

---

[64] *CCC* 1397.

discerning the body eats and drinks judgment upon himself" (1 Cor 11:29). If we recognize Christ's presence in the Mass and then deny His presence in the poor, we risk the condemnation of those who did not serve His needs in the least of His brethren: "Depart from me, you cursed, into the eternal fire prepared for the devil and his angels; for I was hungry and you gave me no food, I was thirsty and you gave me no drink" (Mt 25:41–42). In Luke's parallel passage, we find a striking Eucharistic connection. Those who are denied entrance into the Kingdom say to Christ, "We ate and drank in your presence," and yet He still tells them that "I do not know where you have come from" (Lk 13:26–27). Consider the significance of this for receiving the Eucharist! We may think we are good Catholics or even that our salvation is secure because we partake of the Holy Eucharist, and yet Christ warns us that if we ignore Him in the world then He will not recognize us. As we have seen throughout this book, a fruitful reception of the Eucharist requires living a Eucharistic life, living out the gift we have received.

Jesus deliberately becomes vulnerable, even in a position of need, through the poor, inviting us, His disciples, to express our love for Him. Drawing upon biblical imagery, Gary Anderson points out that God allows us to repay our debts to Him through the poor. He mentions that the early Church considered this a "sacramental act," with the poor as a "mediator of the Godhead."[65] The Church has understood this work of charity as an extension of Christ's own self-offering in the Mass: "In almsgiving, the layperson has

---

[65] Anderson, *Charity*, 7; 9.

the opportunity to participate in this divine act by that mercy."[66] Charity manifests the fruits of the Eucharist, expressing in action the presence of Jesus in the soul. An unknown Dutch painter captured this connection in his portrayal of the corporal works of mercy, the actions Jesus described in Matthew 25 pertaining to judgment, including feeding the hungry. The loaves and fish in the bottom left of the image point to these actions as an extension of Jesus Himself feeding us and then sending us out to feed others. The corporal works of mercy manifest the love and mercy that we have received from God, extending our communion with Jesus to others. If God feeds us, then we must help quench the hunger and thirst of others.

Painter of the Haarlem School,
The Seven Corporal Works of Mercy, 1580

[66] Anderson, 8.

Acts of charity recognize the bond of unity we have with others as members of the same body. As Christ's followers and members of His body, we cannot think solely of ourselves, as has become so common in our culture that views everyone as anonymous individuals. As William Cavanaugh explains, through the Eucharist, "the very distinction between what is mine and what is yours breaks down in the body of Christ."[67] God bestows gifts on us to be used for others, as there is a real bond of justice and charity uniting Christians together. We belong to each other and are responsible for one another. The pain of one member belongs to another, for, "If one member suffers, all suffer with it" (1 Cor 12:26). To share in Christ's love is to share in the sacrifice He made of himself, which considers the good of others more than one's own needs.

The Brothers Grimm relate a traditional folktale that expresses this responsibility and common bond, "God's Food," a name that in itself points to the Eucharist. The deeply challenging and moving story is short enough to repeat in its entirety:

> Once there were two sisters; the one had no children and was rich; the other had five children, was a widow, and was so poor that she no longer had enough bread to feed herself and her children. In distress she went to her sister and said, "My children and I are starving. You are rich; give me a bite of bread." The rich but hard-hearted woman said, "I don't have anything in my house either," and with angry words she sent the poor

---

[67] Cavanaugh, *Being Consumed*, 56.

woman away. Some time later the rich sister's husband came home and wanted to cut himself a piece of bread, but when he cut into the loaf, red blood gushed from it. When his wife saw this, she became horrified and told him what had happened. He hurried away and wanted to help. When he entered the poor widow's room, he found her there praying. She was holding the two youngest children in her arms; the three oldest ones were lying there dead. He offered her food, but she answered, "We no longer need earthly food; God has filled three already, and will hear our prayers as well." She had hardly uttered these words when the two small ones stopped breathing, whereupon her heart broke too, and she sank down dead.[68]

A connection exists between the spiritual and earthly food we eat. Just as Christ wants everyone to commune with Him in the gift of His body, so He wants His followers to commune with others by ensuring that they are also fed. Giving away our earthly food becomes a sign and fruit of the spiritual food that we have received.

Christian charity is not simply about relieving the temporal needs of others. For those in need, who suffer and may even feel despair, acts of charity manifest God's love and care for them. We cannot separate the material and spiritual elements of human life, of course, so meeting the needs of the body takes on a spiritual character in affirming the innate dignity of each person and God's love for them. The connection between the Eucharist and meeting material needs

---

[68] Grimm, "God's Food," 434.

can be seen even in something that we take for granted: the Sunday collection. If we truly feel that God is caring for us at the Mass, giving us His own self to satisfy our needs, then we should be inspired to give to others in return, repaying our debt to God (see 2 Cor 8). We tend to think of our money solely as our own and what we do with it a personal matter. The Church teaches us, however, that everything we have is a gift from God and we owe a portion of it back to Him, traditionally a tenth or tithe, as a matter of justice and an opportunity to glorify God.

Our material goods provide us a chance to honor God and serve the needs of others. Tithing and almsgiving offer us an opportunity to express Christ's charity as an extension of the communion He offers us. We cannot fully participate in the Holy Sacrifice of the Mass if we neglect others' sufferings. Charity is the chief fruit of the Eucharist, leading us to put the good of others before ourselves, imitating God's own love. This supernatural charity should shape all our choices, suffusing them with God's own love. The *Catechism* makes clear that *"the moral life is spiritual worship.* As does the whole of the Christian life, the moral life finds its source and summit in the Eucharistic sacrifice."[69] In charity, the Eucharist shapes life concretely and gives vitality to a truly Christ-like culture. When charity guides all of our actions, our lives become truly Eucharistic.

---

[69] *CCC* 2031.

Living the Mission of the Eucharist

The Eucharist plants a leaven of the divine life within us, allowing God to transform not only our lives but the world itself. Jesus proclaimed that the Kingdom of God was at hand, the radical inbreaking of God into human life. Jesus, the God-man, initiated a revolution in the world, bringing wandering souls back to Himself. In teaching us how to pray, He taught us to ask that God's will be done on earth as on heaven, beseeching also for a daily, supersubstantial bread to live a supernatural life. To live the Kingdom of God now is to put God before all else and to do everything in communion with Him. Living in communion with God will make an impact in the world, acting also as a leaven that inspires others to holiness.

The Eucharist contains within it the spiritual dynamism needed to transform the world. Christ sanctifies His followers so that in making them His temple, they can in turn reclaim the world for Him, making it a tabernacle of His presence. The Second Vatican Council, in its document on the laity, *Apostolicam Actuositatem*, describes the Eucharist's mission in leading Christians to enter into the work of the Kingdom: "The sacraments, however, especially the most holy Eucharist, communicate and nourish that charity which is the soul of the entire apostolate."[70] The unique apostolate of the laity focuses on transforming society by being God's presence within it and building up human culture. The laity are called to go where the Church could

---

[70] Second Vatican Council, *Apostolicam Actuositatem* (November 18, 1965), no. 3.

not go otherwise. They are missionaries because "Christ's redemptive work, while essentially concerned with the salvation of men, includes also the renewal of the whole temporal order."[71] As Salvador Dalí intuited in his rendition of the Last Supper, the Eucharist truly encompasses the whole world in a mystical sense. Jesus is truly present throughout the world in the sacrament, and the grace of this sacrament upholds Christians in their efforts to spread the faith and live in charity. It is up to the laity to bring Christ's presence more explicitly into it through their work and relationships, extending their own Holy Communion.

Salvador Dalí, *Sacrament of the Last Supper*,
1955. National Gallery of Art.

The Eucharist provides the nourishment Christians need for their work in the world, feeding them with the sustaining

---

[71] *Apostolicam Actuositatem*, no. 5.

power of God's divine life. J. R. R. Tolkien expressed this truth poetically in *The Lord of the Rings*, a work of a Catholic imagination that uses fantasy to convey the deeper truths of human life. In a way parallel to the Eucharist, Tolkien describes how a simple waybread, the lembas made by the elves for their journeys, had the power to sustain those who consumed it in difficult moments, even without any other food: "The lembas had a virtue without which they would long ago have lain down to die. It did not satisfy desire, and at times Sam's mind was filled with the memories of food, and the longing for simple bread and meats. And yet, this way bread of the Elves had potency that increased as travelers relied upon it alone and did not mingle it with other foods. It fed the will, and it gave strength to endure, and to master sinew and limb beyond the measure of mortal kind."[72]

The more we rely on the Eucharist, the more it will sustain us. Or as Tolkien himself explains, "The only cure for sagging or fainting faith is Communion."[73] The Christian life requires this supernatural food to provide a unique strength from which the laity will find inspiration and courage to renew the world.

What can Catholics really accomplish in the world? The Church has laid out its body of social teaching to call the faithful to work for the common good, presenting principles to guide the family, economics, education, and political life. Pope Benedict XVI affirms that "in a particular way, the Christian laity, formed at the school of the Eucharist, are

---

[72] Tolkien, *The Return of the King*, 227.
[73] Tolkien, *The Letters of J.R.R. Tolkien*, 338.

called to assume their specific political and social responsibilities."[74] There are notable examples even from recent history of Catholics making significant contributions to society, such as Venerable Robert Schuman, who helped found the European Union to promote peace, the Solidarity movement inspired by John Paul II that brought down Communism in Poland, and doctors seeking to help the vulnerable, such as Venerable Jerome Lejeune. Catholics have made significant impacts in educating the poor, defending the unborn, caring for the sick and elderly, and working to end human trafficking. God inspires this work through many hardships and persecutions. The Eucharist calls for a political order that protects the vulnerable and truly serves all, an economy of gift and love, education that forms the person in truth, goodness, and beauty, and a family life that nourishes children and enables them to thrive in the world.

Entire social programs flow from the Eucharist simply by applying its logic and grace to the challenges and opportunities at hand in society. Gift and sacrifice—these Eucharistic principles provide the Christian *agenda*—literally, what must be done. First of all, we need Christian culture to take root in the family, a sanctuary of the Christian life, with the domestic church making Christ present in the home. Pope Saint John Paul II saw the family as closely linked to the Eucharist, even as "the very source of Christian marriage. . . . In the Eucharistic gift of charity, the Christian family finds the foundation and soul of its 'communion'

---

[74] Pope Benedict XVI, *Sacramentum Caritatis*, no. 91.

and its 'mission.'"[75] The school should serve as an extension of the home. Catholics schools bring children into contact with the Truth itself and help them learn to recognize the truth of creation as an expression of the Word by whom all things were created. The Eucharist is the heart of the Catholic school, forming its distinct culture and animating all of its instruction. Catholic students should learn how to become disciples of Christ and to discern a vocation of service in the world.

Work foundationally builds culture, applying human creativity to shape nature and supply for the needs of society. Connecting work to the Eucharist, the monks, once again, model how the *opus Dei* of worship (the ultimate work of praising God) should shape the daily work of labor. Work supplies the necessary support for the Mass in many ways, bringing forth the needed matter, building the space and furnishing it, and supporting the whole life of the parish. For a Christian, work should also flow from prayer, inspiring a creative sacramentality that expresses the interior life and commitment to serve in tangible ways. Ultimately, we should work out of charity, providing for the material needs of our families, society, and the whole Church, as well as helping the less fortunate—all for the glory of God. Likewise, a Christian should approach politics as a means to protect human dignity, supply for the needs of society, and to achieve the common good. The Eucharist inspires us to work for peace because it is Christ's

---

[75] Pope John Paul II, *Familiaris Consortio*, no. 57.

sacrifice, the one who laid down His life to reconcile all people to God and to one another.

In building a Christian culture in the world, the laity follow the kingship of Christ. Christ reigns over the world from the right hand of the Father, though He does so in silence, visiting His faithful in the quiet presence of the Eucharist and living in them in a special way. This sacramental presence expresses His desire to reign in and through the hearts of those who love Him. He enlivens His followers in His Eucharistic presence, calling them to reign with Him even now: "You made them a kingdom, and priests to serve our God, and they shall reign on the earth" (Rv 5:10). This reigning, however, is one of service and self-sacrifice, which Christ manifested on the cross, inaugurating His reign. Jesus calls all of His followers to be martyrs (literally witnesses) to His reign and to exercise a kingship of service to others.

The greatest act of Christian kingship may be helping someone experience God's love, especially when it requires a sacrificial gift of self. The task of evangelization, the spreading of the good news of salvation, entrusted to the Church calls all Christians to draw others into communion with our Eucharistic King. Evangelization serves as the greatest act of service to the King and the greatest act of charity to those who receive the message: "Go therefore to the thoroughfares, and invite to the marriage feast as many as you find" (Mt 22:9). Those who have received the sublime gift of the Eucharist and realize its greatness want to share it with as many people as possible. "The more ardent the love for the Eucharist in the hearts of the Christian people, the more clearly will they recognize the goal of all mission: *to bring Christ to others.*[76] We are sent forth from the Mass on mission, *ite Missa est*, to bring its gifts into the world and draw others back to the source of this gift, God Himself. The mission of evangelization will bring about the Church's renewal in exercising faithfulness to the mandate given to her by Jesus, and also the world, as it will be renewed from within through the Eucharistic presence of Christ. Just as Mary brought Christ to Elizabeth, "the first Eucharistic procession in history" according to Pope Benedict XVI, so too must we become living monstrances, allowing Christ's presence to transform others through our witness.[77]

[76] Pope Benedict XVI, *Sacramentum Caritatis*, no. 86.

[77] Pope Benedict XVI, "Address during the Prayer Meeting in the Vatican Gardens for the Conclusion of the Marian Month of May," May 31, 2005, https://www.vatican.va/content/benedict-xvi/en/speeches/2005/may/documents/hf_ben-xvi_spe_20050531_rosary-may.html.

13

The Heart of the World: How the Eucharist Can Save Civilization

Jesus gave us the Eucharist not to build a civilization but to make us one with Him. Does that mean that we should avoid renewing our civilization, leaving it for someone else? No, it does not. Even if our ultimate goal lies in heaven, we have seen that our faith should guide us to live in a way that flows from our faith. If our efforts of living a Eucharistic life are successful, we will impact others. The fruits will be local, confined mostly to the circle of our family, friendships, and work. We may never live to see a Eucharistic-centered civilization come to life again, but we can lay the foundation for this rebuilding project through our own prayer and work. Like the *ora et labora* of the monks of old, our homes can serve as oases of a true spiritual life in a barbaric world. This godless world may be fine for many who do not see the need for salvation. On the outside, technology continues to develop at a staggering pace, new advances in medicine prolong life, and poverty is declining throughout the world. On the other hand, everyone seems to realize that the cornerstone of civilization is missing. Our civilization continues to experience a spiritual malaise, having no real purpose except acquiring wealth or inventing the latest device. Ultimately, our society needs God to rediscover who we are and where we are going. The Eucharist truly can reanimate it, restoring its lost vitality and vigor, and help us to order our material goods to higher purposes. More than ever, the Church needs renewal from within, particularly a Eucharistic renewal. For when the Church is renewed, society will be renewed, supernaturally guided in rediscovering its even most basic, though lost, natural goods.

The Precondition: Renewal in the Church

The Eucharist is the heart of the Church, and the Church is the heart of the world. This is not simply a pious sentiment but one of the deepest truths that govern reality. The life of the Church directly relates to the life of the world by upholding it through prayer and communicating a hidden life to it through her worship. God sustains all things in being, and the more attuned we are to Him, the more rightly ordered we will be. The Eucharist is truly the most powerful means of attuning all things to God. There are 1.34 billion Catholics in the world. If they were truly to live as tabernacles of God's Eucharistic presence in the world, just imagine what the fruits would be.

Although the Church has been founded for the salvation of souls, its mission also includes the renewal of human society. In the modern world, we tend to think of the spiritual and temporal as completely apart, but just as we ourselves are body-soul unities, so we cannot divorce our interior life from the exterior life. Our society is currently sick, and its greatest problem is not economic, political, or environmental—it is the absence of God from our civilization. The Church, therefore, holds the key to the inner renewal of our civilization upon which its long-term exterior health depends as well. Pope Leo XIII, in his encyclical *Immortale Dei*, describes how the mission of the Church reaches also to the renewal of civilization:

> The Catholic Church, that imperishable handiwork of our all-merciful God, has for her immediate and natural purpose the saving of souls and securing our happiness in heaven. Yet, in regard to things temporal, she is the source of benefits as manifold and great as if the chief end of her existence were to ensure the prospering of our earthly life. And, indeed, wherever the Church has set her foot she has straightway changed the face of things, and has attempered the moral tone of the people with a new civilization and with virtues before unknown. All nations which have yielded to her sway have become eminent by their gentleness, their sense of justice, and the glory of their high deeds.[78]

The Eucharist, as the true heart of the world, gives the greatest meaning to everything, not just to things in the Church. What has more power to renew politics, economics, education, leisure, and the family than the Lord's sacramental presence in the world? As the most powerful force in the

---

[78] Pope Leo XIII, *Immortale Dei*, no. 1.

universe, it has the spiritual energy needed to rebuild that can actually address the problem that is causing civilization to crumble. Saint Clare drove the Saracens away by simply holding a monstrance before them. Do we believe the Eucharist can defeat the Church's enemies of today, the new barbarians at the gate, not by driving them away but by converting them from within?

Cavalier d'Arpino, *St. Clare with the Scene of the Siege of Assisi*, 17th century

Because the world has lost its moral compass, it needs God more than anything else. Would anyone deny this? And yet, when the Eucharist is proposed as the antidote to feed the spiritually hungry, many people balk and claim that it is an overly pious solution. Religion is the true heart of any civilization, and so the renewal of our own civilization depends upon turning back to its Lord, sacramentally present, though largely ignored, within it.[79] Can we find a political or economic solution to the world's problem? If we think so, then we are giving into the secular thinking that has rejected God to begin with. Imagine being a doctor and having the medicine that a patient needs, though holding it back. As Catholics, we may be embarrassed to tell the world that we truly have the answer for each individual and for our society as a whole, although we have to offer it!

For the Church to transform the world, we first need to renew the life of every Catholic. We ourselves have abandoned the bread of life and become spiritually anemic. Even if, as Joseph Ratzinger predicted, the Church is going to become smaller, while also becoming more faithful, a dedicated minority can enliven the whole. Cardinal Robert Sarah laments that the crisis of Western culture has reached into the Church, disabling us from serving as agents of change: "Christians have abandoned their mission, and the decadence of the West is the result. They no longer look to heaven. They are taken hostage by the new paradigms. They make themselves worldly."[80] If we are like the world, we cannot change it. We need a concerted effort from Catholics, uniting us together in a common goal to save our culture

---

[79] As Joseph Ratzinger points out, "with the exception of modern technological civilization, there is no such thing as faith devoid of culture or culture devoid of faith." "Christ, Faith, and the Challenge of Cultures," Meeting with the Doctrinal Commissions of Asia, Hong Kong, March 3, 1993, https://www.vatican.va/roman_curia/congregations/cfaith/incontri/rc_con_cfaith_19930303_hong-kong-ratzinger_en.html.
[80] Sarah, *The Day Is Now Far Spent*, 286.

and to begin the great work of rebuilding. We can create dedicated circles of building Christian culture through stronger Christian community and witness.

For Catholics to serve as agents of change for civilization, a more radical Christian life is needed that embraces a mission of prayer, penance, and witness. The Eucharist teaches us a spirituality of sacrifice and communion. On the first point, if we are too worldly, it means that we have a stronger attachment to earthly goods and pleasures than to spiritual goods. Sacrifice gives up these good things in order to put God first. Sacrifice also enables us to enter into the spiritual mission of penance, making reparation for not only our sins but also the sins of others. The message of Fatima calls for penance and making "everything a sacrifice," which was linked also to reparation against the regular sins and neglect of the Eucharist in the Church, as we see in the prayer taught to the children by an angel: "I offer You the most precious Body, Blood, Soul, and Divinity of Jesus Christ, present in all the tabernacles of the world, in reparation for the outrages, sacrileges, and indifference with which He Himself is offended." We have to remove the obstacles that impede the Eucharist's power from flowing in our lives and from the Church to the world. Trusting in the power of Jesus's sacramental power, on the other hand, teaches us the centrality of prayer and penance in upholding and transforming the world.

Like an anchor in the midst of a storm, the Eucharist establishes our true identity as members of the Body of Christ and children of God during these unsettling times. The unity of the Body provides a transcendent source of peace and communion that overcomes the wounds and divisions of our culture, played upon by the machinations of identity politics. Cardinal Sarah gives the example of his native Guinea, where not only Europeans and Africans worshipped together but also various tribes. In this context, the Church looked to the Eucharist "to make us blood brothers, one family, one people, one race, that of the children of God."[81] If we are focused on ourselves or even just our own nation or ethnicity, we will miss the greater unity brought by Christ that does not dissolve distinctiveness but integrates it into a larger whole. Without a deeper source of unity, we are increasingly pitted against one another, consuming one another's flesh, through various forms of exploitation, even as Christ offers His own flesh to satisfy us. Catholics should find their deepest identity in communion with God, which opens doors to serving and working with others. Communion is the deepest reality of human life, rooted in God's own triune communion within Himself, and He wants His Church to draw all people to participate in His communion.

Culture cannot survive without cult, and as a civilization experiences greater disintegration, holiness comprises the Church's greatest answer to rebuilding culture. The liturgy itself stabilizes culture and provides an oasis for the spiritual life. It should radiate the greatest beauty found in a world that has become far too ugly. Even here, though, we see a need for renewal, as Father Aidan Nichols explains, "The 're-enchantment' of the Catholic Liturgy is the single most urgent ecclesial need of our time."[82] If the Eucharist is the heart of

---

[81] Sarah, *God or Nothing*, 32.
[82] Nichols, *Christendom Awake*, 21.

the world, it pulsates from the liturgy, supplying it with a spiritual lifeblood of Christ's divine presence. Yet, the spiritual anemia of Catholics stems ultimately from a horizontal and mundane worship that is more focused on the worshipper and one's own feelings than a transcendent encounter with God. It is from this source that Catholics themselves become agents of renewal, as Nichols once again explains, "The primary offering we make is not self-sacrifice but the offering of Christ in the Mass. There can be no offering of ourselves, our souls and bodies, except with that. . . . The Eucharist empowers us to die daily to self, to offer ourselves to the Father."[83] Living united to Christ's offering makes our daily lives supernatural, suffusing the ordinary with God's divine life. All that contradicts the sacredness of the Mass needs to be driven out of the Church like Christ did with the money changers at His temple: regular Eucharistic abuses, ugliness in song and decoration, sacrilegious communions (including by public sinners such as politicians), and the human centered approach to worship.

The Eucharist gives us courage to live as a sign of contradiction in a world coming apart at the seams. It reminds us that all is possible with God, while nothing is possible without Him. Like the disciples at the miracle of the dividing of loaves, some might be tempted to ask if we have too little to give, "what good are these for so many" (Jn 6:9). The Eucharist is the little spark of change in the world. Faith tells us that God's ways often overthrow the logic of the world, even in the Church at times, helping us to recover the true primacy of the

---

[83] Nichols, 243–44.

spiritual life. If the Church is the soul of the world, then she must think with the mind of Christ, not according to human logic. As a prophetic voice, the Church and her members point back to God, echoing the crowds assembled to greet John Paul II during his visit home to Communist Poland, "We want God!" A living and vibrant faith that makes God present is what enables the Church to be "a creator of culture in its very foundation," a role it has served since the beginning.[84] The Church does not create culture by planning out solutions to practical problems; rather she creates culture by making "the redeeming sacrifice of her Bridegroom a part of human history and makes it sacramentally present in every culture," and transforming it from within.[85]

Within the Church's role in creating culture, we play a crucial part in extending the fruits of Eucharistic Communion into the world. I know it can sound too ambitious to speak of building an entire civilization centered on the Eucharist, but think back to how the monks played a critical role in rebuilding civilization after the fall of the Roman Empire. The monastery became a center of culture by putting God first and ordering everything else around this priority. Putting God first does not mean giving up on culture, as from the monastery grew the nourishment of both soul and body, with libraries, hospitals, and even universities, alongside of baking bread, aging cheese, cultivating the vine, and brewing beer. The monks continue to remind us of what matters most, which is why Cardinal Sarah thinks

---

[84] John Paul II, Speech to UNESCO, June 2, 1980.
[85] Pope Benedict XVI, *Sacramentum Caritatis*, no. 12.

that "the renewal will come from monasteries."[86] We can at least say that renewal will come from strong spiritual centers that model an integrated Christian life and offer a radical witness to the world. The renewal of the world must come from the renewal of the Church. The fight for civilization is a spiritual battle, and only the Church can adequately fight back against the growing evil in the world.

John Senior describes the intertwined nature of spiritual and cultural renewal:

> It is not enough to keep the Commandments, though we must; it is not enough to love one another as ourselves, though we must. The one thing needful, the *unum necessarium* of the Kingdom, is to love as He loves us, which is the love of joy in suffering and sacrifice, like Roland and Olivier charging into battle to their death defending those they love as they cry "Mon joie"; that is the music of Christian Culture. These devils in the nation and in the Church who murder children and disgrace the Bride of Christ can only be driven out by prayer and fasting. Impurity results in breaking the Commandments, but in essence it is a misdirection of love. We shall never drive it out—all attempts to solve the crisis in the Church are vain—unless we consecrate our hearts to the Immaculate Heart of Mary, which means not just the recitation of the words on a printed card, any more than fasting just

---

[86] Sarah, *The Day Is Now Far Spent*, 112. John Senior echoes this sentiment, "Of course the simplest, most practical restoration of Christian Culture will be the reestablishment of contemplative convents and monasteries." *The Restoration of Christian Culture*, 62.

means eating less, but a commitment to her interior life. We must descend for a certain time each day into the cellar of wine–if He will draw us there–where, alone with Him, we are inebriated by His love.[87]

And in another passage:

Our Lord explains in the Parable of the Sower that the seed of His love will only grow in a certain soil–and that is the soil of Christian Culture, which is the work of music in the wide sense, including as well as tunes that are sung, art, literature, games, architecture–all so many instruments in the orchestra which plays day and night the music of lovers; and if it is disordered, then the love of Christ will not grow. It is an obvious matter of fact that here in the United States now, the Devil has seized these instruments to play a danse macabre, a dance of death, especially through what we call the "media," the film, television, radio, record, book, magazine and newspaper industries. The restoration of culture, spiritually, morally, physically, demands the cultivation of the soil in which the love of Christ can grow, and that means we must, as they say, rethink priorities.[88]

Senior gives us a rallying cry to reclaim our culture from the evil influences which have laid hold of it. Although it is primarily a spiritual battle, calling for intense prayer and fasting to cast out obstinate demons, it also entails tilling the soil of culture and planting the seeds of rebirth.

---

[87] Senior, *The Restoration of Christian Culture*, 18.
[88] Senior, 21.

Picking Up the Pieces of Civilization

Humpty Dumpty, that sign of fallen humanity, could not be put back together again, having shattered into pieces. Putting our culture together again may seem similarly futile, yet we have faith that the Lord can restore our culture through the divine power of the Eucharist. As we have traced throughout this book, there are certain consistent elements required by every culture: nature, people, common practices and institutions, and shared beliefs. When a culture reaches a high level of organization and expression, particularly through the systematic governance of the city (*civis*), it becomes a civilization. And all of these elements of civilization's life can be viewed in relation to the Eucharist's power of renewal.

In the Eucharist, God comes to us so that we may be drawn into His divinity, and yet, when it comes to its power to transform civilization, it is the restoration of our humanity that forms the basis of the reinvigoration of the world. Sin makes us less human, less dignified, but God wants to heal and elevate our nature, including our social life. When we look at the elements that make up culture, we see a profound crisis affecting all aspects of civilization. This is why many people, including Pope Saint John Paul II, speak of the rise of an anti-culture alienated from nature, undermining human dignity, breaking social bonds, and denying God His proper honor.[89] The Eucharist, in presenting Christ's perfect humanity to us, restores our own humanity and begins the

---

[89] Pope John Paul II, "The Pontifical Council for Culture's Work Now and Plans for the Future," January 16, 1984.

process of reordering the goods of our personal and social lives. Jesus makes "all things new" (Rv 21:5).

To rebuild a Christian culture, the Church needs to focus on recovering the basic lost goods of human nature that provide the necessary soil upon which grace builds. Cardinal Sarah presents the stakes of the vital task:

> I am convinced that Western civilization is going through a lethal crisis. It has reached the limits of self-destructive hatred. . . . Today, too, the Church preserves what is most human in man. She is the guardian of civilization. In the first centuries of our era, the bishops and the saints were the ones who saved the cities that were threatened by the Barbarians. The monks were the ones who preserved and transmitted the treasures of ancient literature and philosophy. More profoundly, the Church makes herself the guardian of human nature. . . . Bishops do not seek to take control over consciences. They take seriously their mission as *defensor civitatis*, defenders of cities and of civilization!"[90]

Western civilization is experiencing a fatal malaise, a sickness of soul, that could easily lead to a complete collapse. The interior collapse of the ultimate guiding spiritual vision has already extinguished civilization in the deepest sense. When we think of what the end of civilization looks like, we might think of the final painting in Thomas Cole's series *The Course of Empire*, but we are finding out that barbarism can coexist with a high level of technological development.

---

[90] Sarah, *The Day Is Now Far Spent*, 158–59.

A barbarian is essentially characterized not by a simplicity of material culture but by a lack of true civilization, without a noble vision of human life and a personal cultivation of virtue. If we looked at the spiritual landscape of the modern world, it might look like Cole's painting *Desolation*, with the remnants of past civilization still present, even if largely overlooked and overgrown. Our task now is to put the pieces back to together and revivify them through the divine life of the Eucharist.

Thomas Cole, *Desolation*, 1836

The Eucharist offers a sacramental vision of life that treats the human person and even the world itself as laden with profound spiritual worth. The Eucharist reminds us that Jesus offered His life for each one of us, giving Himself as a divine gift (with the Church as the guardian and steward of His sacred mysteries). The sacrament stimulates a culture of life by affirming the dignity of each person as made in the image and likeness of God and called to a heavenly vocation of eternal happiness. The Eucharist is a gift meant to enable this dignity and vocation to shine forth in each person's life. At the same time, the Eucharist calls us to help others find their identity and worth. Society, too, must reconstitute itself on the essential foundation of the human person as spelled out by John Paul II in *Evangelium Vitae*:

> Christ's blood reveals to man that his greatness, and therefore his vocation, consists in the sincere gift of self. Precisely because it is poured out as the gift of life, the blood of Christ is no longer a sign of death, of definitive separation from the brethren, but the instrument of a communion which is richness of life for all. Whoever in the Sacrament of the Eucharist drinks this blood and abides in Jesus (cf. Jn 6:56) is drawn into the dynamism of his love and gift of life, in order to bring to its fullness the original vocation to love which belongs to everyone (cf. Gen 1:27; 2:18–24). It is from the blood of Christ that all draw the strength to commit themselves to promoting life.[91]

The Incarnation and Jesus's continuing gift of Himself in the Eucharist helps us to rediscover the nature of the human person and the call to give oneself as a gift for others. In fact, we can say that it overturns the idols that we have set up. The Eucharist can return things to right order, destroying the false worship of our society and restoring things to their right order.

---

[91] Pope John Paul II, *Evangelium Vitae*, no. 25.

We have parodied the Eucharist by seeking a false communion, a false consumption by which we eat and drink ourselves into oblivion, seeking to escape others and reality.[92] We have distorted our bodies, no longer seeing them in the image and likeness of God but as our own creation that can be remade at will. Rather than embracing a love that moves us out of ourselves, we have turned inward in this false communion, using the bodies of others for our own selfish pleasure, refusing to give, sacrifice, and bear fruit. We have initiated a false worship, placing material things above the spiritual, adoring our wealth and the domination of nature and others. All of this reveals the true spiritual combat for the life of our civilization. We have engaged in a serious iconoclasm, breaking the images established by the Creator, and now we must work to restore the lost beauty and goodness. We have to reunite what we have broken, bringing faith back into the center to heal and restore the image of God in us that we have defaced.

The dignity of the human person as the height of God's creation points also to the fundamental vocation given by God to be His stewards and exercise dominion over the world. This task has been disrupted in daily life through a profound alienation from nature, with modern culture falling into abstraction and artificiality. Human beings have become overly dependent on mass production and removed from their direct dependence upon the land, from which our own bodies have arisen, having been made from the dust

---

[92] One of the greatest false communions of history, communism, still threatens us. It seeks to make all equal, although at the expense of the true dignity and transcendence of the person.

of the earth. A renewed civilization will have to recognize that the spiritual reality of creation is the foundation not only for human life but also for the original covenant that God made with humanity. Since the bread and wine come from the fruits of the earth and human work, the Eucharist is a constant reminder of this reality—one of thanksgiving. Our Eucharistic thanksgiving should shape the way that we eat and drink, pointing to the dependence we have on natural goods that come to us as gifts from God. All of our eating and drinking can be sacramental in this sense, giving thanks and praise to God and reconnecting us to the foundation of culture in God's work of creation. Wendell Berry, the great advocate for a more human and sustainable culture, points to the latent spiritual reality of our eating and drinking: "To live, we must daily break the body and shed the blood of Creation. When we do this knowingly, lovingly, skillfully, reverently, it is a sacrament. When we do it ignorantly, greedily, clumsily, destructively, it is a desecration. In such desecration we condemn ourselves to spiritual and moral loneliness, and others to want."[93] The Eucharist teaches us that everything in our culture has spiritual value. However, when we turn it away from God and the good of others, we desecrate it.

In many ways, modern culture is a vast experiment, seeking to recreate humanity apart from God and strong relationships with others. In other words, modern culture wishes to create hell on earth, while Catholic culture desires to create a civilization mirroring heaven. Can human beings truly

---

[93] Berry, *The Gift of Good Land*, 281.

be autonomous, a law and end unto themselves? If we are to overcome this spiritual rebellion, we will have to overcome the spiritual isolation of this individualism by reestablishing strong relational bonds, particularly within the family and local community (both of which have become imperiled in our anti-culture). The Eucharist can teach us about the nature of marriage, sexuality, and family life, not as self-serving ends that meet one's own needs but as profound gifts of self. Only in complete gift of self for the good of the other do we see fruitfulness and joy. There is nothing more needful for the health of society and the Church then strong family life, which provides the first and longest lasting formation in how to live.[94] In communion with others, virtue is more easily perfected and vice is more readily overcome.

The family is truly the domestic church that prepares Catholics to receive the Eucharist and to live in it faithfully. The parish extends the domestic church into a broader family gathered around the celebration of the Eucharist. Catholic culture depends upon the instantiation of the faith in the community, depending upon the concrete coming together of the community around the Body and Blood of Christ,

---

[94] Cardinal Sarah again points to the monastery as an inspiration for how to live the Christian life: "The world is organized against God. Our communities must organize themselves, not by being content to make some room for him, but by putting him at the center. I am struck when I see that many Christian families choose to settle near a monastery or a vibrant parish. They want to live by the rhythm of the Church and to make their existence a true liturgy. They want their children not only to have abstract Christian ideas but to experience concretely a milieu imbued with the Divine Presence and an intense life of prayer and charity." *The Day Is Now Far Spent*, 303.

something that cannot be done virtually. To be Catholic is not to be a member of a global organization but to celebrate the Eucharist within one particular community, a circle of a revivified culture not only for the parish but the entire surrounding society. Parishes will provide new life for the Church and world if they overcome a spiritual consumerism—where people come to meet an obligation and leave— by drawing people together into meaningful relationships that actively translate faith into life.

Education is the transmission of culture to the next generation. It is an expression of hope in the future that a civilization possesses some intellectual and spiritual goods that can shape the life of young people. This reflects Remi Brague's definition of civilization as sharing in certain ways of thinking and living: "What we call culture or a civilization is a definite set of answers that distinguish a right way and a wrong one."[95] The suicide of our own civilization could be seen in nothing more than our refusal to pass on our way of life, in refusing to have children at all and also in negating any definite meaning or purpose in education. Catholics recognize that we have received a great legacy in our ecclesial tradition—the great fruits of Western civilization, art, learning, the saints, and especially the handing down of the Eucharist itself—and that we have the responsibility of transmitting these fruits into the future. Our schools should be places where the treasures of civilization are preserved rather than destroyed, as we see happening intentionally in our society, and especially in public education, as a form of

---

[95] Brague, *Curing Mad Truths*, 72.

hatred of Western civilization. In Ray Bradbury's dystopian novel *Fahrenheit 451*, the "fireman" and bookburner Montag realized the burning of the treasure of civilization had to stop: "Somewhere the saving and putting away had to begin again and someone had to do the saving and keeping, one way or another, in books, in records, in people's heads, any way at all so long as it was safe, free from moths, silverfish, rust and dry rot, and men with matches."[96] Catholics have to educate in the truth, refusing to go along with lies (2 Cor 13:8), that negate our own culture, by passing on the great wisdom of Christ.[97]

The Eucharist itself teaches us how to live. It focuses us on the importance of presence and sacrifice for others. If our bodies are meant to be gifts to be received and then given, if we are to receive the gift of the presence of others, then we have to accept our own limits, be inconvenienced, and learn to depend on others. In our anti-culture, we have given into the supremacy of ease and distraction, constantly saturated by technology, which creates a buffer through which we view others (or not) and which filters our experience of reality. The concrete experience of the Eucharist, Jesus's own physical presence, reminds us of the need to be present, to gaze directly at reality, and to give of ourselves in tangible ways.

---

[96] Bradbury, *Fahrenheit 451*, 134. Brague speaks of the need to conserve: "In fact, conservative people are simply conscious of the weight that lies on the shoulders of man as a free being. They know that whatever bears the stamp of humanity, such as historical achievements, depends on the will of people to uphold them. If this will should fail, those achievements would crumble down and disappear forever" (114).

[97] Cardinal Sarah even says that "Christian culture is the love of a wisdom embodied by a man, the Son of God." *The Day Is Now Far Spent*, 271.

Jesus calls us to a healthy detachment from the things of this world, a perennial truth but one even more pressing in a technological world. Rather than using technological devices as limited tools, we have been manipulated by their omnipresence and pulled into the mass control and manipulation of the media and propaganda. We have become susceptible to a psychological oppression that shapes the way that we view ourselves, others, and society. Our civilization has become unmoored by any spiritual principles that could guide how we use technology, and we can see that, without a proper moral compass, technology often is used in destructive ways. Looking at the dominance of technology, we could echo Christopher Dawson insight that "we have discovered that evil too is a progressive force and that the modern world provides unlimited prospects for its development."[98] We have accepted massive changes in technology uncritically, "But the change has been too sudden for men to adapt themselves to the new conditions. . . . . For humanity cannot save itself by its own efforts."[99] Only the Eucharist, Christ Himself, can save us and serve as our compass, pointing us to the need for presence above devices, logical thinking (rooted in the Logos) to counter ideology, and a gift of self rather than distraction.

The same kind of moral compass and accepting of limits is needed in economics. Once again, the Eucharist reveals our purpose in life. Our anti-culture focuses on wealth and profit as the goal of economics, although if we literally think

---

[98] Dawson, *The Judgment of the Nations*, 4.
[99] Dawson, 5.

of why we work, we come back to the basic reality of caring for the needs of ourselves, our families, and those in need. John Senior exhorts us, "We must inscribe this first law of Christian economics on our hearts: the purpose of work is not profit but prayer, and the first law of Christian ethics: that we live for Him and not for ourselves. And life in Him is love."[100] Work and prayer; it brings us back to the monastery. The two need to be united in ordering everything we do to the glory of God. The Eucharist leads us to turn the fruits of our work to the needs of others. Jesus Himself points to the folly of the man who stuffed his barns full and could not enjoy the harvest after his death: "So is he who lays up treasure for himself, and is not rich toward God" (Lk 12:21). As Christians, we should be laying up treasure in heaven, saying no to unbounded wealth and the alleged power it gives us. Wealth is not a true end; it is a means that, when used rightly, can help us to pursue higher goods. We should put our money where it matters most, with a human-centered economy that cares for those in need, respects the environment, and gives glory to God.

In terms of politics, the Eucharist opposes the movement toward a mass State that subsumes the person into its own ends. The State does not exist as an end in itself either. Rather, it depends upon a vision of life that seeks the common good while upholding each person's dignity, which is why our spiritual vacuum is so dangerous. Simply recognizing the profound limits of politics presents one of the most important aspects of the renewal of our civilization. One of the greatest

---

[100] Senior, *The Restoration of Christian Culture*, 18.

threats today comes from the all-encompassing state that dominates every aspect of life, controlling economics, education, and communication, and limiting religious freedom. The early Christian community had to face the challenge of Caesar, claiming the right of divine worship and seeking to stop the Eucharistic celebration, where Christians claimed allegiance to a higher king. Nations such as China, North Korea, Pakistan, and Saudi Arabia, among others, have likewise sought to stop or seriously curtail the celebration of the Eucharist, a phenomenon that also reached the West in recent years in the name of health. Without a true spiritual guide, the state often identifies earthly realities as the highest good: power, wealth, or health, although with these mundane horizons actual human beings are often treated as disposable goods in light of the utility of the whole. The unity inspired by the Eucharist sees every person as a transcendent good that has a role to play for the greater good, even if in a hidden way, such as with the disabled or suffering.

Although the Church has been frequently accused of limiting our freedoms, modern society itself has enslaved humanity in the name of freedom. The modern liberal order was founded upon the notion that individual freedom is the greatest good, although this order has imploded on this metric alone, descending into the mass control and manipulation by government bureaucracy, mega-corporations, and media. This illusive freedom has become an empty goal with no intrinsic meaning as we do not know what it is for. Unlike in the ancient world, where the faith was received as a source of true freedom, liberating from the darkness of sin and the meaninglessness of a world bound by death, today freedom has become so open ended that it actually paralyzes, particularly by returning to the bondage of sin as an illusion of happiness. The Eucharist offers true freedom: freedom from an obsession with one's own desire, freedom from a blind search for meaning, and freedom from having to create one's own identity. In the Eucharist, Christ gives us the freedom to know the truth and to love freely what is good. Although our world seeks a false freedom of restraint from anything outside of the self, Jesus is the source of the true freedom that is found in the pursuit of the highest goods and giving oneself to others in love. Jesus frees us from the oppression of evil both within our souls and in our civilization. When He comes to us in the Eucharist, He comes to reclaim His own, helping us to "be free indeed" (Jn 8:36).

A Civilization Revitalized

I truly believe that, unless the world ends soon, Christian culture will rise again. Things might get worse first, with the Church keeping the seeds of civilization alive, as we see in Walter Miller's post-apocalyptic novel *A Canticle for Leibowitz*, where, after nuclear war, the monks once again keep faith and learning alive. This is simply what the Eucharist does on earth; in the midst of cultural ebbs and flows, it slowly changes everything! We should not conceive of a new civilization as an imposition of the Christian faith or the Church on the world. God, even though He is omnipotent, does not force Himself on us, and He gives a wide berth to our freedom. He wants us to become fully alive and for human institutions to achieve justice in accordance with nature's real goods. Because the Eucharist is the heart of the Church as well as the heart of the world, it enlivens the secular realm to achieve its end: the common good of society.

A new civilization will not occur by chance. It will arise through the slow toil of Christians working to make all things new, inspired and strengthened by the presence of Jesus within them. This is how Jesus changes the world: one person at a time. The United States bishops explained this ripple effect in their document on Eucharistic revival, "The Mystery of the Eucharist in the Life of the Church": "The personal and moral transformation that is sustained by the Eucharist reaches out to every sphere of human life. The love of Christ can permeate all of our relationships: with our families, our friends, and our neighbors. It can also reshape the life of our society as a whole. Our relationship with Christ is not restricted to the private sphere; it is not for ourselves alone" (§35). A civilization revitalized by the Eucharist would recognize the worship of God as its highest good, as a source of life beyond itself upon which it depends, while drawing from this strength the ability to rightly order the things of the world in justice and charity.

The Eucharist can save civilization by providing the spiritual ability to restore order and sanity to our culture. Its power is primarily an interior one, which is needed to overcome the moral and spiritual vacuum of our culture. We celebrate the liturgy for its own sake, not as a means to a practical end. It remains a sign that our ultimate good rests beyond this world in the eternal Sabbath of God. The goal of the Eucharist, therefore, is not a new civilization but communion with God. The goals of civilization, on the other hand, can be realized through the power of the Eucharist, which promotes a right order and harmony in human life. If we seek to restore things by our own power, we will fail, but with the help of the true king of the world, we can transmit the power of God's healing truth and love. The goal of a new Christian civilization is not a theocracy, as the Church has always recognized the distinct and separate legitimacy of the political order. The cathedral cannot replace the city hall, although it should serve as the true center of the city and its constant reference to what matters most.

The culture of Christendom was not a single political entity. Dawson explains how "the medieval Church was not a state within a state, but a suprapolitical society of which the state was a subordinate, local, and limited organ. Ideally there was one great society—that of the Christian people—with a twofold hierarchy of spiritual and temporal ministers."[101] A Christian civilization is not run by the Church, as it arises when members of the Church permeate society with Christian values through their leadership and work. It is a matter not simply of having enough Catholics in influential positions, as we already have that to no good effect, but of allowing Jesus to act through the daily fidelity and influence of ordinary Catholics. Originally, Christian civilization arose through the providential encounter of the Gospel with the culture of the ancient Mediterranean, primarily Greek philosophy and Roman law, which was transmitted to the new peoples of Europe, the barbarians. There is nothing particular in this culture to Europe, per se, as a similar pattern of education

---

[101] Dawson, *The Judgment of the Nations*, 67.

and justice can arise anywhere in the world. There is not one particular way of doing things in a Christian society, not one particular culture or politics, but a Christian way of living that transforms how we think and all that we do.

A new Christian civilization will not be ethnic or national. It will arise from the same kind of spiritual society of Christians who live their faith in a radical way, looking to the kingdom of heaven while doing their best to serve within this world. Very cautiously, we can envision how things might progress in the coming decades. Western society will continue to grow more and more secular and experience social decline, with low birth rates that necessitate more immigration and an erosion of the traditions of Western Europe and North America. At the same time, the global south—Latin America, Africa, and Southeast Asia—will continue to grow in the Christian faith. Some of its countries will stabilize and develop and perhaps even become major international players. Major questions include whether or not the faith will continue to grow in China and South Korea, whether the Church can stop hemorrhaging members in Latin America, and if Eastern Europe can preserve its Christian heritage. With the shift in Christian demographics to the south, we can also wonder if the West might be rejuvenated as younger Christian countries take the lead. Africa, in particular, offers some hope for the growth of Christian culture. As Philip Jenkins describes in *The Next Christendom*, "The number of Africans claiming to be Catholic is already approaching 200 million. . . . By 2050, Africa will have more Catholics than Europe."[102] In the global south,

---

[102] Jenkins, *The Next Christendom*, 73.

"all too often the Catholic Church occupies such a prominent role because it is literally the only institution that can hope to speak for ordinary people, and this is especially true in nations in which the mechanisms of government and civil society have virtually collapsed."[103] Jenkins reflects on the phrase "God goes where He is wanted," for as the West becomes more secular, the Church continues to grow elsewhere.

Faith necessarily creates culture by making spiritual realities visible to the world, although we have to have faith first in order to rebuild civilization! Dawson rightly recognizes that wherever it arises, "the return to Christianity is therefore the indispensable condition for the restoration of a spiritual order and for the realization of the spiritual community which should be a source of new life for our civilization."[104] T. S. Eliot articulates a similar point: "However bigoted the announcement may sound, the Christian can be satisfied with nothing less than a Christian organization of society—which is not the same thing as a society consisting exclusively of devout Christians. It would be a society in which the natural end of man— virtue and well-being in community— is acknowledged for all, and the supernatural end—beatitude—for those who have the eyes to see it."[105] Eliot posits the two essential goals: acknowledging and living the goods of nature, while ordering them to an ultimate goal beyond this world. Since we have experienced what Nietzsche called an inversion of all values, a restoration of Christian civilization would entail a reversion once again, turning the world upside down (Acts 17:6) so that

---

[103] Jenkins, 179.
[104] Dawson, *The Judgment of the Nations*, 110.
[105] Eliot, *Christianity & Culture*, 27.

it will land on the right side again—valuing humility over pride, sacrifice over selfishness, leisure over frenetic busyness, and gift over consumption.

In terms of working for natural goods, Christians can cooperate with all those of good will, especially our fellow Christians. The Eucharist inspires us to upend the culture of death by emphasizing the intrinsic value of life. Pope Benedict XVI's exhortation *Sacramentum Caritatis* relates, "The food of truth demands that we denounce inhumane situations in which people starve to death because of injustice and exploitation, and it gives us renewed strength and courage to work tirelessly in the service of the civilization of love."[106] The word *love* has been eviscerated of meaning. Rather than a feeling that seeks one's own fulfillment, true love sacrifices for the good of the other. A Christian society has to reject harmful lies and refuse to offer a public place to evil. In fact, precisely out of love, it must refuse to affirm evil as good while protecting the vulnerable from the exploitation of our technological society. As Jérôme Lejeune aptly put it, "The quality of a civilization is measured by the respect that it has for its weakest members."[107] A Christian civilization is marked by love, creating an environment that makes it easier to be good, because it seeks after the right goals, ones that lead to the flourishing of the human person.

A Christian civilization embraces a greater simplicity because it does not seek an earthly utopia or the recreation of humanity (as in the satanic project of transhumanism). It puts

---

[106] Pope Benedict XVI, *Sacramentum Caritatis*, no. 90.
[107] Quoted in Sarah, *The Day Is Now Far Spent*, 190.

earthly goods in the right perspective as limited and ordered toward higher things. The virtue of religion, the virtue that gives God what He is owed and orders all things to Him, is a civic virtue because God is the origin and end of all earthly goods. A healthy society honors God and lives in a way pleasing to Him, which also leads to the happiness of its citizens. A Christian civilization holds the faith in honor, seeks solutions inspired by it, and unites people together in pursuit of the highest goods. In overcoming secularism, it allows for a public exercise of faith, not simply a private one that struggles to express itself in a consistent and fully fledged way. Like the spires of Sagrada Familia in Barcelona, Christian civilization can rise in the modern world, not simply as a return to the past. It will be a new creation, drawing upon the great legacy of Christian culture and expressing it a new way, incorporating the genuine advances of the modern world while integrating them into a deeper vision of human life.

Would a civilization shaped by the Eucharist be triumphal or self-sacrificial? Jesus's words remain valid, "From the days of John the Baptist until now the kingdom of heaven has suffered violence, and men of violence take it by force" (Mt 11:12). Christians will always remain signs of contradiction, reminding the world that it must look beyond itself. The Eucharist points to the deepest dignity found only in following Christ, taking up our cross daily, even to the point of death. Like the dramatic concluding scene of the movie *The Mission*, where the missionary Father Gabriel sacrifices his life while processing with the monstrance, our Eucharistic witness may cost us our lives. Christian civilization may arise like it did the first time: through the blood of martyrs, who witnessed that

there was something worth dying for. From the throne of the
cross, Christ has the answer to every problem facing humanity, though He usually responds silently and humbly, transforming people from within. Christian culture must remain
eschatologically focused, pointing beyond itself to the true
realization of human life found only in heaven. Like we see in
Davidson Knowles's painting *The Sign of the Cross*, depicting
the suffering of early Christians, Jesus continues by our side,
accompanying us through the trials of the world and beckoning us to the full communion we will have with Him in
heaven, eating and drinking at His table. Standing at an open
door, He knocks: "Behold, I stand at the door and knock; if
any one hears my voice and opens the door, I will come in to
him and eat with him, and he with me" (Rv 3:20).

Davidson Knowles, *The Sign of the Cross*, 1897

Conclusion

Ite Missa Est

Fixed in Hope

When the Mass ends, the *ite missa est*, translated loosely as "go the Mass has ended," constitutes a sending forth on mission (indicated by the Latin *missa*). This does not entail leaving our Eucharistic encounter behind; rather, we are called to take this presence into the world. Even in the midst of suffering, persecution, and weakness, the Eucharist should give us hope. God has become man, entwined Himself with us for eternity, and even enters into a marital union through this communion, anticipating our eternal happiness as a kind of down payment. The sending forth at the end of Mass should give us hope, as Jesus assures His Church, "Lo, I am with you always, even until the end of the age" (Mt 28:20).

The modern world, with its intense optimism in material progress and technology, suffers from a deep interior despair. The theological virtue of hope expresses confidence that God, who is all good, will lead us to what is good, even when we undergo hardships. Christians give witness to the world that there is reason to hope, even when things seem to fall apart. The real presence of Jesus in the Eucharist gives us this confidence because God's perfect goodness has come to us and entered within us. Pope Benedict XVI speaks of the need for this spiritual confidence: "It is important to know that I can always continue to hope, even if in my own life, or the historical period in which I am living, there seems to be nothing left to hope for. Only the great certitude of hope that my own life and history in general, despite all failures, are held firm by the indestructible power of Love, and that this gives them their meaning and importance, only this kind of hope can then give the courage to act and to persevere."[108]

Even when Church members or her leaders seem to contradict the holiness and mission given to her by Christ, the Eucharist should give us confidence in Christ's unfailing presence. Saint John Bosco had many dreams of important consequence, but one stands out. He once dreamt of the Church facing imminent shipwreck on a hostile sea, although the barque of the Church was suddenly saved by sailing through two pillars: one with Our Lady on top under the title "Mary, help of Christians" and the other adorned by the Eucharist, with the inscription "Salvation of the Faithful." Devotion to the Eucharist and praying the rosary will preserve the Church and her faithful in these difficult times. We have to stay focused on Jesus and rooted in divine worship, like the faithful so actively engaged in Jasiński's depiction of the Mass. The liturgy is our refuge, not to escape society, but to be refreshed, helping us to stay firm through the many trials we must face. Yes, with Christ's real presence in us, He can help us conquer the world (see Jn 16:33).

---

[108] Pope Benedict XVI, *Spe Salvi*, no. 35.

Zdzisław Jasiński, *Palm Sunday*, 1891

Jesus promised in the book of Revelation, "Behold, I make all things new" (Rv 21:5). Although this work will be complete only at the end of time, even now He begins to make all things new. He gives new birth in Baptism and healing in confession. In the Eucharist, He gives the food that enables growth and interior transformation. His real presence in the Eucharist will continue to reform the Church and make her new, raising up saints to witness to the power of His holiness, hidden in the Blessed Sacrament. He will make society new by guiding the faithful in their work and mission, giving them the waybread to do what they could not do on their own. And by transforming the matter of bread and wine into His body and blood, Christ gives a glimpse of His power to transform all things, perfecting even the elements of the universe.

The celebration of the Eucharist as a moment of festive worship points to the very purpose of our existence. We see its fulfillment in the new and eternal festivity of the wedding feast in heaven, to which we are all called, as the bride: "Blessed are those who are invited to the marriage supper of the Lamb" (Rv 19:9). The heavenly assembly still worships the Lamb who was slain, though, seeing the Lord face to face leads to an interior union more complete than the Eucharist on earth. Nevertheless, even in heaven, the natural foundations of eating and drinking will remain as tangible means of communion: "To the thirsty I will give water without price from the fountain of the water of life"; "on either side of the river, the tree of life with its twelve kinds of fruit, yielding its fruit each month (Rv 21:6; 22:2). God will fulfill and perfect every natural good and will bring His work of salvation to completion in making all things new.

A New Creation

The Eucharist's power to transform lives is obvious. The lives of the saints are proof as well as the graces many of us have received. And yet, the Eucharist's power is not limited solely to inspiring saints; rather, it can perfect and transform the whole cosmos. Just as the bread and wine become the body and blood of Christ, so these divine elements transform the Christian who receives them into Christ. This divine food serves as a pledge for the resurrection of the body, when it will take on the characteristics of Christ's own perfected body— no longer suffering and assuming characteristics of the spirit, such as luminosity and agility. The Eucharist makes eternity present in the world not only by making God present sacramentally within it but also in demonstrating the world's own future glory in time. God's work of re-creation, begun in the Resurrection, will reach its fulfillment in the resurrection of all the dead and the transformation of the heavens and the earth. As depicted powerfully in Matthias Grunwald's Isenheim altarpiece, the glorious Christ, who so patiently hid Himself through the centuries in the Eucharist, will triumph over all His enemies, destroying sin and death. In the large halo surrounding Christ, you can see a cosmic power radiating from Him that will serve as the source of this renewal.

Matthias Grünewald, *Resurrection*, 1512–16

In the fullness of time, there will be a new heaven and a new earth as God's grace fulfills and perfects the physical universe. The Eucharist begins this perfection in making God present through created things and provides the first instance of Jesus making "all things new" (Rv 21:5). Pope Benedict XVI points this out in *Sacramentum Caritatis*: "The substantial conversion of bread and wine into his body and blood introduces within creation the principle of a radical change, a sort of 'nuclear fission,' to use an image familiar to us today, which penetrates to the heart of all being, a change meant to set off a process which transforms reality, a process leading ultimately to the transfiguration of the entire world."[109] Christ's resurrected humanity, enthroned in heaven, also makes a place for human nature and material goods in glory. In the renewal of creation, Christ will become "all in all" (1 Cor 15:28). The Eucharist, therefore, represents the pinnacle of creation, pointing to the very purpose of the world and human life: to glorify God and to embody His presence.

In writing about the care of the environment, Pope Francis looks to the Eucharist as the source of its greatest dignity and promise of its future glory:

> It is in the Eucharist that all that has been created finds its greatest exaltation. Grace, which tends to manifest itself tangibly, found unsurpassable expression when God himself became man and gave himself as food for his creatures. The Lord, in the culmination of the mystery of the Incarnation, chose to reach our intimate

---

[109] Pope Benedict XVI, *Sacramentum Caritatis*, no. 11.

depths through a fragment of matter. He comes not from above, but from within, he comes that we might find him in this world of ours. In the Eucharist, fullness is already achieved; it is the living centre of the universe, the overflowing core of love and of inexhaustible life. Joined to the incarnate Son, present in the Eucharist, the whole cosmos gives thanks to God. Indeed the Eucharist is itself an act of cosmic love: "Yes, cosmic! Because even when it is celebrated on the humble altar of a country church, the Eucharist is always in some way celebrated on the altar of the world." The Eucharist joins heaven and earth; it embraces and penetrates all creation. The world which came forth from God's hands returns to him in blessed and undivided adoration: in the bread of the Eucharist, "creation is projected towards divinization, towards the holy wedding feast, towards unification with the Creator himself."[110]

The ultimate fulfillment of our lives within the new creation also gives us hope. As we work out our salvation in fear and trembling, in our humble weakness, we can have confidence that God will use these small seeds and cultivate them into perfection. The union and happiness for which we are striving now will become a reality. God will become all in all, and we will become fully who God has meant us to be, restoring us through the power of the Eucharist and moving us toward the renewal of creation.

---

[110] Pope Francis, *Laudato Si'*, no. 236, quoting Pope John Paul II, *Ecclesia de Eucharistia* (17 April 2003), no. 8; Pope Benedict XVI, "Homily for Corpus Christi," June 15, 2006.

A Final Invitation

This book's aim is to lead Catholics to a deeper knowledge and love of the Holy Eucharist, especially at Mass. From the Mass, we then seek to abide with His Eucharistic presence at all times. Its central contention has been that the Eucharist is something not just to be believed but to be lived, as "the source and summit of the Christian life."[111] The Christian life flows from communion with Christ, which intends to shape our whole life, inspiring the practices that make up a Christian culture.

In forming this way of life, we have to translate the interior into the exterior, although the interior always maintains the priority. You can have exterior habits that are lifeless if they do not flow from genuine communion with God. The three most important interior habits are faith, hope, and charity, because, as Saint Paul said, "these three endure" even when all else fades away (1 Cor 13:13). These theological virtues (virtues that relate directly to God) are the fuel to give real life to a Eucharistic culture, enabling us to live in relationship with God at all times. We need these virtues to live in daily communion with God, as they make it possible, in an abiding way, to know Him, to love Him, and to live in hope with Him.

Faith helps us to see everything differently, with the vision of God. Through it we assent to all that God has revealed to us about Himself and His plan of salvation. It is in faith that we know with confidence that Jesus is truly present in the Eucharist. As a virtue, faith is a habit, and it enables us to keep Jesus ever before our eyes. It also enables us to see

---

[111] *CCC* 1324.

everything with a sacramental imagination, as an opportunity for grace. Through faith, we can relate everything in our lives to its eternal significance, moving us either closer or further away from God. Faith opens up to us an entire supernatural world that surrounds us, helping us to live grounded in a reality larger than ourselves. At the same time, faith must be exercised in order to grow. To help increase our faith in the Holy Eucharist, I have provided a list of recommended books to continue learning about Jesus's Eucharistic presence (see appendix I).

In coming to know Jesus more deeply through faith, we are moved to love Him more. The theological virtue of charity enables us to love God and others with His own love. This divine love moves us to choose God above all things, to put Him first, and to serve others before ourselves. Prayer expresses our love for God and draws us into a closer communion with Him. We need this love to receive the fruits of the Eucharist and must seek out communion with Jesus and open ourselves to the graces He wants to give. It should also bring us joy to know that God has given us the greatest gift of Himself in the Eucharist, enabling us to live with, in, and through Him. Believing in the power of the Eucharist and embracing Jesus in love will enable the Eucharist to transform our lives. Making acts of faith and love at Mass help in receiving the Eucharist more fruitfully (see appendix II for some suggestions). We can also offer acts of love to honor His real presence in the Blessed Sacrament.

The relationship we have with Jesus that flows from faith and charity gives us hope and confidence that Christ is always with us, drawing us to Himself at every moment and leading us to heaven. We don't wander this world like barbarians in search of the next passing treasure, harming others to get what we want. No, our greatest treasure is the Holy Eucharist, which alone provides meaning and purpose for our lives. Jesus invites us to trust in Him, knowing that through our communion with Him He animates our actions from within. The theological virtue of hope gives us assurance that God will fulfill His promises and that we will reach heaven if we abide with His Eucharistic presence through His grace. It should inspire us to give up the false promises of the world that hold us back from laying hold of the highest goods. The saints give us examples of how the hope of the Christian life can be realized concretely. They show us the power of the Eucharist to transform life and to make us holy. It can work its gentle power on each one of us, transforming us more and more into the image of Jesus.

Jesus invites us, "Come to me all you who are weary and burdened, and I will give you rest" (Mt 11:28). He awaits us in the Eucharist, inviting us to come to Him, to encounter Him, to be fed by Him, and to live always in communion with Him. By His wondrous humility in the Holy Eucharist, Jesus makes Himself available to comfort and to strengthen us. Douillard depicts this solicitude movingly in his painting *Viaticum*, showing a faithful priest making his final entrance into a home to bring the sacrament at the moment of death. Jesus accompanies us throughout our journey of life, carrying our crosses with us, but most especially at the hour of death—leading us to our everlasting home.

Alexis-Marie-Louis Douillard, *Viaticum*, c.1875

Mankind cannot save civilization; only Jesus truly present in the Holy Eucharist can. God Himself gave us the Holy Eucharist to remain with us until the end of time. And Jesus wants to transform the heart of culture by first transforming our hearts so that we might set the world on fire with the His Eucharistic love. At the same time, Jesus reminds us that our true community, our true home, exists elsewhere—in heaven, the place where the angels and saints unceasingly worship before the Lamb of God. In heaven, Jesus's real presence in the Holy Eucharist will no longer be hidden or necessary, because He will appear in all of His splendor and glory. While we are still pilgrims on this earth, may Jesus's Eucharistic Presence become the source and summit of the Christian life within every soul and every civilization.

Appendix I

Recommended Books

Anderson, Gary. *Charity: The Place of the Poor in the Biblical Tradition*. New Haven, CT: Yale, 2013.

Aquinas, Saint Thomas. "The Holy Eucharist." In *Summa Theologiae*. Volume 4. New York: Benziger Brothers, 1948.

Barron, Robert. *Eucharist*. Park Ridge, IL: Word on Fire Institute, 2021.

Bux, Nicola. *No Trifling Matter: Taking the Sacraments Seriously Again*. Brooklyn: Angelico Press, 2018.

Carstens, Christopher. *A Devotional Journey into the Mass: How the Mass Can Become a Time of Grace, Nourishment, and Devotion*. Manchester, NH: Sophia Institute, 2017.

Cavanaugh, William. *Being Consumed*. Grand Rapids, MI: Eerdmans, 2008.

Corbon, Jean. *The Wellspring of Worship*. San Francisco: Ignatius, 2005.

Cruz, Joan Carroll. *Eucharistic Miracles and Eucharistic Phenomena in the Lives of the Saints*. Charlotte, NC: TAN, 1991.

Dauphinais, Michael and Matthew Levering. *Rediscovering Aquinas and the Sacraments*. Chicago: Hillenbrand Books, 2009.

Dawson, Christopher. *The Judgment of the Nations*. Washington, DC: Catholic University of America Press, 2011.

Eymard, Saint Peter Julian. *How to Get More Out of Holy Communion*. Manchester, NH: Sophia, 2000.

Guardini, Romano. *Spirit of the Liturgy*. In Joseph Ratzinger. *Spirit of the Liturgy: Commemorative Edition*. San Francisco: Ignatius, 2019.

Hahn, Scott. *Consuming the Word: The New Testament and the Eucharist in the Early Church*. New York: Image, 2013.

———. *The Fourth Cup: Unveiling the Mystery of the Last Supper and the Cross*. New York: Image, 2018.

———. *The Lamb's Supper: The Mass as Heaven on Earth*. New York: Image, 1999.

Hourlier, Jacques. *Reflections on the Spirituality of Gregorian Chant*. Brewster, MA: Paraclete, 1995.

Levering, Matthew. *Sacrifice and Community: Jewish Offering and Christian Eucharist*. Malden, MA: Blackwell, 2005.

Marmion, Blessed Columba. *Christ in His Mysteries*. Bethesda, MD: Zaccheus, 2008.

McNamara, Denis. *How to Read Churches: A Crash Course in Ecclesiastic Architecture*. New York: Rizzoli, 2011.

Pitre, Brant. *Jesus and the Jewish Roots of the Eucharist: Unlocking the Secrets of the Last Supper*. New York: Image, 2011.

Pope Benedict XVI. *Sacramemtum Caritatis*. 2007.

Pope John Paul II. *Ecclesia de Eucharistia*. 2003.

Ratzinger, Joseph. *The Feast of Faith: Approaches to the Theology of the Liturgy*. San Francisco: Ignatius Press, 1986.

———. *God is Near Us: The Eucharist, Heart of Life*. San Francisco: Ignatius Press, 2003.

———. *The Spirit of the Liturgy: Commemorative Edition*. San Francisco: Ignatius Press, 2019.

Sarah, Robert. *The Day Is Now Far Spent*. San Francisco: Ignatius Press, 2019.

Stroik, Duncan. *The Church Building as a Sacred Place: Beauty, Transcendence, and the Eternal*. Chicago: Hillenbrand Books, 2012.

Vonier, Anscar. *A Key to the Doctrine of the Eucharist*. London: Burns, Oates, and Washbourn, 1934.

von Trapp, Maria Augusta. *Around the Year with the von Trapp Family*. Manchester, NH: Sophia Institute, 2018.

Appendix II

Prayers[1]

Prayers before Mass and Communion

Prayer before Mass

Eternal Father, I unite myself with the intentions and affections of our Lady of Sorrows on Calvary, and I offer Thee the sacrifice which Thy beloved Son Jesus made of Himself on the Cross, and now renews on this holy altar: To adore Thee and give Thee the honor which is due to Thee, confessing Thy supreme dominion over all things, and the absolute dependence of everything upon Thee, Who art our one and last end. To thank Thee for innumerable benefits received. To appease Thy justice, irritated against us by so many sins, and to make satisfaction for them. To implore grace and mercy for myself, for [any special intentions], for all afflicted and sorrowing, for poor sinners, for all the world, and for the holy souls in purgatory. Amen.

Prayer of Saint Thomas Aquinas

Almighty and Eternal God, behold I come to the sacrament of Your only-begotten Son, our Lord Jesus Christ. As one sick

---

[1] For a reference of common prayers from the Catholic tradition, including most of the prayers in this section, see James Socias, *Handbook of Prayers*, 8th ed. (Chicago: Midwest Theological Forum, 2019).

I come to the Physician of life; unclean, to the Fountain of mercy; blind, to the Light of eternal splendor; poor and needy to the Lord of heaven and earth. Therefore, I beg of You, through Your infinite mercy and generosity, heal my weakness, wash my uncleanness, give light to my blindness, enrich my poverty, and clothe my nakedness. May I thus receive the Bread of Angels, the King of Kings, the Lord of Lords, with such reverence and humility, contrition and devotion, purity and faith, purpose and intention, as shall aid my soul's salvation. Grant, I beg of You, that I may receive not only the Sacrament of the Body and Blood of our Lord, but also its full grace and power. Give me the grace, most merciful God, to receive the Body of your only Son, our Lord Jesus Christ, born of the Virgin Mary, in such a manner that I may deserve to be intimately united with His mystical Body and to be numbered among His members. Most loving Father, grant that I may behold for all eternity face to face Your beloved Son, whom now, on my pilgrimage, I am about to receive under the sacramental veil, who lives and reigns with You, in the unity of the Holy Spirit, God, world without end. Amen.

Prayer of Saint Ambrose

I beg of you, O Lord, by this most holy mystery of Your Body and Blood, with which You daily nourish us in Your Church, that we may be cleansed and sanctified and made sharers in Your divinity. Grant to me Your holy virtues, which will enable me to approach Your altar with a clean conscience, so that this heavenly Sacrament may be a means of salvation and life to me, for You Yourself have said: "I am the living bread that has come down from heaven. If anyone eat of this bread, he shall live forever; and the bread that I will give is my flesh for the life of the world." Most Sweet Bread, heal my heart, that I may taste the sweetness of Your love. Heal it from all weakness, that I may enjoy no sweetness but You. Most pure Bread, containing every delight which ever refreshes us, may my heart consume You and may my soul be filled with Your sweetness. Holy Bread, living Bread, perfect Bread, that has come down from heaven to give life to the world, come into my heart and cleanse me from every stain of body and soul. Enter into my soul; heal and cleanse me completely. Be the constant safeguard and salvation of my soul and body. Guard me from the enemies who lie in wait. May they flee from the protecting presence of Your power, so that, armed in soul and body by You, I may safely reach Your Kingdom. There we shall see You, not as now as in mysteries, but face to face, when You will deliver the Kingdom to God the Father, and will reign as God over all. Then You, who with the same God the Father and the Holy Spirit, live and reign forever, will satisfy the hunger of my soul perfectly with Yourself, so that I shall neither hunger nor thirst again. Amen.

Prayer of Saint John Chrysostom
(recited in the Byzantine Liturgy)

O Lord, I believe and profess that you are truly Christ, The Son of the living God, who came into the world To save sinners of whom I am the first.

Accept me today as a partaker of your mystical supper,
O Son of God,
For I will not reveal your mystery to your enemies,
Nor will I give you a kiss as did Judas,
But like the thief I profess to you:
Remember me, O Lord, when you come in
your kingdom.
Remember me, O Master, when you come in
your kingdom.
Remember me, O Holy One, when you come in
your kingdom.

May the partaking of your Holy mysteries, O Lord,
Be not for my judgment or condemnation,
But for the healing of my soul and body.

O Lord, I also believe and profess, that this,
Which I am about to receive,
Is truly your most precious Body, and your
life-giving Blood,
Which, I pray, make me worthy to receive
For the remission of all my sins and for life ever-
lasting. Amen

O God, be merciful to me, a sinner.
O God, cleanse me of my sins and have mercy on me.
O Lord, forgive me for I have sinned without number.[2]

---

[2] "Prayers and Devotions," *Byzantine Catholic Eparchy of Parma*, https://
parma.org/prayer.

Intention to Receive Communion

O Lord Jesus Christ, King of everlasting glory, behold I
desire to come to Thee this day, and to receive Thy Body and
Blood in this heavenly Sacrament for Thy honor and glory,
and the good of my soul. I desire to receive Thee, because
it is Thy desire, and Thou hast so ordained: blessed be Thy
Name for ever. I desire to come to Thee like Magdalen, that
I may be delivered from all my evils, and embrace Thee, my
only good. I desire to come to Thee, that I may be happily
united to Thee, that I may henceforth abide in Thee, and
Thou in me; and that nothing in my life or death may ever
separate me from Thee.

After Communion and Mass

Anima Christi

Soul of Christ, sanctify me.
Body of Christ, save me.
Blood of Christ, inebriate me.
Water from the side of Christ, wash me.
Passion of Christ, strengthen me.
O good Jesus, hear me.
Within Thy wounds hide me.
Suffer me not to be separated from Thee.
From the malignant enemy, defend me.
In the hour of my death, call me.
And bid me come to Thee.
That with Thy saints I may praise Thee.

Suscipe

Take, Lord, and receive all my liberty, my memory, my understanding, and my entire will, all that I have and possess. You have given all to me. To You, O Lord, I return it. All is Yours, dispose of it wholly according to Your will. Give me Your love and Your grace, for this is sufficient for me. Amen.

Prayer of Saint Bonaventure

Pierce, O my sweet Lord Jesus, my inmost soul with the most joyous and healthful wound of your love, with true serene and most holy apostolic charity, that my soul may ever languish and melt with love and longing for you, that it may yearn for you and faint for your courts, and long to be dissolved and to be with you. Grant that my soul may hunger after you, the bread of angels, the refreshment of holy souls, our daily and supernatural bread, having all sweetness and savor and every delight of taste; let my heart hunger after and feed upon you, upon whom the angels desire to look, and may my inmost soul be filled with the sweetness of your savor; may it ever thirst after you, the fountain of life, the fountain of wisdom and knowledge, the fountain of eternal light, the torrent of pleasure, the richness of the house of God; may it ever compass you, seek you, find you, run to you, attain you, meditate upon you, speak of you and do all things to the praise and glory of your name, with humility and discretion, with love and delight, with ease and affection, and with perseverance unto the end; may you alone be ever my hope, my entire assistance, my riches, my delight, my pleasure, my joy, my rest and tranquility, my peace, my sweetness, my fragrance, my sweet savor, my food, my refreshment, my refuge, my help, my wisdom, my portion, my possession and my treasure, in whom may my mind and my heart be fixed and firm and rooted immovably, henceforth and forever. Amen.

Prayer of Saint Thomas Aquinas

I give thanks to Thee, O Lord, most holy, Father almighty, eternal God, that Thou hast vouchsafed, for no merit of mine own, but out of Thy pure mercy, to appease the hunger of my soul with the precious body and blood of Thy Son, Our Lord Jesus Christ. Humbly I implore Thee, let not this holy communion be to me an increase of guilt unto my punishment, but an availing plea unto pardon and salvation. Let it be to me the armour of faith and the shield of good will. May it root out from my heart all vice; may it utterly subdue my evil passions and all my unruly desires. May it perfect me in charity and patience; in humility and obedience; and in all other virtues. May it be my sure defence against the snares laid for me by my enemies, visible and invisible. May it restrain and quiet all my evil impulses, and make me ever cleave to Thee Who art the one true God. May I owe to it a happy ending of my life. And do Thou, O heavenly Father, vouchsafe one day to call me, a sinner, to that ineffable banquet, where Thou, together with Thy Son and the Holy Ghost, art to Thy saints true and unfailing light, fullness of content, joy for evermore, gladness without alloy, consummate and everlasting happiness. Through the same Christ our Lord. Amen.

Prayer of Saint Padre Pio

Stay with me, Lord, because I am weak and I need Your strength, that I may not fall so often. Stay with me, Lord, for You are my life, and without You, I am without meaning and hope. Stay with me, Lord, for You are my light, and without You, I am in darkness. Stay with me, Lord, to show me Your will. Stay with me, Lord, so that I can hear Your voice and follow you. Stay with me, Lord, for I desire to love You ever more, and to be always in Your company. Stay with me, Lord, if You wish me to be always faithful to You. Stay with me, Lord, for as poor as my soul is, I wish it to be a place of consolation for You, a dwelling of Your love. Stay with me, Jesus, for it is getting late; the days are coming to a close and life is passing. Death, judgement and eternity are drawing near. It is necessary to renew my strength, so that I will not stop along the way, for that I need You. It is getting late and death approaches. I fear the darkness, the temptations, the dryness, the cross, the sorrows. O how I need you, my Jesus, in this night of exile! Stay with me, Jesus, because in the darkness of life, with all its dangers, I need You. Help me to recognize You as Your disciples did at the Breaking of the Bread, so that the Eucharist Communion be the light which disperses darkness, the power which sustains me, the unique joy of my heart. Stay with me, Lord, because at the hour of my death I want to be one with You, and if not by Communion, at least by Your grace and love. Stay with me, Jesus, I do not ask for divine consolations because I do not deserve them, but I only ask for the gift of Your Presence. Oh yes! I ask this of You. Stay with me, Lord, for I seek You alone, Your Love, Your Grace, Your Will, Your Heart, Your Spirit, because I love You and I ask for no other reward but to love You more and more, with a strong active love. Grant that I may love You with all my heart while on earth, so that I can continue to love you perfectly throughout all eternity, dear Jesus.[3]

Daily Prayers

Spiritual Communion Prayer of Saint Alphonsus Liguori

My Jesus, I believe that You are present in the Most Holy Sacrament. I love You above all things and I desire to receive You into my soul. Since I cannot at this moment receive You sacramentally, come at least spiritually into my heart. I embrace You as if You were already there and unite myself wholly to You. Never permit me to be separated from You. Amen.

Fatima Prayer

Most Holy Trinity, Father, Son and Holy Spirit, I adore Thee profoundly. I offer Thee the most precious Body, Blood, Soul and Divinity of Jesus Christ, present in all the tabernacles of the world, in reparation for the outrages, sacrileges and indifferences whereby He is offended. And through the infinite merits of His Most Sacred Heart and the Immaculate Heart of Mary, I beg of Thee the conversion of poor sinners.

---

[3]   Weldon Owen, *Saints*, 287.

Benediction Prayer

May the Heart of Jesus, in the Most Blessed Sacrament, be praised, adored, and loved, with grateful affection, at every moment, in all the tabernacles of the world, even til the end of time. Amen.

O Sacrament Most Holy

O Sacrament most Holy,
O Sacrament Divine,
All praise and all thanksgiving,
Be every moment Thine.

Prayer of Saint Faustina

O Blessed Host, in whom is contained the testament of God's mercy for us, and especially for poor sinners.

O Blessed Host, in whom is contained the Body and Blood of the Lord Jesus as proof of infinite mercy for us, and especially for poor sinners.

O Blessed Host, in whom is contained life eternal and of infinite mercy, dispensed in abundance to us and especially to poor sinners.

O Blessed Host, in whom is contained the mercy of the Father, the Son and the Holy Spirit toward us, and especially toward poor sinners.

O Blessed Host, in whom is contained the infinite price of mercy which will compensate for all our debts, and especially those of poor sinners.

O Blessed Host, in whom is contained the fountain of living water which springs from infinite mercy for us, and especially for poor sinners.

O Blessed Host, in whom is contained the fire of purest love which blazes forth from the bosom of the Eternal Father, as from an abyss of infinite mercy for us, and especially for poor sinners.

O Blessed Host, in whom is contained the medicine for all our infirmities, flowing from infinite mercy, as from a fount, for us and especially for poor sinners.

O Blessed Host, in whom is contained the union between God and us through His infinite mercy for us, and especially for poor sinners.

O Blessed Host, in whom are contained all the sentiments of the most sweet Heart of Jesus toward us, and especially poor sinners.

O Blessed Host, our only hope in all the sufferings and adversities of life.

O Blessed Host, our only hope in the midst of darkness and of storms within and without.

O Blessed Host, our only hope in life and at the hour of our death.

O Blessed Host, our only hope in the midst of adversities and floods of despair.

O Blessed Host, our only hope in the midst of falsehood and treason.

O Blessed Host, our only hope in the midst of the darkness and godlessness which inundate the earth. O Blessed Host, our only hope in the longing and pain in which no one will understand us.

O Blessed Host, our only hope in the toil and monotony of everyday life.

O Blessed Host, our only hope amid the ruin of our hopes and endeavors.

O Blessed Host, our only hope in the midst of the ravages of the enemy and the efforts of hell.

O Blessed Host, I trust in You when the burdens are beyond my strength and I find my efforts are fruitless.

O Blessed Host, I trust in You when storms toss my heart about and my fearful spirit tends to despair.

O Blessed Host, I trust in You when my heart is about to tremble and mortal sweat moistens my brow.

O Blessed Host, I trust in You when everything conspires against me and black despair creeps into my soul.

O Blessed Host, I trust in You when my eyes will begin to grow dim to all temporal things and, for the first time, my spirit will behold the unknown worlds.

O Blessed Host, I trust in You when my tasks will be beyond my strength and adversity will become my daily lot.

O Blessed Host, I trust in You when the practice of virtue will appear difficult for me and my nature will grow rebellious.

O Blessed Host, I trust in You when hostile blows will be aimed against me.

O Blessed Host, I trust in You when my toils and efforts will be misjudged by others.

O Blessed Host, I trust in You when Your judgments will resound over me; it is then that I will trust in the sea of Your mercy.[4]

---

[4]   St. Faustina Kowalska, *Divine Mercy in My Soul*, no. 356.

Bibliography

Ambrose, St. "On the Mysteries." Translated by H. de Romestin, E. de Romestin and H. T. F. Duckworth. In Philip Schaff and Henry Wace, eds. *Nicene and Post-Nicene Fathers, Second Series*. Vol. 10. Buffalo, NY: Christian Literature Publishing Co., 1896.

Anderson, Gary. *Charity: The Place of the Poor in the Biblical Tradition*. New Haven, CT: Yale, 2013.

Astell, Ann. *Eating Beauty: The Eucharist and the Spiritual Arts of the Middle Ages*. Ithaca, NY: Cornell University Press, 2006.

Barron, Robert. *Catholicism: A Journey to the Heart of the Faith*. New York: Image, 2011.

Benedict XVI, Pope. *Sacramentum Caritatis*. February 22, 2007 .

————. *Spe Salvi*. November 30, 2007.

Berry, Wendell. *The Gift of Good Land: Further Essays Cultural and Agricultural*. Berkeley, CA: Counterpoint, 2009.

Bethel, Francis. *John Senior and the Restoration of Realism*. Merrimack, NH: Thomas More College Press, 2016.

Bradbury, Ray. *Fahrenheit 451*. New York: Simon & Schuster, 2018.

Brague, Remi. *Curing Mad Truths: Medieval Wisdom for the Modern Age*. Notre Dame: University of Notre Dame Press, 2019.

Bullivant, Stephen. *Mass Exodus: Catholic Disaffiliation in Britain and America since Vatican II*. New York: Oxford University Press, 2019.

Bux, Nicola. *No Trifling Matter: Taking the Sacraments Seriously Again*. Brooklyn, NY: Angelico Press, 2018.

Cantalamessa, Raniero. *The Eucharist: Our Sanctification*. Collegeville, MN: Liturgical Press, 1993.

Carpenter, Humphrey, ed. *The Letters of J. R. R. Tolkien*. Boston: Houghton Mifflin, 2000.

Carstens, Christopher. *A Devotional Journey into the Mass: How Mass Can Become a Time of Grace, Nourishment, and Devotion*. Manchester, NH: Sophia Institute, 2017.

Cavanaugh, William. *Being Consumed: Economics and Christian Desire*. Grand Rapids, MI: Eerdmans, 2008.

Coakley, John and Andrea Sterk, eds. *Readings in World Christian History, Volume I: Earliest Christianity to 1453*. New York: Orbis, 2004.

Corbon, Jean. *The Wellspring of Worship*. San Francisco: Ignatius, 2005.

Cyprian, St. "Treatise 3, On the Lapsed." Translated by Robert Ernest Wallis. In Alexander Roberts, James Donaldson, and A. Cleveland Coxe, eds. *Ante-Nicene Fathers* Vol. 5. Buffalo, NY: Christian Literature Publishing Co., 1886.

Cyril of Jerusalem, St. "Catechetical Lecture 22." Translated by Edwin Hamilton Gifford. In Philip Schaff and Henry Wace, eds. *Nicene and Post-Nicene Fathers*,

Second Series. Vol. 7. Buffalo, NY: Christian Literature Publishing Co., 1894.

Dawson, Christopher. *The Age of the Gods.* London: Sheed & Ward, 1928.

———. *The Judgment of the Nations.* Washington, DC: Catholic University of America Press, 2011.

———. *Religion and the Rise of Western Culture.* New York: Image Books, 1958.

de Sales, Francis, St. *Introduction to the Devout Life.* Translated by John Ryan. New York: Image, 1972.

Dinesen, Isak. "Babette's Feast." In *Anecdotes of Destiny.* New York: Vintage Books, 1985.

Dostoyevsky, Fyodor. *Demons.* Translated by Robert Maguire. New York: Penguin Classics, 2008.

Eliot, T. S. *Christianity & Culture.* New York: Harcourt, 1976.

Eymard, Peter Julian, St. *How to Get More Out of Holy Communion,* abridged edition. Manchester, NH: Sophia Institute Press, 2000.

Francis, Pope. *Laudato Si'.* May 24, 2015.

Grimm, Jacob and Wilhelm. "God's Food." In *The Complete Folk & Fairy Tales of the Brothers Grimm.* New York: Wisehouse Classics, 2016.

Hardon, John A. *The History of Eucharistic Adoration: Development of Doctrine in the Catholic Church.* Oak Lawn, IL: CMJ Marian Publishers, 1997.

Ignatius of Antioch, St. Roberts, Alexander and James Donaldson, eds. "Letters." In Alexander Roberts, James Donaldson, and A. Cleveland Coxe, eds. *Ante-Nicene Fathers.* Vol. 1. Buffalo, NY: Christian Literature Publishing Co., 1885.

Irenaeus, St. *Against Heresies*. Translated by Alexander Roberts and William Rambaut. In Alexander Roberts, James Donaldson, and A. Cleveland Coxe, eds. *Ante-Nicene Fathers*. Vol. 1. Buffalo, NY: Christian Literature Publishing Co., 1885.

Jackson, John, Keith Propp, Rebecca Jackson, Ares Koumis, Jim Bertrand, and Bob Siefker. *The Shroud of Turin: A Critical Summary of Observations, Data and Hypotheses*. Colorado Springs, CO: The Turin Shroud Center of Colorado, 2017. https://www.shroudofturin.com/Resources/CRTSUM.pdf.

Jenkins, Philip. *The Next Christendom: The Coming of Global Christianity*. New York: Oxford University Press, 2011.

John Paul II, Pope. *Christifideles Laici*. December 30, 1988.

———. *Ecclesia de Eucharistia*. April 17, 2003.

———. *Evangelium Vitae*. March 25, 1995.

———. *Familiaris Consortio*. November 22, 1981.

John of the Cross, St. *The Ascent of Mt. Carmel*. Translated by Allison Peers. London: Burns, Oates, and Washbourne, 1935.

Justin Martyr. "First Apology." Translated by Marcus Dods and George Reith. In Alexander Roberts, James Donaldson, and A. Cleveland Coxe, eds. *Ante-Nicene Fathers*. Vol. 1. Buffalo, NY: Christian Literature Publishing Co., 1885.

Kane, John A. *Transforming Your Life through the Eucharist*. Manchester, NH: Sophia Institute, 1999.

Kass, Leon. *The Hungry Soul: Eating and Perfecting Our Nature*. Chicago: University of Chicago Press, 1999.

Kelly-Gangi, Carol. *365 Days with the Saints: A Year of Wisdom from the Saints*. New York: Wellfleet Press, 2015.

Kowalska, Faustina, St. *Diary: Divine Mercy in My Soul*. Stockbridge, MA: Marian Press, 2005.

Lemna, Keith. *The Apocalypse of Wisdom: Louis Bouyer's Theological Recovery of the Cosmos*. Brooklyn: Angelico, 2019.

Leo XIII, Pope. *Immortale Dei*. November 1, 1885.

Levering, Matthew. *Sacrifice and Community: Jewish Offering and Christian Eucharist*. Malden, MA: Blackwell Publishing, 2005.

Liguori, Alphonsus, St. *Visits to the Blessed Sacrament and the Blessed Virgin Mary*. Charlotte, NC: TAN Books, 2012.

Marmion, Columba. *Christ in His Mysteries*. Bethesda, MD: Zaccheus Press, 2008.

Mechtilde of Hackenborn, St. *The Love of the Sacred Heart*. London: Burns, Oates & Washbourne, 1922.

Newman, John Henry. *Essay on the Development of Christian Doctrine*. New York: Longmans, Green, and Co, 1905.

Nichols, Aidan. *Christendom Awake: On Reenergizing the Church in Culture*. Grand Rapids, MI: W.B. Eerdmans, 1999.

Paul VI, Pope. *Evangelii Nuntiandi*. December 8, 1975.

Philippe, Jacques. *Time for God*. Strongsville, OH: Scepter, 2008.

Pieper, Josef. *In Tune with the World: A Theory of Festivity*. South Bend, IN: St. Augustine Press, 1999.

———. *Leisure: The Basis of Culture*. San Francisco: Ignatius Press, 2009.

Pitre, Brant. *Jesus and the Jewish Roots of the Eucharist: Unlocking the Secrets of the Last Supper.* New York: Image, 2016.

Pius XII, Pope. *Mediator Dei.* November 20, 1947.

Ratzinger, Joseph. *The Feast of Faith: Approaches to a Theology of the Liturgy.* San Francisco: Ignatius, 1986.

———. *The Spirit of the Liturgy.* San Francisco: Ignatius Press, 2000.

——— with Vittorio Messori. *The Ratzinger Report.* San Francisco: Ignatius Press, 1985.

Riddle, M. B., trans. "The Didache: The Lord's Teaching Through the Twelve Apostles to the Nations." In Alexander Roberts, James Donaldson, and A. Cleveland Coxe, eds. *Ante-Nicene Fathers.* Vol. 7. Buffalo, NY: Christian Literature Publishing Co., 1886.

Sarah, Robert. *The Day Is Now Far Spent.* Translated by Michael J. Miller. San Francisco: Ignatius, 2019.

———. *God or Nothing: A Conversation on Faith.* San Francisco: Ignatius Press, 2015.

Schroeder, H. J. *Disciplinary Decrees of the General Councils: Text, Translation and Commentary.* St. Louis: B. Herder, 1937.

Scribner, Charles, III. *The Triumph of the Eucharist.* New York: Carolus Editions, 2014.

Second Vatican Council. *Gaudium et Spes.* December 7, 1965.

———. *Sacrosanctum Concilium.* December 4, 1963.

Senior, John. *The Restoration of Christian Culture.* Norfolk, VA: IHS Press, 2008. San Francisco: Ignatius Press, 1983.

Smith, Scott L. *Lord of the Rings and the Eucharist.* Holy Water Books, 2019.

Staudt, R. Jared. *The Beer Option: Brewing a Catholic Culture Yesterday & Today.* Brooklyn, NY: Angelico Press, 2018.

Thérèse of Lisieux, St. *Story of a Soul.* Washington, D.C.: ICS Publications, 1996.

Thurston, Herbert. "Processions." In *The Catholic Encyclopedia.* New York: Robert Appleton Co., 1911.

Tolkien, J. R. R. *The Letters of J.R.R. Tolkien.* Edited by Humphrey Carpenter. New York: Houghton Mifflin Harcourt, 2000.

———. *The Return of the King: Being the Third Part of the Lord of the Rings.* Boston, MA: Mariner Books, 2012.

von Trapp, Maria Augusta. "The Land without a Sunday." In *Around the Year with the von Trapp Family.* Manchester, NH: Sophia Institute, 2018.

Weldon Owen. *Saints: Inspiration and Guidance for Every Day of the Year: Book of Saints: Rediscover the Saints.* San Rafael, CA: Weldon Owen, 2021.